FIELDING'S
NEW ORLEANS
AGENDA

The Buzz About Fielding

Fielding Worldwide

"The new Fielding guidebook style mirrors the style of the company's new publisher: irreverent, urbane, adventuresome and in search of the unique travel experience."

—*San Diego Union Tribune*

"Individualistic, entertaining, comprehensive."

—*Consumers Digest*

"Guidebooks with attitude."

—*Dallas Morning News*

"Full of author's tips and asides, the books seem more personal and more credible than many similarly encyclopedic tomes."

—*Los Angeles Times*

"At Fielding Worldwide, adventurous might well be the order of the day."

—*Des Moines Register*

"Biting travel guides give readers a fresh look."

—*Houston Chronicle*

"For over 30 years Fielding guides have been the standard of modern travel books."

—*Observer Times*

Fielding's Las Vegas Agenda

"A concise but detailed look at the capital of glitter and gambling."

—*Atlanta Journal Constitution*

Fielding's Los Angeles Agenda

"...contains much more than the standard travel guide. The lists of theatres, sports arenas and attractions are worth the book's price by itself."

—*Baton Rouge Advocate*

Fielding's New York Agenda

"Loaded with advice...puts the whole of the Big Apple in hand."

—*Bon Appetit*

Fielding's Guide to Worldwide Cruises

"One of the year's ten best books."

—*Gourmet Magazine*

"Perhaps the best single source for unbiased cruise information."

—*The New York Times*

"To be all things to all people is impossible, but this book pretty well does it."

—*The New York Daily News*

"You can trust them [Fielding] to tell the truth. It's fun—and very informative."

—*New Orleans Times-Picayune*

"The Bible. If scarcity is any indication of quality, then this book is superb."

—*St. Petersburg Florida Times*

Cruise Insider

"One of the best, most compact, yet interesting books about cruising today is the fact-filled *Cruise Insider*."

—*John Clayton Travel With a Difference*

Fielding's The World's Most Dangerous Places

"Rarely does a travel guide turn out to be as irresistible as a John Grisham novel. But *The World's Most Dangerous Places*, a 1000-page tome for the truly adventurous traveler, manages to do just that."

—*Arkansas Democrat-Gazette*

"A travel guide that could be a real lifesaver. Practical tips for those seeking the road less traveled."

—*Time Magazine*

"The greatest derring do of this year's memoirs."

—*Publishers Weekly*

"Reads like a first-run adventure movie."

—*Travel Books Worldwide*

"One of the oddest and most fascinating travel books to appear in a long time."

—*The New York Times*

"...publishing terra incognito...a primer on how to get in and out of potentially lethal places."

—*U.S. News and World Report*

"Tired of the same old beach vacation?...this book may be just the antidote."

—*USA Today*

"Guide to hot spots will keep travelers glued to their armchairs."

—*The Vancouver Sun*

Fielding's Borneo

"One of a kind...a guide that reads like an adventure story."

—*San Diego Union*

Fielding's Budget Europe

"This is a guide to great times, great buys and discovery in 18 countries."

—*Monroe News-Star*

Fielding's Caribbean

"If you have trouble deciding which regional guidebook to reach for, you can't go wrong with *Fielding's Caribbean*."

—*Washington Times*

"Opinionated, clearly written and probably the only guide that any visitor to the Caribbean really needs."

—*The New York Times*

Fielding's Europe

"Synonymous with the dissemination of travel information for five decades."

—*Traveller's Bookcase*

"The definitive Europe... shame on you if you don't read it before you leave."

—*Travel Europe*

Fielding's Far East

"This well-respected guide is thoroughly updated and checked out."

—*The Reader Review*

Fielding's France

"Winner of the annual 'Award of Excellence' [with Michelin and Dorling Kindersley]."

—*FrancePresse*

Fielding's Freewheelin' USA

"...an informative, thorough and entertaining 400-page guide to the sometimes maligned world of recreational vehicle travel."

—*Travel Weekly*

"...very comprehensive... lots more fun than most guides of this sort..."

—*Los Angeles Times*

Fielding's Italy

"A good investment...contains excellent tips on driving, touring, cities, etc."

—*Travel Savvy*

Fielding's Mexico

"Among the very best."

—*Library Journal*

Fielding's Spain and Portugal

"Our best sources of information were fellow tour-goers and *Fielding's Spain and Portugal*."

—*The New York Times*

Vacation Places Rated

"...can best be described as a thinking person's guide if used to its fullest."

—*Chicago Tribune*

"Tells how 13,500 veteran vacationers rate destinations for satisfaction and how well a destination delivers on what is promised."

—*USA Today*

Fielding's Vietnam

"Fielding has the answer to every conceivable question."

—*Destination Vietnam*

"An important book about an important country."

—*NPR Business Radio*

Fielding Titles

Fielding's Alaska Cruises and the Inside Passage
Fielding's America West
Fielding's Asia's Top Dive Sites
Fielding's Australia
Fielding's Bahamas
Fielding's Baja California
Fielding's Bermuda
Fielding's Best and Worst — The surprising results of the Plog Survey
Fielding's Birding Indonesia
Fielding's Borneo
Fielding's Budget Europe
Fielding's Caribbean
Fielding's Caribbean Cruises
Fielding's Caribbean on a Budget
Fielding's Diving Australia
Fielding's Diving Indonesia
Fielding's Eastern Caribbean
Fielding's England including Ireland, Scotland & Wales
Fielding's Europe
Fielding's Europe 50th Anniversary
Fielding's European Cruises
Fielding's Far East
Fielding's France
Fielding's France: Loire Valley, Burgundy & the Best of French Culture
Fielding's France: Normandy & Brittany
Fielding's France: Provence and the Mediterranean
Fielding's Freewheelin' USA
Fielding's Hawaii
Fielding's Hot Spots: Travel in Harm's Way
Fielding's Indiana Jones Adventure and Survival Guide™
Fielding's Italy
Fielding's Kenya
Fielding's Las Vegas Agenda
Fielding's London Agenda
Fielding's Los Angeles Agenda
Fielding's Mexico
Fielding's New Orleans Agenda
Fielding's New York Agenda
Fielding's New Zealand
Fielding's Paradors, Pousadas and Charming Villages of Spain and Portugal
Fielding's Paris Agenda
Fielding's Portugal
Fielding's Rome Agenda
Fielding's San Diego Agenda
Fielding's Southeast Asia
Fielding's Southern California Theme Parks
Fielding's Southern Vietnam on Two Wheels
Fielding's Spain
Fielding's Surfing Australia
Fielding's Surfing Indonesia
Fielding's Sydney Agenda
Fielding's Thailand, Cambodia, Laos and Myanmar
Fielding's Travel Tool™
Fielding's Vietnam, including Cambodia and Laos
Fielding's Walt Disney World and Orlando Area Theme Parks
Fielding's Western Caribbean
Fielding's The World's Most Dangerous Places™
Fielding's Worldwide Cruises

FIELDING'S
NEW ORLEANS
AGENDA

By
Nan Lyons

Fielding Worldwide, Inc.
308 South Catalina Avenue
Redondo Beach, California 90277 U.S.A.

Fielding's New Orleans Agenda

Published by Fielding Worldwide, Inc.

Text Copyright ©1997 Fielding Worldwide, Inc.

Maps, Icons & Illustrations Copyright ©1997 FWI

Photo Copyrights ©1997 to Individual Photographers

FIELDING WORLDWIDE INC.

PUBLISHER AND CEO	**Robert Young Pelton**
GENERAL MANAGER	**John Guillebeaux**
OPERATIONS DIRECTOR	**George Posanke**
ELEC. PUBLISHING DIRECTOR	**Larry E. Hart**
PUBLIC RELATIONS DIRECTOR	**Beverly Riess**
ACCOUNT SERVICES MANAGER	**Cindy Henrichon**
PROJECT MANAGER	**Chris Snyder**
MANAGING EDITOR	**Amanda K. Knoles**

PRODUCTION

Martin Mancha	**Rebecca Perry**
Ramses Reynoso	**Craig South**
COVER DESIGNED BY	**Digital Artists, Inc.**
COVER PHOTOGRAPHERS —	**Jeff Greenberg/**
Front Cover	**Omni Photo Communications**
Back Cover	**Louisiana Office of Tourism**
INSIDE PHOTOS	**Louisiana Office of Tourism, New Orleans Convention and Visitors Bureau, Inc.**
CARTOONS	***The New Yorker***

Inquiries should be addressed to: Fielding Worldwide, Inc., 308 South Catalina Ave., Redondo Beach, California 90277 U.S.A., ☎ *(310) 372-4474*, Facsimile *(310) 376-8064*, 8:30 a.m.–5:30 p.m. Pacific Standard Time.
Website: http://www.fieldingtravel.com
e-mail: fielding@fieldingtravel.com

ISBN 1-56952-122-0

Printed in the United States of America

Letter from the Publisher

In 1946, Temple Fielding began the first of what would be a remarkable new series of well-written, highly personalized guidebooks for independent travelers. Temple's opinionated, witty and oft-imitated books have now guided travelers for almost a half-century. More important to some was Fielding's humorous and direct method of steering travelers away from the dull and the insipid. Today, Fielding's travel guides are still written by experienced travelers for experienced travelers. Our authors carry on Fielding's reputation for creating travel experiences that deliver insight with a sense of discovery and style.

Designed to save travelers time and money, *Fielding's New Orleans Agenda* cuts to the chase, telling readers all they need to know to "do" the town. Whether you have a day or a week in New Orleans, Nan Lyons will take you straight to all the memorable and off-the-beaten-path places and clue you in to the city's best kept secrets.

The concept of independent travel has never been bigger. Our policy of *brutal honesty* and a highly personal point of view has never changed; it just seems the travel world has caught up with us.

RYP

Robert Young Pelton
Publisher and CEO
Fielding Worldwide, Inc.

Acknowledgments

For service above and beyond, I want to thank Avraham Inlender, Barbara Settanni, and most especially Janet Rodgers, and Tracy and Gary Fullup for being "godparents" who came through not only with tea and sympathy, but with shoeleather and love.

— Nan Lyons

ABOUT THE
AUTHOR

Nan Lyons

Nan Lyons is best known as one of the authors, in collaboration with her husband, Ivan, of the best-selling novel turned movie, *Someone Is Killing the Great Chefs of Europe*, and for travel articles in magazines such as *Bon Appetit*, *Travel & Leisure*, and *Food & Wine*.

Their nonfiction output includes *Imperial Hotel, A Century of Elegance at Tokyo's Imperial Hotel*, and several guides to New York City. Nan Lyons is the author of *Fielding's New York Agenda*, *Fielding's London Agenda*, *Fielding's Paris Agenda* and *Fielding's Sydney Agenda*.

Fielding Rating Icons

The Fielding Rating Icons are highly personal and awarded to help the besieged traveler choose from among the dizzying array of activities, attractions, hotels, restaurants and sights. The awarding of an icon denotes unusual or exceptional qualities in the relevant category.

RATINGS: Fielding Award, Author Selection, Money Saver, Expensive, Quality, Warning, Danger, Inexpensive, Spacious, Cramped, Mild Disapproval, Timesaving

CULTURAL: Museum/Art, Interesting Architecture, History, Book Reference, Artistically Important, Musically Interesting, Cultural Archeology, Crafts, Theater, Festivals

SIGHTS: Picturesque, Great Scenery, Market, Beaches/Resorts, Cultural, Fortress, Castles, Church

WHERE TO STAY: Simple, Luxurious, Cottage, Bed & Breakfast, Scenic, Business, Honeymoon, Château

TRAVEL TIPS: Arrival/Departure, By Air, By Water, By Train, By Car, Bus/Local Transit, Barge, River Boat, Calendar, Itinerary, Compass, Kids

SPECIAL INTERESTS: Nightlife, Singles, Romantic, Nude Beaches, Lecture, Spectacular Cuisine, Wine Tasting, Shopping, Cafe Stops, Gardening, Pro Sports, Mystery, Gambling, Wildlife

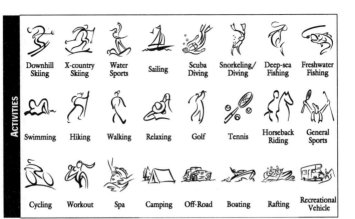

ACTIVITIES

Downhill Skiing · X-country Skiing · Water Sports · Sailing · Scuba Diving · Snorkeling/Diving · Deep-sea Fishing · Freshwater Fishing

Swimming · Hiking · Walking · Relaxing · Golf · Tennis · Horseback Riding · General Sports

Cycling · Workout · Spa · Camping · Off-Road · Boating · Rafting · Recreational Vehicle

Map Legend

Essentials

🏨 HOTEL
⚥ YOUTH HOSTEL
✕ RESTAURANT
Ⓢ BANK
Ⓒ TELEPHONE
Ⓘ TOURIST INFO.
✚ HOSPITAL
🍺 PUB/BAR
♪ MUSIC CLUB
✉ POST OFFICE
Ⓟ PARKING
Ⓣ TAXI
Ⓢ SUBWAY
Ⓜ METRO
Ⓜ MARKET
Ⓢ SHOPPING
Ⓒ CINEMA
♉ THEATRE
✈ INT'L AIRPORT
✛ REGIONAL AIRPORT
✸ POLICE STATION
⚖ COURTHOUSE
🏛 GOV'T. BUILDING
■ ATTRACTION
✈ MILITARY AIRBASE
♟ ARMY BASE
⚓ NAVAL BASE
🏰 FORT
🎓 UNIVERSITY
🎓 SCHOOL

Activities

⌕ BEACH
△ CAMPGROUND
🎋 PICNIC AREA
⛳ GOLF COURSE
🚤 BOAT LAUNCH
🤿 DIVING
🐟 FISHING
🎿 WATER SKIING
⛷ SNOW SKIING
🦅 BIRD SANCTUARY
🐾 WILDLIFE SANCTUARY
🌳 PARK
🏕 PARK HQ.
⛏ MINE
🗼 LIGHTHOUSE
🌾 WINDMILL
⚓ CRUISE PORT
✈ VIEW
⬭ STADIUM
🏢 BUILDING
🐃 ZOO
❀ GARDEN

Historical

⋰ ARCHEOLOGICAL SITE
⚔ BATTLEGROUND
♜ CASTLE
⚲ MONUMENT
🏛 MUSEUM
⚱ RUIN
≋ SHIPWRECK

Religious

✝ CHURCH
☸ BUDDHIST TEMPLE
卐 HINDU TEMPLE
☪ MOSQUE
⛩ PAGODA
✡ SYNAGOGUE
✚ CEMETERY
✡ HEBREW CEMETERY
☪ MUSLIM CEMETERY

Physical

— — — INTERNATIONAL BOUNDARY	🚶 HIKING TRAIL
– – – COUNTY/REGIONAL BOUNDARY	▬▬ DIRT ROAD
PARIS ⊙ NATIONAL CAPITAL	▪▪⊙▪▪ RAILROAD
Victoria ● STATE/PARISH CAPITAL	**RR** RAILROAD STATION
Los Angeles ● MAJOR CITY	⟷ FERRY ROUTE
Quy Nhon ○ TOWN/VILLAGE	— RIVER
⑤ MOTORWAY/FREEWAY	🔴 LAKE
⑯³ HIGHWAY	〽 WATERFALL
1AB FREEWAY EXIT	🐚 CORAL REEF
═══ PRIMARY ROAD	♨ HOT SPRING
═══ SECONDARY ROAD	▲ MOUNTAIN PEAK
▬ ▬ ▬ SUBWAY	◠ CAVE
🚲 BIKING ROUTE	
🚃 TROLLEY/STREET CAR	

©FWI

A WORD FROM THE AUTHOR

The Agenda Series was designed to put the guide back into travel guides. Unlike other guides that are written by committee, I take full responsibility for the personal, candid and sometimes controversial opinions I have expressed in order to provide my readers with the quintessential New Orleans experience.

Today, with travelers having just a few short days to spend on a trip, the only guide that is really useful is one that can distill the hundreds of choices that are available in New Orleans into the very essence of the City.

If an old friend were coming to town everything I would tell them is in this guide. Time is as valuable as money, and you need to know what you can afford to miss and what should be at the top of your agenda. My goal is to be selective, not provide you with endless details and historical minutia. The definition of the word "Agenda" is a list of business to be covered and that is my intention as well.

By exploring New Orleans neighborhoods and listing a shopping and restaurant agenda for each, I have made it possible to construct a relaxed agenda for an afternoon or evening without having to leave the area. I also have suggested one, two, and three day agendas that cover most of what makes New Orleans the most exciting, unique city in the world (I told you I was opinionated).

I am looking forward to putting my years of travel writing and globe-trotting at your disposal, so that at the end of your stay in New Orleans, you'll leave knowing that you have taken away the very best it has to offer.

—Nan Lyons

Stars In The Agenda Guide's Eyes

Just a few words to fully explain the twinkle in our Agenda stars. Since this guide is geared to bring you only the very best a city has to offer, one might question why an additional rating system is necessary. The reason is that even with the "best" there is always finer tuning that might be done. However, this is in no way a competition between us and that adorably, chubby tire guy. So the agenda of the Agenda Stars is really to tell you how to go from best to superb.

★★★	**Superb**
★★	**Excellent**
★	**One of the Best**

The "Best Bite" restaurant choices have not been rated since they are just "drop-in" places as you visit the different neighborhoods of New Orleans. If they're listed in "Best Bites," then of course they're the best.

I value your time too highly to cover every "down and dirty" choice that exists, and then bother to rate it. If it's in the guide, you can bet it has "star power."

—Nan Lyons

AGENDA HERE TODAY— GONE TOMORROW

In the words of Stephen Sondheim "Not a Day Goes By" without a restaurant closing, a new hotel opening, a store changing its address, or all of the above. Trying to keep up with the changes in New Orleans is harder than diapering quadruplets. It's enough to drive any self-respecting travel writer to the nearest mental facility. And so gentle reader, have patience, if there were no changes in New Orleans they'd all still be speaking French.

TABLE OF CONTENTS

LIST OF MAPS

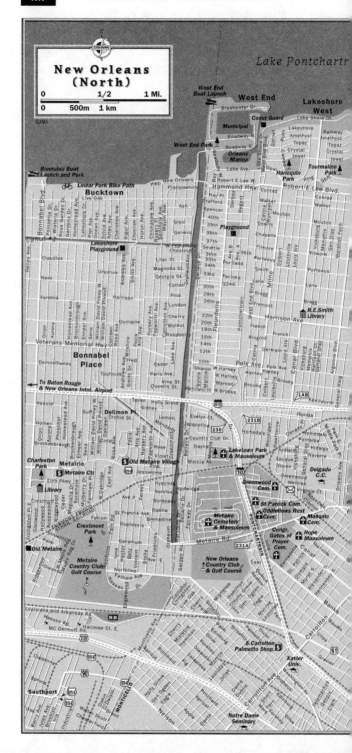

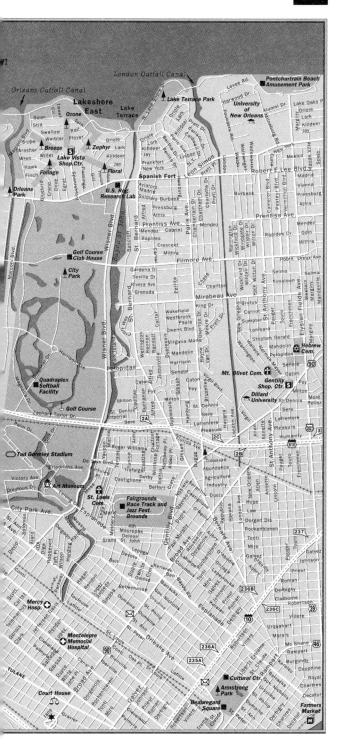

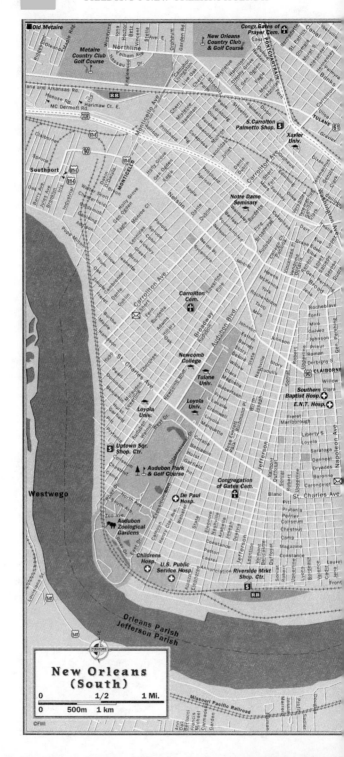

New Orleans
(South)

0   1/2   1 Mi.

0   500m   1 km

©FWI

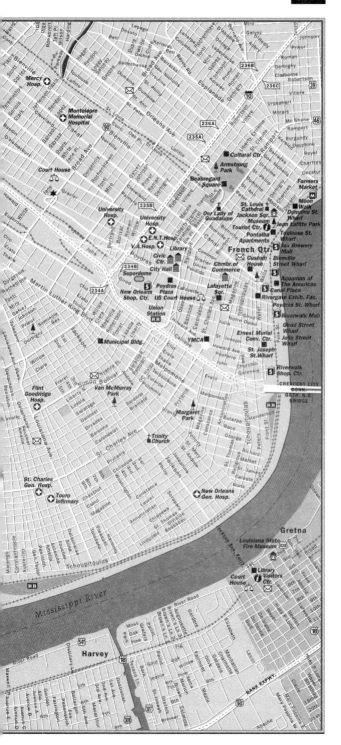

WHAT IS NEW ORLEANS?

Mardi Gras tourists and locals congregate for street parties.

Life in this irresistible city is one perpetual, exuberant, celebration. It sits shimmering in the sun, as if it were a brilliant multicolored fruit aspic. It sports curlicues and filigrees more suited to the art of a pastry chef than an architect. And the whipped cream that tops off this most buoyant of souffles is the endless delight its residents take in their beloved confection.

Not only do the people of New Orleans revel in their own history, culture and endless festivals, they're eager to share this array of riches with the millions of visitors who pass through their city each year. Perhaps the generosity of spirit eagerly extended to tourists is because they themselves are still traveling through the legends that have made New Orleans so provocative.

It would be difficult to find a place more devoted to the sybaritic, sensual and often decadent delights of life than New Orleans. One has only to look at a street map marked by names such as Elysian Fields, Terpsichore, Desire and Erato to understand that it has at its very heart, the pursuit of pleasure.

Nothing about this subtropical city leads you to believe you're in for a typical "down south" experience. To walk through the narrow winding streets of the **French Quarter** is to be reminded of the Left Bank in Paris. Not just because the street signs and the patois of conversation are full of the **Vieux Carré's** French heritage, but because of a European sensibility that hangs in the sultry air like the perfume of chicory. The past is everywhere.

When the population isn't feasting on the diverse ethnic cuisines that New Orleans is so famous for, it's swaying to the sounds of its equally famous music. Rhythm and blues is as much a part of its heritage as the Mississippi. But most of all, the people of New Orleans love a parade. Not only because they host one of the world's most extravagant of spectacles, Mardi Gras, but because they'll parade anytime at all. At the drop of a trumpet they proceed through the street accompanied by the ever-present jazz band that marks festivals and funerals alike. New Orleanians are the proud citizens of the capital of "Laissez Les Bons Temps Rouler." And so, the good times roll on and on and on with the constancy of the Mississippi.

The Big Easy, as it's often called, is anything but. Its spicy temperament thrives on blood lines and lineage, superstition and gossip, position and privilege, but most of all—mystery. New Orleans is a city of secrets. Secret gardens hidden behind high walls, secret societies that were formed centuries ago, and perhaps most of all, a secret longing to return to the past. It's no mere happenstance that Mardi Gras is attended in masks and disguises. Concealment has evolved into an art form here.

That Old Black Magic isn't just a song title in New Orleans. The locals, perhaps because of the exotic nature of their past are still seduced by the romance of superstition. They may laugh about the "hoodoo" of voodoo with the tourists but most of the small groceries in the French Quarter still sell voodoo charms alongside the Diet Coke and the Campbell Soups. The old and the new are forever coming together with a remarkable, fatalistic sense of spirit.

Despite floods and fire, catastrophic epidemics, hurricanes, recessions, depressions, and the see-saw governing of both France and Spain, New Orleans has always been shaped and defined by its disasters. Not only has it survived its vivid history but today it continues to infect its visitors with terminal romanticism. It was no accident that Tennessee Williams created Blanche Du Bois to echo the image of New Orleans' fragile beauty. Like Blanche it believes the past is precious because it leads to the undying optimism of the future. When Blanche stepped off that streetcar named Desire she became the postergirl for New Orleans. Even at its most remarkable it has always depended on the kindness of strangers.

New Orleans Yesterday

Intricate ironwork detailing adorns many buildings.

Louis XIV, when he wasn't having dainty furniture named after him, was a King who enjoyed a new colony with the same gusto he enjoyed a new mistress. Both were wonderfully diverting. To that end explorers were dispatched by the French Court to chart the Mississippi since it was so compellingly close to the gold of Mexico, which just happened to be in the possession of Louis' in-law, the king of Spain. La Salle headed the expedition and his explorations finally resulted in a sizable piece of territory that was sure to entertain the King. Continuing La Salle's quest for gold and glory were the brothers La Moyne, Pierre the Sieur d'Iberville and Jean Baptiste Sieur de Bienville. In 1699 they sailed down to the mouth of the Mississippi and dropped anchor near a tiny bayou (inlet of water), on Shrove Tuesday. Not missing a beat and with an admirable presence they decided to name the spot they first came ashore, Point du Mardi Gras (Trans: Fat Tuesday) in honor of this festive Catholic holiday. Little did they know they were not just honoring the church, but also the hopes and dreams of hundreds of hoteliers in the centuries to come.

The French as well as the Canadians flooded into King Louis' new colony, known as Louisiana, for obvious reasons. They came for all kinds of reasons, some to escape prison, some to work off debts, smugglers for the easy pickings and, of course, that ever-present group of fun seekers, "les femmes des soir." This exotic mix of new colonists were the beginnings of the Creole, Cajun, Spanish and Indian influences in Louisiana. They would blend together deliciously to produce the multicultural society that made the territory totally unique.

No one realized at the time that they were going to be residents of New Orleans until 1718 when it became a city, and was named after the Duc d'Orleans.

By 1762 the king had come to the conclusion that the stories of bayous paved with gold, and diamond alligators were greatly exaggerated. Besides, he had been able to rid himself of the more sordid element of his subjects, so what better time to dump New Orleans on an unsuspecting relative, in this case, Carlos III, King of Spain. Graceful wrought iron grillwork was added to the luxurious mansions, and the flavors of Spain began to mingle with the French accent of the city. Even Napoleon was a player in this game of musical monarchies. The "Short One" had New Orleans ceded to him by Spain like a Cracker-jack™ prize in return for his signature on the treaty of 1800. Since the city was raging with yellow fever at the time, Napoleon in his wisdom let Spain continue to govern his very infectious new colony.

The settlers of New Orleans barely knew which flag was theirs from day to day. However, they were united in one infamous endeavor: slavery. Even though by the early 1800s more than 2000 free people of color were residents of the city, New Orleans was raised, and continued to prosper from the sweat of its slave economy. Every home, with the exception of the poorest shacks, had its own slave quarters out back. Even today, no matter how gentrified they have been made, or charming their uses in today's society, the slave quarters still stand as a reminder of the grim excesses of New Orleans' past.

AGENDA GONE BUT NOT FORGOTTEN!!

When a rich planter came to New Orleans for a couple of days of R&R, it was not only inconvenient but financially inefficient to bring a number of personal slaves with him. Instead, there was a service set up in town where one could obtain a slave for the duration of one's trip. In effect, it was a Rent-a-Slave agency (If only Hertz had been around).

In 1803, without enough cash in the treasury, and without the assistance of American Express or MasterCard, the United States pulled off the greatest real estate deal since the Dutch bought that tacky, annoying little Island in New York for $24.00. James Monroe negotiated the Louisiana Purchase from Napoleon which included 600 million acres stretching from New Orleans to Canada, for about a nickel an acre (eat your heart out Donald Trump), The United States had succeeded in buying over 900 miles for about $15 million, almost as much as Elvis paid for Graceland.

The Americans added yet another color to New Orleans rainbow of cultures and Louisiana gained statehood in 1812. The cosmopolitan, European mecca grew into a rich and privileged city where culture and refinement were as highly prized as the cotton and sugar that brought millions to its economy. It was the civil war that finally stopped New Orleans dead in its tracks. It was occupied for almost three years and when reconstruction began, New Orleans once again changed its character to become a magnet for musicians, extraordinary food, and even more exotic cultures.

New Orleans Today

An aerial view of the Crescent City.

From their soggy vantage point, nearly five feet below sea level, the over 1,200,000 residents of Greater New Orleans have just begun to reach the crest of their "Crescent City." Things of late have definitely been looking up, but that wasn't always the case. For years corruption and vice were served up as casually as shrimp creole and jambalaya. In the 1920s the king of corruption in Louisiana was Huey Long who ruled the state with an iron fist and a velvet tongue. To the hopelessly poor he brought hope along with his personal brand of governing: dictatorship. His unchallenged political machine was responsible for everything both good and bad that happened in New Orleans from the '20s to 1935 when the "Kingfish" was assassinated.

The population in New Orleans today is its own most extravagant gumbo. The spicy mix of Cajun, Creole, Irish, French, African and of late, Asian, Indian and Arab, gives a wild spin to the old notion of southern hospitality as well as down-home cooking. There is no down-home in New Orleans, there is rather down Paris or Madrid or Dublin. Of course there are the fabled signature delicacies that make even a trip to the corner luncheonette in New Orleans an exciting journey. There is no way to visit here without having a "po-boy" sandwich overstuffed with oysters and dripping with sauce, or a cajun gumbo overflowing with sweet crawfish and tender okra. Top all this off with a couple of rich, buttery pralines, and there's no doubt you'll know what it means to miss New Orleans once you've left.

Greater New Orleans is made up of four different parishes (counties): **Orleans**, which takes in the metropolitan city, **Jefferson**, **St. Bernard** and **St. Tammany**. Even though it spreads out to almost 364 miles, only about half is above water. As a result the humidity makes the Amazon rain forest look like an outpost in the Sahara.

The New Orleans that shows its party face to visitors is of course **The French Quarter**, the **Central Business District** (referred to by the natives as the **C.B.D.**) as well as the carefully manicured, genteel, uptown **Garden District**. Despite the fact that the city suffered a massive blow during the '80s when the bottom dropped out of the oil industry, it's beginning to strut its stuff again. New hotels are shooting up all over town and the old **Warehouse District** has become the center of the arts and gallery scene. Artists have begun to transform the spaces with spectacular creativity.

Wherever you look there is growth and change and renewal in New Orleans. That is, with the exception of the city's gigantic casino folly, that "crapped-out" before construction on the doomed horror was even completed. But in most other areas of development New Orleans has been rolling straight sevens. Tourism continues to grow every year and the city's two most famous events, Mardi Gras and the equally medieval celebration of Super Bowl Sunday fills the town with millions of people who spend millions of dollars.

For some bizarre reason the residents of New Orleans seem to take a fiendish delight in bashing their own city. At the drop of a beignet they point out that street crime, drugs and corruption have never been more prevalent. But unlike most other places that have only recently suffered from the scars of urban decay, New Orleans has always been plagued with crime. Ever since it was colonized it's had a violent profile. After all, some of the world's most infamous pirates counted their "pieces of eight" in the **French Quarter**. Smugglers and brigands were the superstars of their time. Unfortunately, crime in the city today may not be quite as swashbuckling and glamorous but it's still a part of daily life here. It is necessary therefore, as in any other urban environment, to be careful. Don't stray into deserted streets late at night and don't walk through the city wearing the contents of Ali Baba's cave. However, that said, New Orleans can be as unique and exciting as a trip abroad. It has color and style, beauty and daring, and last but not least, no matter how much it changes it still has "all that jazz."

Famous New Orleanians

In addition to producing some of the world's finest food and music, New Orleans boasts an impressive roster of native sons and daughters who have made significant contributions in a wide variety of fields.

Person	Famous For
Louis Armstrong	World famous jazz musician.
Truman Capote	Author of *In Cold Blood* and *Breakfast at Tiffany's.*
Kitty Carlisle	Singer, actress, game show personality.
Harry Connick, Jr.	Grammy winning singer, musician.
Ellen DeGeneres	Actress and comedian, star of TV's "Ellen."
Fats Domino	One of the founding fathers of R&B music.
Dr. John	Famous R&B pianist/singer.
Pete Fountain	Famous clarinetist.
George Fort Gibbs	Artist and author of adventure books.
Ellen Gilchrest	Award-winning novelist.
Shirley Ann Grau	Pulitzer prize-winning author of *Keeper of the House.*
Bryant Gumbel	Former host of NBC's "Today" show.
John Hampson	Inventor of venetian blinds.
Lillian Hellman	Author of *Julia* and *The Little Foxes.*
George Herriman	Cartoonist known for "Krazy Kat."
Al Hirt	Renowned trumpet player.
Mahalia Jackson	Famous gospel singer.
Frances Parkinson Keyes	Author of *Dinner at Antoine's.*
Dorothy Lamour	Actress.
Josef Delarose Lascaux	Inventor of cotton candy.
John Larroquette	Emmy award winning actor from "Night Court" and "John Larroquette Show."
Branford Marsalis	Jazz saxophonist, who served as leader of "Tonight" show band.
Wynton Marsalis	Jazz musician, classical trumpet player.
Garrett Morris	Actor/comedian famous for *Saturday Night Live.*
Jelly Roll Morton	Famous jazz pianist.

Fielding NEW ORLEANS

LITERARY TOUR OF NEW ORLEANS

During the 1920s, the French Quarter was to New Orleans what the Left Bank was to Paris. Famous writers including Gertrude Stein, Ernest Hemingway and William Faulkner roamed back and forth between the two writers' enclaves. Today such best-selling writers as Anne Rice and Sheila Bosworth get inspiration from the colorful city.

Mark Twain

Twain's *Life on the Mississippi*, written in 1882, includes chapters filled with his impressions of New Orleans.

Mark Twain

Old Absinthe House

(240 Bourbon Street) Walt Whitman and Oscar Wilde shared more than a few drinks at this legendary bar.

Galatoire's

(209 Bourbon Street) This famous restaurant was featured in "A Streetcar Named Desire," and in Sheila Bosworth's novel, *Almost Innocent*.

WilliamFaulkner

Galatoire's

Old Abisinthe House

IBERVILLE

BOURBON ST.

Anne Rice

Antoine's

(713 St. Louis Street) William Faulkner celebrated his Legion of Honor award from the French government here.

ROYAL

BIENVILLE

CONTI

Herman Grima House

(820 St. Louis Street) This famous landmark was the model for the family home in Anne Rice's book, *Feast of All Saints*.

DECATUR

Omni Royal Hotel

Tennessee Williams, Truman Capote and Lillian Hellman were literary luminaries who stayed here.

Tennessee Williams

632 St. Peter Street

Tennessee Williams lived here while working on his famous play, "A Streetcar Named Desire."

Faulkner House

(624 Pirate's Alley) Now a bookshop, this was once William Faulkner's home in New Orleans.

Lillian Hellman

St. Louis Cathedral

In *An Unfinished Woman* Lillian Hellman told how she ran away from her aunt's house and hid in the cathedral.

623 Bourbon Street

Thornton Wilder spent several months writing at this townhouse during the 1940s. He was also a regular at Antoine's.

Thornton Wilder

O'Henry

William Sydney Porter changed his name to O'Henry when he moved to New Orleans after serving time in a Texas prison.

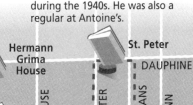

Hermann Grima House

St. Peter

DAUPHINE

TOULOUSE

ST. PETER

ORLEANS

ST. ANN

Antoine's

Omni Royal Hotel

Faulkner House

St. Louis Cathedral

DUMAINE

CHARTRES

Napoleon House Bar

DECATUR

Napoleon House Bar

This bar at *500 Chartres Street* is famous as a literary hangout.

French Market

French Market

Truman Capote was a frequent visitor here and also shopped regularly at the Royal Street Antiques shop. He wrote his first novel, *Other Voices, Other Rooms*, in New Orleans.

Truman Capote

Person	Famous For
Ed Nelson	Actor who starred in "Peyton Place" TV series.
The Neville Brothers	Grammy award-winning musical family.
Mel Ott	Major league baseball player of the 1930s.
Mel Parnell	Boston Red Sox pitcher.
Anne Rice	Author of *Interview With the Vampire*, *The Vampire Lestat* and *Queen of the Damned* among other novels.
Richard Simmons	TV exercise host and nutritionist.
Rusty Staub	Major league baseball player.
Robert Tallant	Author of historical works and fiction.
Jay Thomas	Radio personality and TV actor, star of "Cheers" and "Murphy Brown."
Sara Walker	First black female millionaire in America.
Ray Walston	Star of "My Favorite Martian."
Edward Douglas White	Chief Justice of the U.S. Supreme Court.
Andrew Young	Former U.N. ambassador and mayor of Atlanta.

AGENDA PRIORITIES

The French Quarter has a colorful history.

No matter how sophisticated a traveler you are, it's easy to become overwhelmed by the abundance of "must-see" activities in New Orleans. Part of the problem is that the city keeps changing. There's always something new to do. Just when you think you've covered all the bases, they go and slip in a new jazz club. Then, watch out! Here comes another great restaurant.

Make an agenda by selecting your most important priorities and noting the locations. Then read about the districts in which they're located. See if there are other things of interest to you nearby and estimate how much time you want to spend at each. The goal is to group priorities by districts in order to avoid zig-zagging your way back and forth across the city.

A visit to New Orleans is like being invited to an extravagant banquet prepared by the world's greatest chef. You pick up a plate and head eagerly for the buffet table. The question is, how to sample all those goodies without having to make a second trip? The answer is simple. You can't.

But that doesn't mean you have to go away hungry either. It may take a turn or two around the table before you know what you really want. My suggestion is to be selective: AKA listening to me.

AUTHOR'S NOTE

Unless otherwise stated all hotel and restaurants that appear in the guide accept major credit cards.

The Story Of New Orleans Is The French Quarter

More like a small village that just happens to be located within a city, the **French Quarter** is only about a square mile in size. It is here that New Orleans was born in 1718. From the look of it today the French government has never been replaced, despite the Louisiana Purchase. They are very much present as the arbiters of culture in this open air museum dedicated to the history of the city. In fact, the people who live here have become their own curators. The Vieux Carré Commission was formed in 1936 to watch over and protect the historic integrity of the existing architecture. Today even though the present keeps nudging at the past to step aside, walking through the streets of the French Quarter is like visiting a historical restoration. A blacksmith stoking his bellows or shoeing a horse would scarcely raise an eyebrow. That is not to say you won't stumble upon the odd fast food trap and of course, **Bourbon Street** after sundown is as sedate as a Shriner's convention. Still, the French Quarter is a place to clear your mind of accustomed caveats and give yourself over to the pleasures it will lay before you.

Comfortably commingled with shops and restaurants are superb mansions with sweeping inner stone courtyards. Smaller brick or pastel frame houses festooned with filigreed wrought-iron balconies line the narrow streets. Most of these small luxurious houses have lush hidden gardens with gently flowing fountains. The rooftops with their sloping slate tiles and chimneys form an 18th century outline against a 20th century sky.

The consensus of opinion is that morning is the best time of day to explore the Quarter. The tourist buses have yet to disgorge their daily quotas of polyester pilgrims to clog the narrow streets. The coffee houses are filled with fresh croissants, brioche and most of the locals. This is not a place to spring from your bed and meet the day head on. First, the flowers that cascade from most balconies have to be watered, no matter how much they dampen the unprepared strollers below. Then, on to a favorite cafe or coffee house for a heady cup of chicory-laced coffee colored to a rich caramel by a steaming stream of milk. Next, perhaps a warm crisp beignet smothered in confectioner's sugar and a look at the top story in the *Times-Picayune*, the newspaper of record in New Orleans. By that time one might almost be ready to venture out into the rest of the town. No one actually admits to working in the French Quarter. After all, isn't it the place that makes up for having to suffer the indignity of work. Best of all, not only is it the center of a New Orleanian's universe, it's the official place to party.

Jackson Square is ground zero for the French Quarter. Everything radiates out from the square. **St. Louis Cathedral**, the oldest cathedral in the United States watches over it in elegant splendor (see Sights page 20). Not really a square but more of a rectangle it is enclosed by an iron fence sometimes used to display the work of painters who set up their easels at dawn and remain for the whole day. On either side of the Cathedral stands the **Cabildo** with its graceful stone arches and the **Presbytére**, which started out as a monastery and today after being rebuilt, houses the collections of the **Louisiana State Museum**. Aside from the sidewalk cafes that spill out onto the square there is an ongoing, almost medieval, mix of street entertainment: jugglers, mimes, dancers, rap artists, jazz combos, tarot card readers and off to the side, the Lucky Dog vendor. With a cart shaped like a mobile hot dog, he's a symbolic reminder of how you should feel just being a part of all this infectious pandemonium.

The rest of the **French Quarter** can be covered in about a day, that is, if you don't stop to really experience it. That would be a huge mistake. The Quarter has to be inhaled and savored like fine old cognac. It has to be roamed and explored. My favorite time to walk through the **Vieux Carré** is at sunset when it starts to shake off the constraint of daylight and it embraces the evening with a giddy expectation. It's best to ease into the rhythm of the nightly "celebration" to come. First a ringside table at the **Cafe Du Monde**. Perhaps a bite of beignet to tide you over to your sumptuous Creole feast to come. Then, sit back and watch the world of the **French Quarter** go by. What better time to kick back with the rest of the crowd and let the good times roll.

The Three Top Sights

Mardi Gras

"Throw me Sumpin, Mista!"

There are two distinct ways to approach **Mardi Gras** in New Orleans. One is to make sure your visit is scheduled for any other time of the year and that you are nowhere near the city during this, the most beloved of the endless celebrations in the **Big Easy**. The other is to buy a mask, pack lots of confetti and join in the Mardi Gras madness. To celebrate Carnival in New Orleans is to become an instant part of its history. After all, Mardi Gras is the most legendary event New Orleans has to offer.

Mardi Gras is New Orleans' event of the year.

Fat Tuesday, which is the translation of the French, *mardi gras*, is the climax of the entire Carnival season which traditionally begins on January 6, also known as **Three Kings Day**. It continues in a dizzying round of parties, performances and galas culminating with the Tuesday dawn to midnight extravaganza called Mardi Gras. At the stroke of midnight New Orleans turns back into a predominantly Christian community with the solemn season of Lent before it. What a difference a day makes.

The actual date of **Mardi Gras** varies on the calendar since it's calculated to be 41 days before Easter, which falls on a different day each year. It can occur as early as February or as late as March, so if that's when you're planning to visit you must consult a calendar well before making your arrangements.

AGENDA CRYSTAL BALL

Mardi Gras will take place in

1998	**February 24**
1999	**February 16**
2000	**March 7**

Mystery and secrecy are the best words to describe the origins of Carnival when the French settlers first introduced it to Louisiana. Even the CIA would have been impressed by the masked anonymity of the revelers who in the early 1800s danced through the town illuminated only by blazing torches. The medieval flavor of Carnival gave it a mythic quality that elated the early settlers. When the King of Spain became ruler of New Orleans he had a somewhat more circumspect approach to Catholicism and was horrified by the openly orgiastic celebrations going on the very day before Ash Wednesday, the beginning of Lent. The Spanish monarchy were never noted for being "party animals" so Fat Tuesday was put on a crash diet using healthy portions of contrition. Even the Americans, who finally took control of New Orleans had limited patience with the Creole merriment run amuck, so they continued Spain's ban on masks and costumes until 1827. Little by little the Yankee party poopers relented and masquerading was no longer confined to wolves in sheep clothing; it was legal once more to wear a disguise during Mardi Gras.

Now all that was left was to establish a framework on which to hang this glittering ritual and give it not only mysticism but dignity, respectability and character. Enter the secret societies called the Krewes. Far from being "motley," they were groups that were formed for the benefit of the privileged members of the community. They joined together to march through the streets masking their identities with grand and often bizarre costumes. In the evening they would top off the celebration with a splendid but very exclusive Ball. Only the members and their guests were invited. The very secrecy of the groups permitted them to practice discrimination against religions and ethnic minorities while clothing it with an enigmatic charisma. Sadly, even today, though not many will admit to it, there are still Krewes who manage to keep their ranks closed to certain elements of society.

The **Mystic Krewe of COMUS** was the first to start the tradition of a formal parade in 1856 with theatrical tableaux taking place on floats dragged by horses. They were followed by Rex, a Krewe made up of the business elite in town who decided that for the first time they would parade during the day as a tribute to visiting Russian royalty. The Grand Duke Alexis Romanoff was in town to continue his flaming affair with the musical comedy darling of the stage, Lydia Thompson. Suddenly one of the Rs in Mardi Gras stood for romance.

The city was delighted to be part of this heady drama which could have been called "As the Kremlin Turns." They decided to welcome the Duke by making his favorite song (a tune his lady love made famous) "If Ever I Cease to Love You," the official anthem of Mardi

Gras. Not only that, the Romanoff household colors, green, purple and gold became the recognized colors of Carnival and continue even today. What happened to the Duke and his royal tootsie, you might ask? Well, there was no "Lydia Thompson" ever embroidered on the towels in the Winter Palace.

The city goes all out to make every Mardi Gras float memorable.

The **Parade of Rex** is New Orleans' most extravagant spectacle on Mardi Gras day. It is the central event in all of the festivities and the notable person chosen to be King of Rex is the King of Carnival. There are over 130 Krewes who mount smaller parades and march in different parts of the city. One of the more riotous aspects in this technicolored fantasma is the appearance of the Mardi Gras Indians, marching and singing clubs, usually made up of African Americans. They are known as "tribes." Not only do they add outrageous costumes and headdresses costing thousands of dollars but their rhythms galvanize the already delirious crowds.

What started out as a small, exclusive and hedonistic secret shared by a privileged few is now known all over the world. Millions come to watch, if not participate as New Orleans "loses its mind" once a year. The celebrations that go on in the French Quarter are known for their erotic flavor and their decidedly "lavender" tinge. Transvestites dressed in the most creative and extravagant outfits troop through the Quarter dazzling the crowds. The **Vieux Carré** is known for taking the "Carnal" in Carnival very seriously.

No matter which parade you're watching you probably won't leave empty-handed. The custom is for the masked float riders to throw the begging crowds treasures from their lofty heights. The most common "throws" are bright colored strands of beads or pearls, faux doubloons with the emblem of the Krewes, plastic go cups or panties. Over the years women have become increasingly blatant—flashing their breasts to catch the eye of the throwers. A more modest alternative is to chant the phrase **"Throw me Sumptin Mista"** which dates back to the very first Mardi Gras parades.

The day ends in a sea of confetti, trash, empty liquor bottles and upset stomachs. Everyone staggers home, not to collapse into bed but into their finest evening attire including ball gowns that cost more than the budget of an emerging African nation. No one seems to have heard that song, "The Party's Over" in New Orleans!

(See Mardi Gras Agenda page 204)

Bourbon Street is synonymous with New Orleans jazz.

Bourbon Street

Perhaps too brassy and boisterous, perhaps too honky tonk and down at the heels, it is however, the street that is synonymous with music in New Orleans. It is **Bourbon Street**. And it is still the proving ground for the young jazz musicians of today. Never mind that the tee shirt shops outnumber the blues clubs 10 to one, never mind that sophomoric sightseers careen from side to side spilling margaritas as they go, giving the street its semi-seedy reputation. On **Bourbon Street**, life is still a Cabaret.

The part of **Bourbon Street** that is most famous only runs for about 10 blocks. Despite its name, beer is what you'll probably smell wafting out of the clubs and strip joints that line the street. On both sides of Bourbon there is a raucous mix of blues clubs, jazz joints, cabarets, Cajun dance halls and of course the unavoidable souvenir shops. Here and there you'll find a restaurant that serves the low end of New Orleans specialties but for the most part **Bourbon Street** is for feeding the spirit not the body.

The two most famous landmarks on the street are **Lafitte's Blacksmith Shop** at 941 and the **Absinthe House** at 400. Of the two, Lafitte's is the most historic and dates back to 1772 (see Bars, page 178) The story goes that the superstar pirate, Jean Lafitte, used it as a front to "launder" all his ill-gotten treasure before setting sail again on the *H.M.S. Cutthroat.* Today the weapon of choice here is the Hurricane, a drink that could have blasted Lafitte right out of the water! **Absinthe House** was yet another port in Lafitte's stormy existence. He must have tired of his Blacksmith hideout and in 1805 switched his base of operation to this more sophisticated boîte. Today it's just a creaky place full of atmosphere. Its wallpaper is made up of business cards that cover the place from floor to ceiling. They belong to the generations of "good ole boys" who stopped for a jolt.

Jackson Square

The Baroness Micaela Pontalba's flamboyant life is surely the stuff Movies of the Week are made of. Fabulously wealthy in her own right she married the Duke who just happened to own the choicest real estate parcels in New Orleans. She was not particularly a favorite with her father-in-law who shot her four times in the chest, but failed to kill her. The baroness overcame that annoying but painful experience and went on to put her luxurious stamp on what would become **Jackson Square**, the epicenter of the French Quarter. She "out trumped" Donald by building a group of splendid apartment houses on opposite sides of what was then the Place d'Armes. The Baroness' apartments were as lavish and extraordinary as the woman herself. The balconies gave the residences an even more opulent and exotic look. **The Pontalba Apartments** are still the most valuable real estate in town. Getting a lease on one of its fabled flats is like trying to rent the Oval Office.

The square is filled day and night with people on their way through the **French Quarter** so it is a magnet for street entertainment and razma-taz festivities that give the plaza a European flavor. Old fashioned carriages with drivers only too happy to give you a "tour de Horse" are lined up on the other side of the fence. When night falls and the square is lit by the gas lamps that flicker around its edges, it takes on a particular beauty that makes time stand still.

The 20 Next Best

The Cabildo contains numerous documents and artifacts detailing New Orleans' history.

Cabildo

701 Chartres Street (Jackson Square), ☎ (504) 568-6968.
Tues.–Sun., 10 a.m.–5 p.m. Admission $4 adults, children free.

Not originally meant to be the name of a building, **Cabildo** was the Spanish name for the city council who met there when Spain controlled New Orleans. The stately mediterranean inspired structure has overtones of Renaissance design carried out in its handsome arches which form a covered walkway on **Jackson Square**. All through its history it has been the scene of dramatic events both glorious and infamous. Aside from being the seat of the city council, it was one of the main venues for the slave auctions that were held in New Orleans regularly. However it is best remembered for the signing of the Louisiana Purchase agreement which took place there in 1803. The final transfer of Louisiana to the United States was in a second floor salon overlooking the Square. You could say the Cabildo was the most exclusive store in the world with an entire territory to be signed, sealed and gift-wrapped.

In 1988 the **Cabildo** was almost destroyed by a fire that raged through the upper floors, collapsing the roof. It has since been completely restored. Today it houses among its vast collection, artifacts about the history of New Orleans, as well as a death mask of Napoleon, one of three in existence (the other two are in France). The **Louisiana State Museum** oversees the Cabildo today.

Presbytére

751 Chartres Street, ☎ (504) 568-6968.

Tues.–Sun., 10 a.m.–5 p.m. Admission $4 adults, children free.

The sister structure to the Cabildo, the **Presbytére** was originally built to house the priests of **St. Louis Cathedral** right next door. Before it was ever finished most of it was destroyed by fire. Finally, after the **Louisiana Purchase**, the Americans completed it with great care so that it matched the Spanish Colonial grandeur of the **Cabildo**. Through the years it has been used for various civic purposes until it was finally added to the **Louisiana State Museum** System. It now houses a wonderful collection of decorative arts as well as exhibits on the maritime history of New Orleans and the cultural development of the city.

St. Louis Cathedral

It's the showplace of **Jackson Square**, overlooking the French Quarter and all of the entertainment and gaiety that goes on beneath its gothic spires. It was originally built in 1722 but one of the many fires that seemed to be epidemic in New Orleans razed it to the ground. It was rebuilt in 1794 but J.N.B. de Pouilly remodeled the original design and enlarged it in 1845. Its cool interior is not only beautiful but is a wonderful respite from the hot, sticky chaos of the square outside.

The Cathedral Gardens or their more formal name, **St. Anthony's Gardens**, is a lovely spot behind the church. Standing under the peaceful old shade trees it's hard to believe that this was a favorite dueling spot in the early days of the city. At the side of the Cathedral gardens is one of the tiniest tourist meccas in the city, Pirate's Alley. The story goes that Andrew Jackson himself planned the Battle of New Orleans with someone who just happened to be wearing a gold earring. Good thing Andrew never lived to see the day when most of the male population could be mistaken for Lafitte himself. William Faulkner had a flat at *624 Pirate's Alley* (is that a great address or what?). Today it's **Faulkner House Books**.

The French Market features everything from produce to flea market kitsch.

French Market

Despite sounding like a supermarket in an upscale neighborhood, the historic **French Market**, in the Quarter, was the very beginning of New Orleans' incomparable "food scene." Located at the edge of the **Mississippi** along **Decatur street**, it is a mecca for visitors who love its shops, restaurants, and most of all the **Cafe Du Monde** where its world-famous beignets and café au Lait are synonymous with the social life of the French Quarter.

The **French Market** that exists today is a far cry from the primitive open marketplace used to house the produce that was transported by boat up the river. Originally it was nothing more than the local "7-11" for the Indians who were here long before the French and the Spanish. Once the new arrivals decided they needed a central place to buy produce, they expanded the area. But it wasn't until 1975 that the French Market was gentrified to a fare-thee-well. Today a large section is devoted to a complex of mall stores with eminently forgettable merchandise. At the far end there is a flea market, filled with 24 carat kitsch which leads to a very colorful, if somewhat limited, produce market, with a place for fruit, flowers and stalls devoted to Cajun spices and cookbooks. If you're expecting something like the old Les Halles of Paris you're apt to be disappointed. But if you're up for a little local color and a jazz band or two, the **French Market** is a fast afternoon of fun.

Louisiana Superdome

1500 Poydras Street, ☎ *(504) 587-3810.*
10 a.m.–4 p.m., daily. Admission $6 adults, $4 children.
100,000 (count um) people can cheer their team in this stadium that's just a bit smaller than the state as a whole. The sheer area of the place would bring tears to the eyes of Nero. It's the New Orleans answer to the Colosseum, squared. The enclosed roof brings the height of this mega-stadium to 27 stories and its area covers more than 52 acres. Since it cost over $180 million to build back in 1975, you can bet the city uses it for more than the occasional cat show and ice-skating exhibition. Among other things it's home of the New Orleans Saints football team and if you know who's buried in Grant's Tomb you can figure out where the **Sugar Bowl** is held every year on New Year's Day.

AGENDA FORGETTABLE FACTS AT A GLANCE:

THE SUPERDOME

52 Acres in Total Area

27 Stories in Height

166,000 Square feet of Playing Field

100,000 Seat Capacity

20,000 Tons of Steel Supports

5000 Car Garage

8 Acres of Actual Dome

$180 Million (or so) to Build!!!

Resembling an aluminum flying saucer that has just landed, the big S is more versatile than it looks. Since few events require its total space, the dome can be sectioned off to make more intimate areas of twenty or thirty acres for conventions, Mardi Gras balls, or a Rolling Stones concert.

While I almost never suggest visiting empty arenas for the thrill of imagining what they might look like full (almost as diverting as singing 99 Bottles of Beer), the staggering size of this monumental multipurpose monster should be seen even without its possible 100,000 cheering fans. There are tours of the Dome daily.

St. Charles Avenue Streetcar

Perhaps it doesn't have the recognition factor of that "Streetcar Named Desire" but the **St. Charles Trolley** is one of the loveliest ways to cover the route through the **Garden District**. If Judy Garland were still around, even she would be charmed by this historically listed trolley, a true New Orleans treasure. It dates back to 1850. Not anything like the touristy trams that are sometimes used to cart visitors to sightseeing venues, this is a working streetcar that runs (often S.R.O.) from the **Central Business District**, through the elegant **Garden District** with its stately homes, past **Tulane** and **Loyola universities**, up to **Riverhead** and **Carrollton**. The fare is one of the biggest bargains in the city at only $1. You can use bills (unlike some cranky cities like New York) and it is in operation round the clock. Visitors should use caution late at night while waiting at the car stops because streetcars are few and far between after midnight.

The most convenient boarding stop for the trolley is at **Canal** and **Carondelet Streets** almost the beginning of its run. When you come to the **Garden District** you can hop off, do a bit of exploring and catch another car to continue up the Avenue. The whole 14 mile trip takes about 90 minutes and even if you choose not to get off it's a wonderful way to watch New Orleans pass by.

Audubon Zoo

6500 Magazine Street. ☎ *(504) 861-2538.*
Mon.–Fri., 9 a.m.–4:30 p.m.; Sat.–Sun., 9 a.m.–5:30 p.m. Admission $8 adults, $4 children.

What a surprise! A wonderfully designed, animal friendly, and totally charming zoo in a place known for the creative cooking of its animal population, not the naturalistic presentation of them alive. Well, the **Audubon Zoo**, with more than 1800 animals, is one of the most delightful experiences in New Orleans. Complete with live oak trees covered in spanish moss, the zoo brings the bayou right to the city with its six+ acres of swamp. Enlarged and modernized in the '80s, it is a totally unique exhibit to highlight Louisiana's special terrain. It is also the home of New Orleans' snowy-white albino alligator family. Even though they look stylish enough to have handles and hardware, they are as snappish as their ooze-green relatives. The zoo designers have constructed a network of raised wooden walks to let you get up close and personal with these swamp cuties. There are other denizens of the damp such as snakes and turtles and other creepy crawlies. Back on dry land the environmentally correct habitats of the zoo residents are among the most naturalistic settings for animals found anywhere around the country. One of the best ways to get to the Audubon Zoo is aboard the **James John Audubon Riverboat**. It leaves at various times from the **River View Dock** opposite the Aquarium of the Americas. The overland route is by the bus that runs along **Magazine Street**. Its last stop is the zoo.

Aquarium of the Americas

1 Canal Street (at the River). ☎ *504) 861-2537.*
9:30 a.m.–7 p.m., daily. Admission $11 adults, $6 children.
Water, water everywhere and definitely not a drop to drink but oh, so much to see. Run by the **Audubon Institute** which also is responsible for the marvelous Audubon Zoo, the Aquarium is located opposite even more water, the **Mississippi**. Sea creatures have rarely been exhibited in a more imaginative display. The Marine life of the Caribbean, the Gulf of Mexico, the Amazon Rain Forest and the Mississippi delta itself are on display in amazingly realistic settings. **The Aquarium** is considered one of the five best in the country.

For a real deep sea adventure walk through the 30 foot long see-through acrylic tunnel in the Caribbean exhibit. Fish to the right, to the left and on top makes you feel as if you are snorkeling with your clothes on. The steamy rain forest has waterfalls, tropical birds and exotic flowers as a backdrop for those darlings of the Amazon, the piranhas, who are known to like their steaks really rare. You'll also find a dazzlingly white (they confessed to me that they scrub them down) pair of albino alligators in their **Mississippi Delta Swamp** exhibit.

Royal Street

From one end to the other **Royal** typifies the quintessential shopping street in New Orleans, and even today echoes the antebellum gaiety of the city. But it begins to change character as you walk deeper into the quarter, becoming more serious in quality. Finally toward the end of Royal, antique stores appear that are visited by major collectors from around the country. 17th, 18th, and 19th century antiques, both local and European, are among the most coveted. The more casual part of **Royal Street** which begins at **Canal** is lighter in focus and more buoyant. Souvenir shops vie for space with some of the more contemporary collections of fine furniture, jewelry and of course the legendary **"Brennans,"** breakfast central in New Orleans. As **Royal Street** intersects with **Dumaine**, the **Miltenberger Houses** with their extraordinary iron balconies take you back to the days when the huge fortunes that were made in this port city were spent, one way or the other on **Royal Street**.

Old U. S. Mint

400 Esplanade Avenue.
Tues.–Sun., 9 a.m.–5 p.m. Admission $4 adults, children free.
A better name for this rather architecturally austere, imposing museum would be the "Jazzy" Old U.S. Mint. Not only does it house the memorabilia of the Mint itself but it also houses the **New Orleans Jazz collection** and **Mardi Gras Museum** all under the umbrella of the Louisiana State Museum. That's really putting your money where your mouth is! The Mint itself operated from 1835 to 1909 with a

brief interruption by that dust-up called the Civil War. During the war Confederate troops were locked away in the Mint while the Union soldiers occupied the town.

Today there is very little to remind anyone that the building was used to mint coins for New Orleans. There is only a penny-ante display of coins, but the wonderful jazz collection is money in the bank. There are exhibits about the beginnings of the jazz form, the big band era and even a special room devoted to ragtime. Of course The Mint's most precious of treasures is Louis Armstrong's cornet (trumpet in the old days). Not to be missed is **The Women in Jazz**, displaying pictures of the ladies who sang the blues.

The third and perhaps most entertaining collection under the same roof is the **Mardi Gras Museum** bursting with spangles and memorabilia right down to a scale model of a **French Quarter** street the morning after.

Loyola/Tulane Universities

From the window of the **St. Charles Avenue Streetcar** the Gothic architecture of **Loyola University** makes this a favorite stop for visitors to New Orleans. Actually, it is an embarrassment of rich academic life since **Loyola** is right opposite **Tulane University** which predates Loyola by about 20 years. Unlike its Gothic neighbor, **Tulane** is Roman in style with heroic stone buildings covering its campus.

Loyola was originally started by a small group of Jesuit priests as the College of the Immaculate Conception in downtown New Orleans. When they needed more space they moved up to what was to become **Audubon Park**. The original 69 students, back in 1912, has grown to over 5000 and today it is the largest Catholic university in the south.

Tulane was started by a mere $1 million donation from a New Jersey dentist (go figure). It's made up of 11,000 students, not all of whom play football, and a faculty boasting dozens of Rhodes Scholars. **Tulane** has acquired, over the years the reputation of being "The Harvard of the South."

World Trade Center of New Orleans

A panoramic view of the city spread out before you from the 31st floor observation deck of the Center. Not only is it a chance to see the busy harbor but on a clear day you may not see forever but you can see the **Mississippi** make the bend that gave New Orleans its other most popular nickname (**Big Easy** still wins the day) **The Crescent City**. There are few places to view the city from on high and the sight from the **Trade Center** is really quite breathtaking. The same view but this time seen over the rim of a Martini glass can be had a couple of floors above at Viewpoint, the obligatory revolving cocktail lounge no city should be without.

The Trade Center, despite it's global sounding title is mainly used to house foreign consulates and agencies.

Beauregard-Keyes House, built in 1926, has been restored to all its former grandeur.

Beauregard-Keyes House

1113 Chartres Street, ☎ (504) 523-7257.
Mon.–Sat., 10 a.m.–3 p.m. Admission $4 adults, $1.50 children.

Not only did she have dinner at Antoine's but Frances Parkinson Keyes wrote the famous novel of the same name while she was living in the gorgeous Beauregard-Keyes House. In her spare time she managed to restore the mansion to its former magnificence when she lived there during the 40s. The stately columned house was built in 1826 to be the showplace of its time, by the city's most famous auctioneer Joseph Le Carpentier. During the Civil War it was the temporary residence for General V.G.T. Beauregard.

The house is a true turn-of-the-century beauty with an interior courtyard filled with brilliant flowers and a huge live oak tree. Inside, a tour of the house is highlighted by Keyes' antique doll collection and nearly life-size Victorian dollhouse. If you're fortunate enough to visit during the Christmas season and have children with you, they are invited to bring their own dolls to a splendid holiday tea party. Adults who show up without children are looked upon with suspicion.

The New Orleans Museum of Art contains 46 galleries.

New Orleans Museum of Art

1 Collins Diboll Circle (Lelong Avenue). ☎ *488-2631.*
Tues.–Sun., 10 a.m.–5 p.m. Admission $6 adults, $3 children.
Its benefactor, Isaac Delgado, wealthy merchant, envisioned it as a
neoclassical "temple for rich and poor alike" when he donated
$150,000 to create it, but today **NOMA** has nearly tripled the size of
the original Beaux Arts building with three new additions and a $23
million renovation. It was named after its generous benefactor when
it was erected in 1910 and remained the Isaac Delgado Museum of
Art until its expansion in 1970 when trustees voted to rename their
new world-class institution **The New Orleans Museum of Art**.

The 46 galleries of the museum are spread out over three floors and
contain some 35,000 works valued at a "cool" $200 million. There
are also additional floating galleries for rotating exhibits. Some of the
highlights are an outstanding collection of decorative arts including
the history of glassmaking from the time of the ancient Egyptians.
The French heritage of New Orleans is highlighted with a superb display of 18th and 19th century furniture including the re-creation of
both a Louisiana bedchamber and a Federal parlor. Another outstanding offering is the Art of the Americas collection. Both Asian and
Oceanic Arts are well represented along with European painters of the
13th through 18th centuries. One of the newest and most fascinating
of the galleries is devoted to the museum's exquisite collection of the
works of Peter Carl Faberge, jeweler to the Russian Royal family.

NOMA sits in sparkling white splendor amid the green meadows of
City Park. A romantic tree-lined avenue is the approach from within
the park so that a visit is not only a cultural enrichment, but has the
added bonus of feeling like a day in the country.

Magazine Street

It's called the "street of dreams" and within the length of its six miles,
running from **Canal Street** up to **Audubon Park**, it is packed with

more antique shops, restaurants, crafts galleries, and treasures than most high-profile pirates ever saw in their lifetimes. **Magazine Street** is so addictive they may just have to come up with a twelve step program for "Magazine-aholics." I myself fought as hard as I could to withstand its insidious undertow but I was powerless against the lure of store upon store with everything from trendy trash to museum-quality acquisitions.

Magazine Street got its name not from a periodical but from the arsenal that was once located on the stretch of **Magazine** nearest to **Canal Street**. It ambles along with shops bunched together between residential areas. Since it runs for miles the best way to do it is in sections. Just board the **Magazine Street** bus which runs its length and ends at the zoo. Trying to incorporate both at one shot is myopic madness. What the bus does afford is the chance to hop off when the shopping looks the "hottest." There are some great holes-in-the-walls for a quick po-boy sandwich along the way. (See Garden District, page 89.) Since there are sometimes stretches of questionable residential areas be cautious. When the stores thin out, get back on the bus until you see the next clutch of shops.

AGENDA PRIORITIES

Honey Island Swamp

What better way to understand the beginnings of New Orleans than to explore what its first settlers found when they arrived from France. No sidewalk cafés, not a Chanel boutique in sight, just lots of primeval ooze and a reptile community capable of having supplied shoes and handbags to the entire French court. However, today we like to think we live in a kinder, gentler world, but that shouldn't discourage us from invading the bucolic space of these mega-monsters for a quick look-see. It's a short drive to the **Honey Island Swamp** (there are others but this is one of the closest to the city (see tours page 197) or you can be picked up by one of the gazillion tour operators who ply these murky waters. By no means attempt to solo in the swamp. The very beauty of it is its timeless, mysterious and potentially dangerous terrain. The creepy-crawlies who have much more right to be there are best seen as your boat glides by. You can take a half day tour and cover just enough of the 70,000 acres of protected wildlife to see what a pristine paradise it is. There is nothing that compares with watching a nine foot gator swim gracefully up to the boat to get a better look at his day's "entertainment." The swamp is also a place to see bald eagles, herons, egrets, and if you're extremely lucky, snakes, who manage to sleep a great deal.

AGENDA ALLIGATOR CONFIDENTIAL

If you are ever in a tight situation with one of those toothy tootsies you have only to reach into a bag of marshmallows and float one out upon the water. The Big Green One will glide over and daintily down it with great aplomb. An alligator's favorite treat is a snowy-white marshmallow (for God's sake don't toast it!).

Old Ursuline Convent

1114 Chartres Street. ☎ *(504) 529-3040.*

Tours at varied hours. Admission $4 adults, $2 children.
The old in its name is to be taken very seriously. It is not only the oldest building in New Orleans but in the whole of the Mississippi valley as well. Built in 1745, it was a home for the Sisters of St. Ursula who came to New Orleans in 1727 to serve as nurses and teachers for the French colony. The structure itself is the only building left that characterizes Creole architecture. It looks "governmentally" Caribbean in design. Most of the children of the wealthy were educated by the sisters, but it was also the first school to educate African Americans as well as Native Americans. A church was added in 1845 which still continues to hold services. The Convent has, over the years, served as a refuge for the people of the city. They gathered there the night before the fierce **Battle of New Orleans** in 1815. To this day it is believed that the prayers said that evening miraculously saved the city.

Bayou St. John

Pilot House, 1440 Moss Street, ☎ (504) 482-0312.
Can anyone call a trip to New Orleans a success without actually seeing a real live bayou? **Bayou St. John** is the last one existing in the city today. As the song goes "son of a gun, we'll have great fun on the Bayou." Actually the word bayou comes from the Indian and means small creek or stream. **Bayou St. John** which was considerably larger than a stream was the way small boats originally made their way to New Orleans loaded with freight from the steamboats traveling on **Lake Pontchartrain**. It sounds romantic enough to be located miles from the city, but in truth all you have to do is follow **Esplanade Avenue** all the way, past **St. Louis Cemetery** #3 to **Moss Street** which runs alongside the Bayou. Some of the most beautiful houses in New Orleans line the banks of the waterway and today small pleasure boats have taken the place of the ships bringing supplies to the city. One of the most prized reminders of New Orleans' glittering society is the **Pilot House**, home of James Pilot, the first real mayor of New Orleans. The house, built in 1799 is done in the style of a West Indies plantation and has been restored to make it an enthralling place to walk through. It's possible to follow Bayou St. John all the way to Lake Pontchartrain where you'll find some fine restaurants, picnic areas and weather permitting, swimming. It's about five miles out to the lake so you'll have to drive or call a cab.

Preservation Hall

726 St. Peter Street, ☎ (504) 522-2841.
8 p.m.–midnight. Admission cover $3.
726 St. Peter Street is the most hallowed center of jazz anywhere in the world. No jazz musician worth his mouthpiece hasn't at one time played there or longed to play there. It's filled with rock-hard benches that force you to sit up straight and devote yourself to the greats and the near-greats who have come to entertain both you and themselves. The Hall was opened in 1961 but by now it's an institution that has given birth to its own legends. No food or liquor is sold, although you can get a drink from one of the bars on the street and sip it while you listen, but you'd better do it before the doors open. If you don't line up at least 30 to 45 minutes before the 8 p.m. opening, you won't even be able to get a seat on one of their torturous benches.

Don't expect fancy light shows or flashy costumes. This should be regarded as a pilgrimage to the altar of real New Orleans jazz!

New Orleans' aboveground cemeteries are architectural wonders.

Cities of the Dead

No, I'm not referring to those enormous monuments the Ancient Egyptians built to house their egomaniacal rulers, I'm talking about the cemetery scene in New Orleans. Someone once said that the best architecture to be found in New Orleans is in its burial grounds. They were not exaggerating.

Because the city is below sea level the phrase "Dead and Buried" really meant that you might be dead but you couldn't actually be counted upon to stay buried. Coffins that were soundly entombed could be seen a short time later floating down the street after a heavy rain. This made mourning a full-time occupation. The only way to insure that the dear departed really did so was to start the custom of aboveground burial. Though they began as simple stone containers no bigger than a tiny dollhouse, in time the tombs became more and more elaborate until the design and carving on some of them were true works of art. They grew in size as well with the more imposing structures resembling mini-temples. Some come complete with stained glass, some with intricately fashioned wrought iron gates. One of the most famous of the tombs has the statue of a dog lying outside the entrance, waiting through all eternity for his master.

There are more than 42 cemeteries within New Orleans but the ones most visited and by far the most fabulous are **St. Louis Number I**, **Number II** and even though it's more modern, **St. Louis Number III**. Number I is right in the **French Quarter** and has the most eerie flavor. The tombs here go back to the 1700s and even though most are over-grown and quite dilapidated they have a strange dignity. Because of their age they tend to be smaller and seem to suggest a tiny city of tiny unseen people. To add even more atmosphere, Marie Laveau, the infamous voodoo priestess, is buried here. Her tomb is covered with voodoo symbols, messages and charms. She may still be carrying on business as usual from the great Beyond.

The other cemeteries are even more ornate and dramatic. They could almost be classified as outdoor museums. They are to be seen no matter how brief your visit to New Orleans may be, but they are not to be seen alone. There is nothing to fear from the spirit world, it's the real world that's the problem. Unaccompanied visitors to the cemeteries have been the victims of muggings and worse, so use extreme caution and go in a group or on a tour.

HOTELS

Maison de Ville Hotel in the French Quarter exudes elegance.

Your Hotel

I am not, and never have been, a member of the "who cares where you stay—how much time do you spend in your room anyway?" club. If some of you, like me, are official collectors of hotels as treasured travel memorabilia, then that's one of the reasons I have avoided including some obvious members of the chain gangs, despite the security blankets with which they make their beds. A truly New Orleanian hotel is at least as quintessential a city experience as a good beignet.

Each of the hotels in this section have been stayed in, or at least visited and rooms inspected. I decided not to include a number of hotels for a variety of maddeningly idiosyncratic reasons ranging from too damn institutional, (**The New Wyndham River Front**, the **Inn on Bourbon street** (It's right on Bourbon Street for heavens sake), the **Monteleone** (Tour Bus Heaven) and on and on. Simply, there are too many great hotels in New Orleans to start out making compromises.

How to Select a Hotel

My choice is based upon three golden rules:

1. When it's time to rest my weary bones, I think my weary bones deserve the best my money can buy.

2. Location, location, location. Since the easiest way to get around the city is on foot, stop and think about the pleasures of being able to walk back to your hotel after a business meeting. It's a lot simpler than dealing with traffic. Try not to stay in the **Garden District** if you plan to go to **The French Quarter** on a daily basis. But no matter where you are, check out transport services, if any, offered by the hotel.

3. The least expensive room in the best hotel is usually better than the most expensive room in a moderate hotel. A good hotel buys you a good concierge, sophisticated business systems, and many extra services and facilities that may even wind up saving you money.

AGENDA TIP

Assuming you've made the perfect choice, you should still take a peek at some other hotels when you're in town. I usually hotel hop for drinks or breakfast. Who knows? The next time you plan a trip, your first choice may be booked solid.

How to Make a Reservation

First, unless your travel agent can do better than the listed or "rack" rate, get yourself another travel agent. Or call up yourself and ask about special deals and weekend or airline-sponsored packages. It's often possible to get a corporate rate just by asking for it. Many hotels cut rates by half on the weekend to fill rooms vacated by captains of industry. However, in New Orleans tourism keeps hotels full almost all the time with the exception of the unbearably hot summer when the best hotel deals are possible. If you're attending a conference, there may be a discount even if you make your own reservation. And sometimes, you can get a special rate just by a little discreet bargaining.

If all else fails, you may want to try a hotel consolidator. You'll have to forgo your wish list but you can sometimes get an astonishing bargain: **Room Exchange**, ☎ *(800) 846-7000*, **New Orleans Discount Hotel rates**, ☎ *(800) 964-6835*. Another terrific resource in New Orleans is the **Housing Bureau**, ☎ *(504) 566-5021*, as well as the **New Orleans Tourist and Convention Commission**, ☎ *(504) 566-5011*.

AGENDA CAVEAT

Do not use the hotel's 800 number. Call direct. 800 numbers will get you the rack rates only! When you call direct to the hotel you can inquire about special rates and any packages the hotel is promoting. The last thing you want to do is reach some telemarketing nerd in North Dakota who wouldn't know his arm from his armoire.

If you have preferences about type of bed, high floor vs. low floor, front views (noisy) or back (quiet), special views, not wanting to be near elevators or service areas, whatever—let them know when making your reservation.

If you ask at this time, it's a request. If you wait until after you've arrived, it's a complaint. And why start off by complaining if you don't have to.

Try to get your requests in writing, although that doesn't mean they've been guaranteed. Then call the front desk a couple of days before you arrive. Ask them to check your reservation for your special requests.

Be sure you've guaranteed your time of arrival. No hotel is obliged to hold a reservation past the appointed hour. Therefore, you'll have to book with a credit card or a deposit. That's the only way you can rest assured.

That is, if you can forget about hotel service charges, parking fees, and a whopping 11% plus $1–$3 per day room tax, an Orleans Parish tax which is automatically added no matter what rate you've been quoted.

Call or fax the concierge as soon as you know which restaurants, shows, or exhibits you want to visit. Explain clearly that you will express your gratitude upon arrival. Then call back to make certain it's all been done or whether you need some alternatives. The idea is to take care of this on home time, reserving precious travel time for travel.

Hotels

New Orleans is a city of festivals, celebrations, parades, monster sports events and some of the best food in the world. Now you may well ask, where do they put all the people who come to watch New Orleans as it revels in its endless calendar of events? Well, the truth is gentle reader, New Orleans is at the moment,

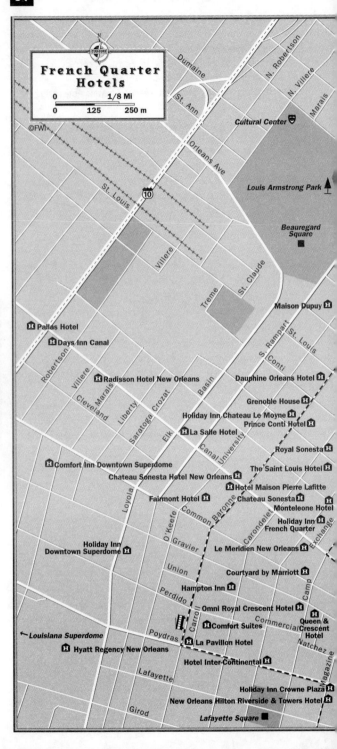

French Quarter Hotels

0   1/8 Mi
0   125   250 m

©FWI

Dumaine

N. Robertson

N. Villere

Marais

St. Ann

Orleans Ave

St. Louis

10

Cultural Center

Louis Armstrong Park

Beauregard Square

Villere

Treme

St. Claude

Maison Dupuy

Pallas Hotel

Days Inn Canal

S. Rampart

St. Louis

S. Conti

Robertson

Villere

Marais

Cleveland

Liberty

Saratoga

Crozat

Basin

Radisson Hotel New Orleans

Dauphine Orleans Hotel

Grenoble House

Holiday Inn Chateau Le Moyne

Prince Conti Hotel

Elk

La Salle Hotel

Canal

University

Royal Sonesta

Comfort Inn Downtown Superdome

The Saint Louis Hotel

Chateau Sonesta Hotel New Orleans

Hotel Maison Pierre Lafitte

Loyola

Common

Baronne

Chateau Sonesta

Monteleone Hotel

Fairmont Hotel

Carondelet

Holiday Inn French Quarter

O'Keefe

Gravier

Le Meridien New Orleans

Exchange

Holiday Inn Downtown Superdome

Union

Courtyard by Marriott

Camp

Perdido

Hampton Inn

←Louisiana Superdome

Carroll

Omni Royal Crescent Hotel

Commercial

Queen & Crescent Hotel

Comfort Suites

Poydras

La Pavillon Hotel

Natchez

Hyatt Regency New Orleans

Hotel Inter-Continental

Magazine

Lafayette

Holiday Inn Crowne Plaza

New Orleans Hilton Riverside & Towers Hotel

Girod

Lafayette Square

Rathbone Inn

Sun Oak

Empress Hotel
Charlene's Club & Guest House

Melrose Mansion Hotel

French Quarter
Courtyard Hotel

The Frenchman

Girod House

French Quarter
Suites

The Courtyards Guest House

La Maison
Guest House

N.O. Guest
House

Royal Barracks Guest House

Marigny Guest House

Sun and the
Moon B&B

LaMothe House

Landmark French
Quarter Hotel

P.J. Holbrook's Olde Victoria Inn

Hotel St. Pierre   Le Richelieu in the French Quarter

Lafitte Guest House

A Creole
House

Ursuline Guest House

French Quarter Guest House

Soniat House

Rue Royal Inn

Hotel Villa Convento

Nine-O-Five Royal Hotel

St. Peter's
Guest House

Bon Maison Guest House

Chateau Motor Hotel

The Cornstalk
Hotel

Hotel Provincial

Olivier House
Hotel

Bourbon Orleans Hotel

Rue Dumaine Guest House

Place d'Armes Hotel

Hotel St. Marie

Hotel Maison de Ville

Best Western Inn

Jackson Square Museum

Omni Royal Orleans Hotel

St. Ann-Marie Antoinette Hotel

Hotel St. Helene

Hotel de
la Poste

Napoleon House

Historic French Market Inn

Bieneville House Hotel

Mississippi River

Hotel Chateau Dupre
New Orleans Marriott Hotel

Westin Canal Place

Canal St. Ferry

ITT Sheraton New Orleans

Doubletree Hotel

Pelham Hotel

Windsor Court Hotel

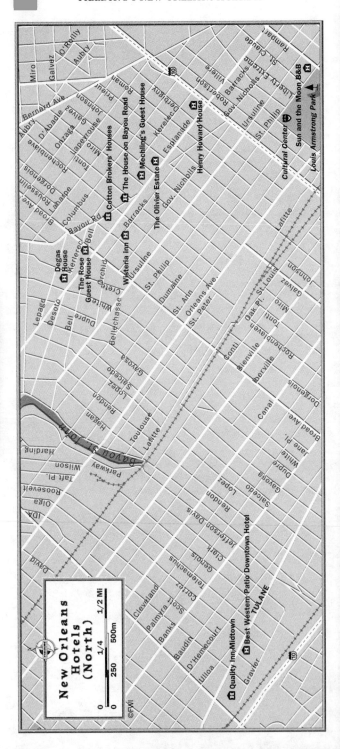

New Orleans
Hotels
(North)

HOTELS

New Orleans Hotels (South)

1/4 Mi   1/2 Mi
0   250   500 m

Mississippi River

CRESCENT CITY CONN.
GRTR—N.O. BRIDGE

Hotels

- Southern Nights B&B
- Hilton Riverside & Towers Hotel
- Lafayette Hotel
- YMCA Int'l Hotel
- Holiday Inn Select
- Holiday Inn Crown Plaza
- Hostelling Int'l Marquette
- Quality Inn Maison St. Charles
- Prytania Inns
- Fairchild House B&B
- St. Charles Guest House
- St. Vincent's Guest House
- McKendrick-Breaux House
- The Pontchartrain Hotel
- The Prytania Park Hotel
- Whitney Inn
- Avenue Plaza Hotel & Spa
- Garden District B&B
- Sully Mansion
- The Josephine Guest House
- La Maison à l'Avenue Jackson
- Marquette House New Orleans Int'l Hostel
- Ramada Plaza Hotel-St. Charles
- Ramada Inn St. Charles
- Columns Hotel
- Mandevilla B&B
- B&B As You Like It
- B&W Courtyards B&B
- Annabelle's House B&B
- Park View Guest House
- St. Charles Inn
- Audubon Park & Golf Course

hotel-poor. Not necessarily in quality but there are just not enough rooms to satisfy the clamor during **Jazz Fest**, **Super Bowl**, **Sugar Bowl** and of course **Mardi Gras**. In fact, during these peak times most hotels require reservations at least a year in advance and a minimum of a three to five night stay. Aside from the lack of accommodations, there is also a scarcity of hotels in the "world class" tradition. With the exception of a few marvelous choices in the Grand Hotel category, New Orleans is best represented by its charming jewellike townhouses or old mansion accommodations in the **French Quarter**.

New Orleans has tried its best to preserve the atmosphere of its past in everything but its prices. The "Paris" of the Gulf coast has tailored hotel rates to match those of its ancestors abroad. Luxury hotels have crept past the $200 mark and far more modest accommodations can still mean triple digits. To add insult to larceny, during **Super Bowl** or **Mardi Gras** even those substantial figures double. Mon Dieu! **Fat Tuesday** gets fatter every year.

There are few moderately priced hotels in New Orleans that you're apt to remember fondly. But they do exist, although the one's I've chosen are for the most part outside the "tres" expensive French Quarter. Really cheap hotels in New Orleans usually come equipped with hot and cold running roaches and certainly could never appear in any travel guide of mine.

If all else fails contact: **New Orleans Housing Bureau**, ☎ *(504) 566-5021;* **New Orleans Tourist and Convention Commission**, ☎ *(504) 566-5011.*

Top Agenda Hotel Choices

Major credit cards accepted unless otherwise stated.

The Grand Hotel Experience	
Fairmont	**$225–$350**
Intercontinental	**$225–$750**
New Orleans Hilton Riverside	**$225–$1870**
Omni Royal Orleans	**$185–$389**
Westin Canal Place	**$239–$329**
Windsor Court Hotel	**$235–$590**

The "Baby" Grands	
Lafayette	**$145–$450**
Omni Crescent	**$259–$450**
Le Pavilon	**$110–$395**
Palma	**$150–$375**
Pontchartrain	**$130–$260**

The Eccentrics

House on Bayou Road	$175–$270
Maison De Ville	$185–$425
Maison Dupuy	$175–$240
Melrose Mansion	$250–$375
Soniat House	$145–$235

The Suite Life

Comfort Suites	$114–$165
Embassy Suites	$189–$320

Budget Bests

Columns	$60–$150
Girod House	$135–$225
Le Richelieu	$95–$150
Loyola University	$20–$30
Oliver House	$120–$295
Tulane University	$50–$75
Y.M.C.A. International Hotel	$30–$45

HOTELS

Columns Hotel   **$60–$150**   ★ ★

3811 St. Charles Avenue, New Orleans, LA 70115; ☎ *(504) 899-9308.*
Why do the words kinky, punk, offbeat, eccentric, all seem to symbol-
ize the character of this very intriguing hotel? One of the reasons
could be that the great director, Louis Malle, thought the very same
thing when he chose **The Columns** as the site to shoot *Pretty Baby* a
film highlighting the decadence of turn-of-the-century New Orleans.

The heroic columns that adorn the front of the sweeping veranda are
how the mansion got its name back in 1883. The lobby is straight out
of a Tennessee Williams play with a staircase that any actress would
give her Tony to descend. Dark mahogany everywhere including the
rooms upstairs which may have seen better days but are still comfortable and sometimes even quite grand.

If you're looking for a Holiday Inn, pass the Columns by but if you're
in the mood for adventure on a budget, you've arrived! 19 rooms.
Credit Cards: All Major.

Fairmont Hotel   **$225–$350**   ★ ★

123 Baronne Street (at University Place) New Orleans, LA 70140;
☎ *(504) 529-7111, (800) 562-1003; FAX: (504) 529-4775.*
This New Orleans landmark celebrated its 100th anniversary a few
years ago and today the Fairmont, though a bit past its golden prime
is still going strong. Its colorful history as the Grand Hotel of New

Orleans made it the subject of Arthur Hailey's novel *Hotel*. Aside from that, eight U.S. Presidents have stayed beneath its gilded roof.

What becomes a legend most is a lobby with huge golden columns, even larger crystal chandeliers and an ornate ceiling inlaid with gold. The Fairmont's famous Sazerac Bar, home of its famous Sazerac cocktail (a lethal mix of rye whiskey and bitters in secret proportions) was also home to Huey Long whose meetings were as much of a secret as the proportions of the Sazerac.

The rooms, which number over 750, are wonderfully old-fashioned with high ceilings, armoires and rich draperies. The marble bathrooms are a joy and some of the suites have wonderful claw-footed free-standing tubs with elegant brass reading racks. The Fairmont's ongoing restoration is devoted to preserving its original classic charm. 750 rooms. Credit cards: All Major.

AGENDA TRIVIA TRIFLE

The word cocktail was born when an apothecary named Antoine Peychaud served his famous "medicinal" concoction of whiskey and bitters in an egg cup which in French is called une coquetier. For the customers who couldn't Parlez Francaise, after a few drinks it become cock-tail. And so, without that harmless slip of the tongue in 1870, none of us would have had to suffer through over 100 years of boring cocktail parties.

Girod House   **$135–$225**   ★

835 Esplanade Avenue, New Orleans, LA 70116; ☎ *(504) 522-5214; FAX (504) 522-7208.*

This all suite guest house is on the wide, tree-lined **Esplanade Avenue**, perhaps not in the center of the French Quarter but near enough to walk over and far enough to enjoy the peaceful neighborhood just a few blocks away.

The 1833 townhouse is a three story residence that owners, Francis and Rodney Smith, who also own the fabulous **Soniat House**, have divided into charming separate suites and one knockout duplex apartment. Breakfast goodies are provided so that you can prepare it in your very own kitchen. The rates at **Girod House** make it possible to have a splendid little apartment at the price you'd pay for a routine hotel room. 6 suites. Credit Cards: All Major.

Hotel Inter-Continental   **$225–$750**   ★★★

444 St. Charles Ave., New Orleans, LA 70130; ☎ *(504) 525-5566, (800) 327-0200; FAX: (504) 523-7310.*

Glass and granite both characterize the Inter-Continental and the business side of New Orleans. Located on **St. Charles Avenue**, the 20th century look of the hotel is highlighted by the 19th century trolley that clangs its way up the avenue below it.

The rooms themselves are deeply comfortable, contemporary, and roomy enough for an added semi-sitting room. There are extravagantly done suites on the Governor's floor which is the Inter-Continental's version of executive V.I.P. suites. They offer a private lounge, breakfast, and cocktails in the P.M. All those fun privileges come at a sobering price. 480 rooms. Credit Cards: All Major.

House On Bayou Road $175–$270   ★ ★ ★

2275 Bayou Road, New Orleans, LA 70119; ☎ (504) 945-0992; FAX: (504) 945-0993.
Something very special is going on out on **Bayou Road**. That may sound like the ends of the earth to anyone who wants to be surrounded by the **French Quarter** while they're in New Orleans. In truth **Bayou Road** is just a five minute cab ride from the Quarter to the edge of **Esplanade Avenue**, but in that short space of time you can have the opportunity to experience the delights of an exotic 18th century "petite plantation." If you are a collector of unique travel experiences you might want to explore this very special place.

Canopy beds, swagged draperies mixed with Louisiana Primitive furniture carry on the plantation style. Fresh flowers are everywhere. If you can tear yourself away from the luxury of your room there is a full plantation breakfast served in the dining room. Another perk is the resident cat who looks like the real owner to me. 4 rooms, 2 cottages. Credit Cards: All Major.

Lafayette Hotel $145–$450   ★ ★ ★

600 St. Charles Ave., New Orleans, LA 70130; ☎ (504) 524-4441, (800) 733-4754; FAX: (504) 523-7327.
A "Boutique Baby" with just the right amount of "petite luxe" to make it a perfect choice for someone who's looking for small and perfect. The Lafayette, having just gone through a stem to stern $6 million update is both. It's also only five blocks from the Superdome and within a beignet's throw of the **French Quarter**. The tiny lobby is more like the entrance to a townhouse than a hotel. There's no lounging around because your room is too lovely to want to leave. Some have floor to ceiling windows that open onto tiny balconies but all have exquisite details such as really good books on the shelves, first-rate botanicals on the walls and sybaritic marble baths with brass and mirror. The Lafayette is that "secret find" everyone wants for their little black hotel books. Try not to tell too many other people. 44 rooms. Credit Cards: All Major.

Le Pavillon $110–$395   ★ ★

833 Poydras Street, New Orleans, LA 70140; ☎ (504) 581-3111, (800) 535-9095; FAX: (504) 523-7434.
Once upon a time, the magnificent edifice of the Pavillon was the reason it was referred to as The Belle of New Orleans. There is simply no way to pass the sparkling white columned hotel with its turn-of-the-century appeal, even though today it's apt to be more frequented by lawyers in the area than the upscale visitors that crowded its lobby in the early 1900s. But that was then and this is the now of a super-glitzy renovation. However within all its new flash are touches of the past, such as the marble railing that was originally in the Grand Hotel in Paris. For my "Ripley Believe it or Not entry," the management serves milk and peanut butter and jelly sandwiches in the lobby at bedtime. Children can be seen under the heroic crystal chandeliers, in their P.Js, munching away. There's more to the Pavillon than meets the eye.

HOTELS

Upstairs the rooms are rather routine and though comfortable, nothing to worry the "Ritz." It's the suites which are so sumptuous and unique that "jaw dropping" is the order of the day here. One in particular, the "Antiques Suite" could have been furnished straight from Buckingham Palace. The suites are remarkably reasonable and if they happen to be vacant the management is open to negotiation. 226 rooms. Credit Cards: All Major.

Le Richelieu   **$95–$150**   ★★

1234 Chartres Street, New Orleans, LA 70116; ☎ (504) 529-2492 (800) 535-9653; FAX: (504) 524-8179.

One of the best choices in the **French Quarter** for a touch of class without "sticker-shock." There are 86 Victorian bedrooms done with great flair, each one with individual decor. Le Richelieu is a great favorite of "celebs" who are passing through and find the personal touch of owner Frank Rochefort irresistible. We certainly know that he can keep a secret, since Paul McCartney was ensconced in one of his yummy suites for two months while he was cutting an album. Paul is not one to mix and mingle around the pool.

The rooms, aside from being romantically Old World (some even with balconies), are right up to the moment in the things that really count such as small fridges and ceiling fans to cool off those sultry New Orleans breezes. 88 rooms. Credit Cards: All Major.

Maison De Ville   **$185–$425**   ★★★

727 Rue Toulouse, New Orleans, LA 70130; ☎ (504) 561-5858, (800) 634-1600; FAX: (504) 528-9939.

Toulouse Street is one of the loveliest in the **French Quarter**, and one of the things that contributes to its elegance is the Maison De Ville. Maison De Ville translates from the French into townhouse, which it was in the 1800s. Both the main house and the original slave quarters behind have been turned into one of the most impressive small mansion hotels in New Orleans. It seems hard to believe that the noise and crowds of the **French Quarter** are just outside the door. The Maison De Ville also owns the **Audubon Cottages**, named after the famous ornithologist who wrote part of his *Birds in America* series while staying there. Another of the Maison De Ville's famous guests was Tennessee Williams. They say he wrote part of "A Streetcar Named Desire" in room number 9, but if he had worked on that play in all the hotels he's been placed at, the play would have had 32 acts.

The courtyard of the Maison is lush with tropical vegetation and could be a patio in the Caribbean. The rooms themselves are breathtaking, furnished with handsome antiques, rich carpets, and brocades. Some have fireplaces, all are opulent. The cottages are even more luxurious with terra-cotta tiled floors, lavish suites, private gardens and a pool. Breakfast is served in the elegant parlor as well as drinks and good conversation. Maison De Ville is the last word in civilized travel. 23 rooms. Credit Cards: All Major.

Maison Dupuy   **$175–$240**   ★

1001 Rue Toulouse Street, New Orleans, LA 70112; ☎ (504) 586-8000 (800) 535-9177; FAX: (504) 525-5334.

The pleasant, well-run Maison Dupuy, in the French Quarter may not be one of the landmarked, historic properties but the large rooms are nicely done with an emphasis on comfort. Some have balconies that overlook the pretty inner-courtyard, filled with hibiscus, banana and orange trees, and the well-priced suites come with full kitchens.

The seven restored townhouses that were joined to make the Dupuy are just a couple of blocks from **Bourbon Street** so if you're planning a jazzy trip you couldn't be better located. 198 rooms. Credit Cards: All Major.

Melrose Mansion $250–$375 ★★★

937 Esplanade Ave., New Orleans, LA 70116; ☎ *(504) 944-2255; FAX: (504) 945-1794.*

Mansion hotels have been raised up to an art form in New Orleans but even within this luscious category the Victorian Melrose Mansion stands on its own. Melvin Jones, its loving owner has restored it to its 1884 magnificence and watches over it today as its benevolent dictator. The Melrose is for the incurably romantic and the terminally discerning.

The rooms and suites that are at the top of the staircase have each been named and decorated in their own unique style. You could opt for Miss Kitty's room which originally was the home of a tenant who was a burlesque dancer and whose lover was a sea captain. It's done in shades of beige with an iron bed and a huge armoire, a balcony overlooking the avenue and a complimentary wet bar. The most lavish accommodation at the Melrose is the Donecio Suite with sumptuous furnishings and a four-poster that's perfect for the honeymoon set.

Downstairs in the antique and crystal-filled parlor both an elegant breakfast and afternoon drinks are served.

In keeping with the Melrose's dedication to living in the "grand" manor, a limousine will pick you up at the airport and drive you back, that is if you can bear to leave all this grace and glory. 8 rooms. Credit Cards: All Major.

New Orleans Hilton Riverside $225–$1870 ★★

2 Poydras Street (at the river) New Orleans, LA 70140; ☎ *(504) 561-0500, (800) HILTONS; FAX: (504) 568-1721.*

It goes on and on and on just like the **Mississippi** alongside which it has been "evolving" since 1977. The Hilton, at the present, boasts more than 1600 rooms, and who knows how many more to come. If you're looking for warmth and intimacy look further. But let's not be too hasty here, The Hilton leads directly into Riverwalk, a covered mall that makes it possible to escape the blistering summer heat without losing sight of Ole Man River.

Both the Hilton and Riverwalk were part of an unbelievable catastrophe that occurred when a freighter traveling up the Mississippi crashed into the river side of the hotel as well as the outdoor promenade of Riverwalk. Sadly, there were serious injuries as well as millions in damages to both. The good news is that the Hilton has made an amazing recovery and today there is almost no evidence of the recent disaster.

While I myself have never been a fan of the Hilton cookie-cutter look, the Hilton Riverside has views that are breathtaking. The rooms that face the river are palatial with a cozy French farmhouse look. Even more luxurious are the rooms and suites on the tower floors which are private from the rest of the hotel with their own concierge and other rarefied perks. The Hilton Riverside in its high-rise, lowrise, mega-roomed, gardened, fountained splendor is very nearly its own Disney-land. 1602 rooms. Credit Cards: All Major.

Olivier House $120–$295   ★

828 Toulouse Street, New Orleans, LA 70112; ☎ *(504) 525-8456; FAX: (504) 529-2006.*

The Danner family who own this 1896 mansion that is listed in the National Historic register, run it as a home away from home complete with family members playing games in the parlor. Olivier House has long been a favorite with Europeans who visit the **French Quarter** because of its authentic feeling of the past. It isn't perfection but it is comfortable and stylish with high ceilinged spaces and antique-filled guestrooms. Actors passing through town love this place for its dedication to La Vie de Boheme. The tropical courtyard is the place to make new friends and future anecdotes. 42 rooms. Credit Cards: All Major.

Omni Royal Crescent $259–$450   ★★

535 Gravier Street, New Orleans, LA 70130; ☎ *(504) 527-0006; FAX: (504) 523-0806.*

Located at the edge of the **Central Business District**, The Omni is a short stroll to anywhere. It is a prime example of the direction the newest of hotels are heading—small and smaller, plush and plusher, high-tech and "techier." You can almost hear someone in the background shout "Honey, I've shrunk the hotels."

With only 98 jewel-like rooms the Omni is a prime example of boutique over behemoth. While the rooms upstairs are not cavernous, they are super comfortable, done in charming iron-frame beds, draped for drama with diaphanous swags. The marble baths are designed for creature-comfort as well as convenience. As a definite nod to the coming millennium, rooms have fax capability. As the trite yet true saying goes "Good things come in small packages." 98 rooms. Credit Cards: All Major.

Omni Royal Orleans $185–$389   ★★

621 St. Louis Street, New Orleans, LA 70140; ☎ *(504) 529-5333, (800) THE-OMNI; FAX: (504) 529-7089.*

In the 1800s, the **St. Louis Exchange Hotel** was the last word in Grand Luxe accommodations. The **French Quarter** revolved around the famous and infamous auctions that were held in the majestic high-domed space in the center of the hotel. Both art and real estate were auctioned but the sales that drew the biggest crowds were the slave auctions. It wasn't the Civil War that put an end to the St. Louis Exchange's more odious practices, but a hurricane, which blew it down. In its place and with architecture to rival the finest hotels on the Rue de Rivoli in Paris, stands the Royal Orleans, an almost exact replica of the old St. Louis, and now part of the Omni group. Right off **Jackson Square**, it rises like a white marble confection to overlook the French Quarter.

The lobby is aglitter with crystal chandeliers, marble floors and a grand staircase. It's very turn-of-the-century romantic and its guest rooms continue the romance. Though some could use a sprucing, for the most part they're plush and comforting. Even if you opt not to stay at the "Royal O," at least have a drink at the rooftop bar that gives you a beautiful sweep of the **French Quarter**, looking even more French from on high. 346 rooms. Credit Cards: All Major.

| **Pelham Hotel** | $150–$375 | ★ |

444 Common Street, New Orleans, LA 70130; ☎ (504) 522-4444, (800) 659-5621; FAX: (504) 539-9010.
What was once a sprawling office building has been elegantly converted to a hotel of grand proportions despite its small number of accommodations, 60 in all. But with 14 foot ceilings and regal English decor, the rooms have a stylishly customized look. Though not in the **French Quarter** the Pelham has the flavor of the Old South, perhaps because it stands on what was once the Bienvielle Plantation. Today the area is part of the **Central Business District**. The Pelham is just a hop, skip and a mint julep away from the **Riverwalk Shopping Center**, **Magazine Street** and the **Convention Center**. A word of caution to the claustrophobic: the rooms that do not face the front of the Pelham have NO WINDOWS!!! Unless your favorite animal is the mole be sure to book a room that has a big glass thing with light coming through (just in case reservations does not remember the word for it). 60 rooms. Credit Cards: All Major.

| **Pontchartrain** | $130–$260 | ★★ |

2031 St. Charles Ave., New Orleans, LA 70140; ☎ (504) 524-0581, (800) 777-6193; FAX: (504) 529-1165.
The glamour of the 30s can still be felt within the elegant halls of the Pontchartrain. Every celebrity who passed through the city in the boom days before World War II stopped here. The Pontchartrain was synonymous with taste and style. Sitting on **St. Charles Avenue** at the beginning of the **Garden District** it reeks of the good life.

The property has the ambiance of a small European hotel. Moorish in design, the outside is lit by gaslights which make it all the more imposing in the evening. Within the lobby there are antiques, fine art, dignified columns and a graceful vaulted ceiling. Even the inside of the elevator makes a statement with its hand-painted floral decorations. The Pontchartrain is "class" all the way.

Upstairs the most charming accommodations are the suites, each done in a different style and each named for a different star that was a guest of the hotel. My favorite was the Ginger Rogers; you could almost hear her tapping out the "Carioca" (not a sign of Fred anywhere). If you're lucky enough to visit off-season, the suites are almost half the regular rate. Wherever you stay at the Pontchartrain you'll get star treatment. 102 rooms. Credit Cards: All Major.

| **Soniat House** | $145–$235 | ★★★ |

1133 Chartres Street, New Orleans, LA 70116; ☎ (504) 522-0570; FAX: (504) 522-7208.

If when choosing a hotel you prefer deluxe surroundings, sumptuous rooms filled with precious antiques, the very essence of the historical past of the city and superb service dedicated to the smallest detail of comfort, then you might want to get in touch with Soniat House.

Considered a Guest House, Soniat House is much closer to a small European luxury hotel. It is incomparable in its decor and truly lavish appointments. The owners, Rodney and Francis Smith have spent years and bushels of dollars to make their property a legend in its own time. The two townhouses that make up the hotel are directly opposite each other behind tall gates on **Chartres Street**, in the heart of the **French Quarter**. Both date back to the middle of the 1800s and both, as many of the fine old mansions of the Vieux Carré, give not a clue to the elegance that lies behind their locked gates.

The courtyard of both houses come equipped with fountains, fish, birds, gorgeous flowers and in the evening an honor bar is set up for one of the most elegant "happy hours" in town. But what good is all this glorious gift wrapping if the rooms themselves are not the icing on the cake. They are! All 24 of them are elegantly furnished and filled with treasures that the Smiths have collected over the years. There are some smaller cozier rooms off the courtyard that bring to mind an old country inn, but for the most part the rooms are of heroic proportions, with sky-high ceilings. A breakfast of delectable home-made biscuits and café au lait is served in the garden or in your room for mega-pampering.

The Smiths have provided a fabulous background to enjoy the rest of the French Quarter. If that were not enough, they also provide a staff of 20 to see that Soniat House will become an indelible memory. 31 rooms. Credit Cards: All Major.

Westin Canal Place $239–$329 ★★

100 Iberville Street, New Orleans, LA 70130; ☎ *(504) 566-7006; FAX: (504) 553-5120.*

If the Westin is your accommodation of choice then you'll be sitting on top of the world, at least the world of New Orleans. Located just outside the French Quarter off **Canal Street**, the Westin doesn't even begin until the 11th floor, for goodness sakes! And then its sprawling lobby crammed with marble, heroic flower displays and antiques looks out onto a panorama of both the **Mississippi** and the city. The river is particularly heart-stopping at this altitude. The reason the Westin starts on the 11th floor is that it sits atop the nifty **Canal Place Shopping Centre** which translates into movies, theatre and the occasional Gucci loafer.

The rooms at the Westin are rather matter-of-fact deluxe. They may be short on antebellum charm but they're exceptionally long on views and excellent service. 437 rooms. Credit Cards: All Major.

Windsor Court Hotel $235–$590 ★★★

300 Gravier Street, New Orleans, LA 70130; ☎ *(504) 523-6000, (800) 262-2662; FAX: (504) 596-4513.*

Simply the finest in the city. The Windsor Court in my opinion is the only true world class luxury hotel in New Orleans. In a city that has a European flavor to begin with, the Windsor Court is closest to the

"Grand Hotels" abroad. Like a well-oiled piece of intricate machinery, it hums along with quiet precision.

Owned by Orient-Express hotels, it is devoted to the same Old World luxury that has made their trains symbolic of the haute-monde of the world. You can feel its dedication to elegance and quality as soon as you step across the Windsor Court's plushly carpeted threshold. The lobby is cool, exquisite and filled with art treasures. In fact the art collection that is displayed throughout the hotel is worth more than $8 million. But man does not live by art alone.

Upstairs the Windsor Court's rooms carry out the promise of its luxurious public spaces. They are oversized, furnished as befits the graciousness of the Old South, with carved canopy or four-poster beds. All of them face either the **Mississippi** or the City. The bathrooms would make Scarlett O'Hara green with envy, not to mention the incomparable service that goes with them. "Courtliness" is right up there with Godliness at the Windsor Court. 324 rooms. Credit Cards: All Major.

The Suite Life

Embassy Suites New Orleans $189–$320 ★ ★

315 Julia Street, New Orleans, LA 70130; ☎ (504) 525-1993, (800) EMBASSY; FAX: (504) 522-3044.

If you're looking forward to an "art attack" in New Orleans then Embassy Suites has one of their no-nonsense, spacious suites for you right in the middle of the **Warehouse/Gallery District** on trendy Julia St. Not only that, but they throw in breakfast and two hours of complimentary drinks in the evening as well. The **Warehouse District** is where all the "cool" things are happening today in the Big Easy. In fact, the whole area including the **Convention Center** only a few blocks away makes the scene there "hot" right now. The suites are very comfortable and make any visit much easier if you're traveling with the wee ones. All the suites come with microwaves and coffee makers. 282 suites. Credit Cards: All Major.

Comfort Suites $114–$165 ★

346 Baronne Street, New Orleans, LA 70112; ☎ (504) 524-1140, (800) 228-5150; FAX: (504) 523-4444.

Baronne Street, while not right in the middle of the French Quarter is only a few short blocks, so you can have your gumbo and eat it too by spreading out in a suite. While not as high-tech or squeaky-new as Embassy Suites, Comfort accommodations are just what their name implies—comfortable. A tiny fridge, microwave, coffeemakers and free local calls are part of this very good deal. 102 suites. Credit Cards: All Major.

Budget Bests

Tulane University $25–$50 ★

Office of Housing, Tulane University, 27 McAllister Drive, New Orleans, LA 70118; ☎ (504) 865-5724.

Perhaps you may not want to enroll in classes, but Tulane has a super program for visitors of all ages in on-campus housing (both small suites and apartments). Of course they go like hotcakes so book as early as possible. Credit Cards: Not accepted.

Loyola University   **$25–$50**   ★

Conference Director, Office of Student's Affairs, PO Box 126, Loyola University, New Orleans, LA 70118; ☎ (504) 865-3735, 3622.
Your basic dorm arrangement with about 100 or so spaces available to all ages from June 1 to August 1. Credit Cards: Not accepted.

Y.M.C.A. International Hotel   **$25–$50**   ★

920 St. Charles Avenue, New Orleans, LA 70130; ☎ (504) 568-9622.
Fifty or so teeny, tiny rooms with air conditioning and T.V. Bare bones are the watchwords here, but the good news is that you can use the Y's health facilities and pool, gratis. Credit Cards: All Major.

Bed and Breakfasts

Bed & Breakfast, Inc.—Reservation Service

1021 Moss Street, Box 52257, New Orleans, LA 70152-2257
☎ (504) 488-4640; FAX: (504) 488-4639; Toll Free: 1-800-729-4640.
Credit Cards: Not accepted.

New Orleans Bed & Breakfast

Sarah-Margaret Brown
Box 81163, New Orleans, LA 70182
☎ (504) 838-0071, 838-0072; FAX: (504) 838-0140.
Credit Cards: Not accepted.

"My, oh, my! What a fascinating guy you are, Vincent! But now, if it's not too much trouble, I'd like you to take my order."

Drawing by Mankoff; ©1995 The New Yorker Magazine, Inc.

AGENDA TRAVEL ADVISORY

New Orleans' streetcars are a fun way to get around town.

Travel to New Orleans couldn't be easier. In terms of accessibility, **The Big Easy** more than lives up to its name. You can arrive with not a trace of "travel trauma" in 2 to 3-1/2 hours from major gateways in the United States. European visitors can fly direct from London, the gateway city for British Airways, Lufthansa, Swiss Air and T.W.A. There also may be other options that have become available after we went to press.

The choice of airlines to New Orleans for U.S. passengers go on and on. Whatever airline you decide to use, there are numerous flights into the city, so that planning a schedule for your

Agenda will be a snap. Below I've listed some of the most reliable choices.

Delta	☎ *(800) 221-1212*
Continental	☎ *(800) 525-0280*
Southwest	☎ *(800) 435-9792*
TWA	☎ *(800) 221-2000*
United	☎ *(800) 241-6522*
American	☎ *(800) 433-7300*

AGENDA FUSS–BUDGET ALERT

Some airlines have day-of-departure or day-prior-to-departure reduced fares for Johnny-Come-Latelys. If you're flexible you can save enough for a jazzier time in New Orleans

Getting to New Orleans

The major airport that serves the city is **Moisant International Airport**. ☎ *(504) 464-3547*. It's about 15 miles from the city and with moderate traffic you should site the "Crescent City" in about 20 minutes. There are several convenient options for getting into town.

By Taxi

This is the best option for those with heavy baggage and light coping abilities. Use only a metered cab and if at all possible opt for a **United Cab**, hands down, the most reliable, courteous taxi company in New Orleans. Expect to pay $20–$23 (three people or more, $8 per person. ☎ *(800) 323-3303/522-9771*.

By Bus

There is regular bus service from the airport to the **Central Business District (Tulane Avenue)** every 10 minutes during rush hours (6–9 a.m., 3–6 p.m.) and at other times every 25 minutes. Buses run from 6 a.m. to 6:20 p.m. The fare is (at press time) $1. ☎ *(504) 737-7433/737-9611*.

By Airport Shuttle

Somewhere between the taxi and the bus the shuttle vans hold about six people (although they go so frequently that I have never had more than four in my group. They're comfortable, chatty (all kinds of information is traded back and forth between passengers) and the trip costs a modest $10.00. You are dropped directly at your hotel in about 40 minutes. Shuttle desks are located throughout the airport. ☎ *(504) 522-3500*.

By Limousine

Olde Quarter Livery, ☎ *(504) 595-5010*. About $40 to your hotel.

Forget about everything that sounds daunting or confusing. You're in New Orleans—what else matters.

That said, the happy, secure traveler doesn't live by admiration for fascinating cities alone. The best thing to focus on when beginning the heroic task of trying to see all of New Orleans is that you can't possibly achieve that in just a day or two. The best to be hoped for on a short stay is to absorb a few of the many flavors that New Orleans sets before you. Then, you can call them up when you return home and smile.

New Orleans is the perfect city for walking, strolling, striding or standing because all of these activities prepare you for what this city does better than any other, balcony sitting. The Orleanians have developed the ritual of an aperitif taken from a balcony overlooking the **French Quarter**, into an art form. What better reward could one have after a hard day of seeing the sights than a romantic rest stop and a long, cool drink.

When you are rested and ready for public transportation, the colorful streetcars, with their wooden seats and old-fashioned pull-cords are the oldest transportation in the city and the easiest to negotiate. The bus system is equally accessible. Trust me, New Orleans is small enough to make you feel at home by the end of your first day, and packed with so much to do you'll hardly know where to begin. But before you go in search of your first beignet you'll need:

1. A plan.
2. A map.
3. Comfortable shoes.
4. An umbrella.

New Orleans Traffic Golden Rules

Unlike most other crowded cities, New Orleans has no rush-hours to be noted and avoided. New Orleans' traffic is horrendous all day.

Arrival to New Orleans by Train

Amtrak services New Orleans from New York, Miami, Los Angeles, Chicago. Trains arrive at **Union Terminal** which is located in the **Central Business District** at *1001 Loyola Avenue;* ☎ *(800) 872-7245.*

Arrival to New Orleans by Car

If you've decided to rent a car at the airport just follow the signs to the city. You will be looking for Interstate 10 (I-10) which will lead right into the city. But getting there is the least of your problems. Keep in mind that there is a parade a minute in New Orleans even when it's not **Mardi Gras**, **Superbowl** or **Jazz Fest**. Even if you survive the town's parade fixation, the number of drunk-driving arrests is fast approaching the amount of the national debt. Still want more reasons to say "Taxi." Meter-

Maids in New Orleans write tickets with methodical efficiency and parking fees at your hotel are likely to be in the $15–$20 per night range. It costs almost as much for your car to cool its weary engine as it does for yours!!!

Getting Around New Orleans

The first thing to remember is to forget all normal thoughts about North, South, East and West—the most important landmark in the city, albeit the wettest, is the river. New Orleanians when asked for directions, will tell you that your destination is "upriver" or "downriver" which must have meant a lot to Mark Twain but will put most visitors "at sea." Then there's the enigmatic "lakeside" which can translate into just about anywhere above the south shore of **Lake Pontchartrain**. The best way to lay out the city in your mind is to think of **Canal Street** as a line of division. Most of what you'll be doing in New Orleans will take you into the **French Quarter** which is laid out in a rectangle six by twelve blocks. This is considered "downriver" from Canal. Upriver from **Canal Street** (on the other side) is the **Central Business District**, the locals refer to it as the CBD. In that direction you'll find most of the large convention hotels and the **Superbowl**. The lakefront will require a car or a cab to reach but it's worth the effort to sample some of the wonderful restaurants that are found there.

Beware of New Orleans' Summer

Very few places in the U.S. are quite as uncomfortable as New Orleans from June through September. The climate is reminiscent of hell with humidity. Now, there are people (and certain swamp creatures) who thrive on subtropical, rainforest conditions during the day and a sultry, steamy breeze in the evenings but for most of us, New Orleans seems as comfortable as the bottom of a terrarium, during its summer months. The good news is that the facts of summer life have led hotels to make their rates as air-conditioned as possible.

Do not even think about walking around in the summer months without a hat, or in fact walking around at all during the heat of the day. Save major sightseeing for the mornings or late afternoons. It's also apt to rain for a short period many times a day so an umbrella is more important here than London. Do not under any circumstances wear a plastic raincoat or you will be reduced to a small puddle of water and your family will never hear from you again. As Mr. Porter once wrote "It's Too Damn Hot!"

How to Take the Streetcar

Often! It's really fun because far from being a tinker-toy kept up for the tourists, it's really a working tram. The two most used lines are the **St. Charles Avenue Streetcar** which takes about 1-1/2 hours up **St. Charles** to **Palmer Park**, the other, the **Riverfront Streetcar** travels a route along the **Mississippi** from the **French Quarter** up to the **Warehouse District**. Both streetcars only take exact fare. (Dollar bills are fine.)

St. Charles Streetcar

24 hours a day–$1 fare.

Riverfront Streetcar

Mon.–Fri., 6 a.m.–midnight, Sat.–Sun., 8 a.m.–midnight–$1.25 fare.

How to Take the Bus

Buses are amazingly frequent and terribly obliging for visitors. They have been known to pick up passengers between bus stops and wait forever if they see you trying to figure out where to get on. Drivers will announce your stop without a murmur. The bus that goes up and down **Magazine Street** is particularly frequent since the area is so popular with tourists making the antiques scene. The Canal Line goes up **Canal Street** from the river all the way to **Lake Pontchartrain**. Buses run 24 hours a day. The fare is $1 exact (dollar bills are ok) and 10¢ if you need a transfer.

The VisiTour Pass is the way to go if you intend to hop on and off public transportation during the course of your stay, taxis are "farely" expensive. The pass is available either for one day's unlimited travel at $4 or for three consecutive days at $8. You can obtain the passes all over, in shops, your hotel or from the RTA Rideline, ☎ *(504) 569-2700.*

Drawing by S. Gross; ©1995 The New Yorker Magazine, Inc.

How to Take a Taxi

Taxis can be easily found cruising most of the areas visitors frequent. There is rarely a problem finding a cab in the **French Quarter** or on **Canal Street** or outside most hotels. But in other areas you should not depend on hailing a cab in the street. However, it's customary for restaurants and shops to call a cab for you as a matter of routine. Taxis rarely take more than a few minutes to arrive so it's unlikely that you'll be inconvenienced at all. The most dependable of all the cab services is **United Cab Co.**, ☎ *(504)*

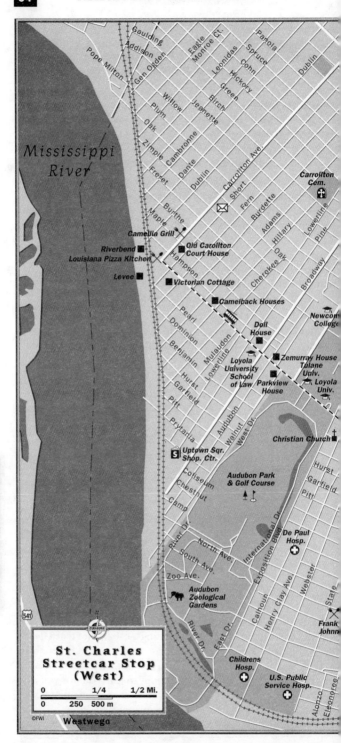

Mississippi River

Carrollton Cém.

Camellia Grill
Riverbend
Louisiana Pizza Kitchen
Levee
Old Carollton Court House
Victorian Cottage
Camelback Houses
Doll House
Newcomb College
Zemurray House
Tulane Univ.
Loyola University School of Law
Parkview House
Loyola Univ.
Christian Church
Uptown Sqr. Shop. Ctr.
Audubon Park & Golf Course
De Paul Hosp.
Audubon Zoological Gardens
Childrens Hosp.
U.S. Public Service Hosp.
Frank Johnn

St. Charles Streetcar Stop (West)

| 0 | 1/4 | 1/2 Mi. |

| 0 | 250 | 500 m |

©FWI Westwega

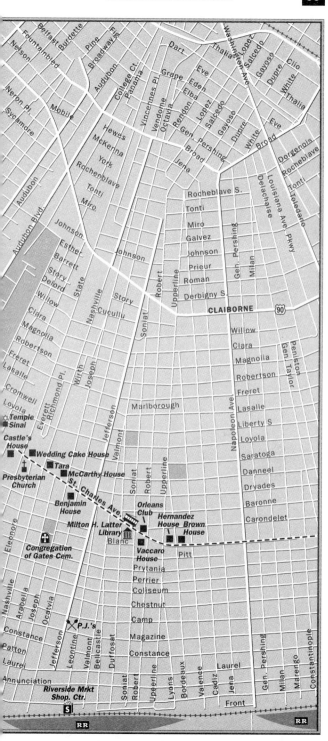

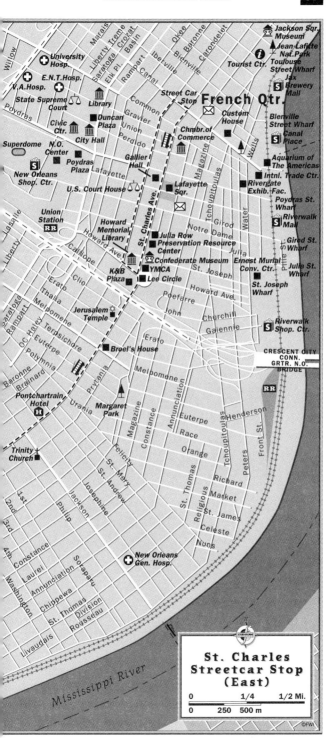

St. Charles
Streetcar Stop
(East)

| 0 | 1/4 | 1/2 Mi. |
| 0 | 250 | 500 m |

©FWI

522-9771. Everyone in the city swears by United as I did myself. The drivers were particularly polite and pleasant. Rates as of press time were $1.70 for the meter drop and $1 per mile as you go. (There is a 50¢ charge for each additional passenger.

AGENDA THREE FOR THE ROAD ALERT

During special events (of which there are many) such as **Jazz Fest** *or* **Mardi Gras** *cabs charge a flat $3 per person (or the price on the meter if it happens to be greater). If they quote you a price that equals the price of a ticket on the Concorde, call the Taxicab Bureau,* ☎ *(504) 242-2600.*

For any questions about transportation either to New Orleans or around the city the people to turn to are:

New Orleans Metropolitan Convention and Visitors Bureau
☎ *(504) 566-5011; (800) 672-6124.*
Web site HTTP://WWW.NAWLINS.COM

NEW ORLEANS BY DISTRICT

Artists frequently set up their easels at Jackson Square.

The French Quarter

The city of New Orleans was born in what is today the **French Quarter**. The tiny colony that was called LA Nouvelle Orleans is best remembered by what is left of it in the **Vieux Carré**. It's no surprise that when you walk its streets you are at once seduced by its irreverent grasp of the present and its glorification of the past.

The French Quarter seems to have more to do with Paris than with New Orleans. In fact, at the height of its wealth and power in the early 1800s it was often referred to as Paris on the **Mississippi**. The sophisticated and cultured lifestyle that comes from its brilliantly mixed society of European, African, Caribbean, French Canadian and lastly American ancestry makes the **French Quarter** as exotic as a trip abroad.

The Old World look of the Quarter or **Vieux Carré** (old square) comes from its resolve to preserve what's left of its history. Unfortunately most of the original architecture of the early French Colony was destroyed by the many fires that occurred at the end of the 1700s. What remains today only dates back to the 19th century. But the irresistible wrought-iron balconies that festoon the small buildings and the charming Creole cottages iced with gingerbread that line the streets could be filled with the turn-of-the-century gentry discussing the pros and cons of the **Louisiana Purchase**.

What gives the **French Quarter** the look of a prosperous Caribbean port city is its diverse styles of architecture. As in most things that New Orleanians hold dear, romanticism is the form that function gives way to. The small **Creole cottages** that line the streets of the **Faubourg Marigny** have slanted roofs with tiny chimneys. These modest houses are interspersed with grander, more elegant **Creole townhouses**, often *pied a terres* for wealthy plantation owners who came to mix and mingle with New Orleans' jet set. Most of them have the extraordinary ironwork gates and balconies that are so identified with the look of New Orleans. One of the most fanciful examples of cast-iron art is the **Cornstalk Fence** with its ears of corn alternating with morning glories, at **915 Royal Street**. Today some of the most beautiful of the townhouses have been turned into sumptuous hotels and guest houses and some were converted to mini-museums such as the **Beauregard-Keyes house** on **Chartres Street**, the **Gallier House** on **Royal Street**, and the **Hermann-Grima** mansion on **St. Louis Street**.

The reason the **French Quarter** remains such a historic treasure is directly due to efforts of the **Vieux Carré** Commission who strictly regulate what is built, how high buildings may rise (not very) a virtual ban on the use of neon, (except on **Bourbon Street** with its carefully planned naughtiness), the replacement of ordinary street lamps by gas, to softly illuminate the street and the exclusion of traffic lights except at the edges of the Quarter.

The streets of the **Vieux Carré** are laid out in an easy to follow grid with **Jackson Square** (see sights page 18) at its center. One of the main arteries is **Royal Street**, home of major antique dealers who attract major collectors from all over the world. Aside from the obvious advantage of being able to exercise your charge cards up and down Royal, there is also the most famous breakfast in all of New Orleans to sample, Brennens (see restaurants page 142) Right across the street the **Louisiana Supreme Court Building** is supremely elegant in white marble and granite. A little farther down Royal, the **Court of Two Sisters** at No. 613 was the 18th century home of Emma and Bertha Camors who ran a little shop together until they died. Today, it's a wonderful place for a jazz brunch.

There is also a bonafide haunted house (one of the few that wasn't created by Anne Rice) at No. 1140 Royal, that belonged to Delphine La Laurie. She was not known for being an "equal opportunity employer" and kept her slaves chained at the top of the house. She finally burned her candle at both ends one too many times and almost burned the house down. Her infamous "toys in the attic" were discovered. (and you thought New Orleans was just fun and gumbos).

Court of The Two Sisters offers a great jazz brunch.

Chartres Street is much calmer than Royal perhaps because its most famous landmark is the **Old Ursuline Convent** (see sights page 27). The pace is much more leisurely. In the morning its residents eat breakfast on their second-floor verandas or at **La Marquise**, a tiny coffee shop. At the corner of **St. Peters Street** (616) and Chartres stands **Le Petit Théatre du Vieux Carré**. This tiny exquisite playhouse is the oldest community theatre in the U.S. It was founded in 1916. They still do new productions every year as well as children's plays. One of the most intriguing places on **Chartres Street** (No.514) is the **New Orleans Pharmacy Museum**. Not a place to have your prescriptions refilled but a museum with a sometimes fascinating, sometimes bizarre and occasionally horrifying collection of cure-alls and surgical tools. "The Cabinet of Dr. Calegari" seems like a 7-11 by comparison.

AGENDA BORE-ING STORY

In New Orleans in the early 18th century, they used a "Trephination Drill" to bore a hole into the skull of someone known to suffer from serious headaches. The method was the last word in releasing the "demons" causing the headaches. Unfortunately it was the last word for the patient as well.

Napoleon House is also found on **Chartres Street** at No. 500. It looks almost exactly as it did in 1797. It was built by a group

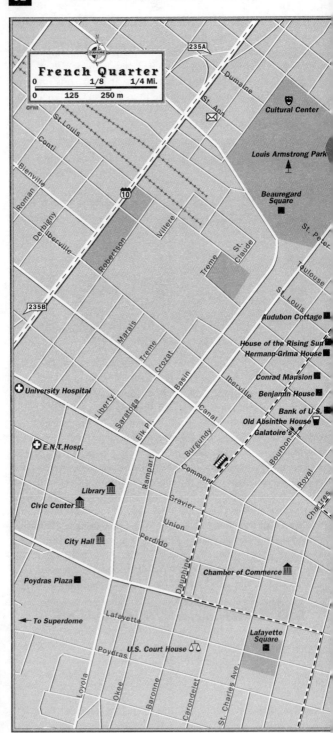

French Quarter

0   1/8   1/4 Mi.

0   125   250 m

©FWI

Dumaine

St. Ann

Cultural Center

Louis Armstrong Park

Beauregard Square

235A

St. Louis

Conti

Bienville

Roman

Delbigny

Iberville

Robertson

Villere

Treme

St. Claude

St. Peter

Toulouse

St. Louis

Audubon Cottage

House of the Rising Sun

Hermann-Grima House

Conrad Mansion

Benjamin House

Bank of U.S.

Old Absinthe House

Galatoire's

Marais

Treme

Crozat

Basin

Iberville

University Hospital

Liberty

Saratoga

Elk Pl.

Canal

Burgundy

Bourbon

Royal

E.N.T. Hosp.

Rampart

Common

Chartres

Library

Civic Center

Gravier

Union

City Hall

Perdido

Chamber of Commerce

Poydras Plaza

Dauphine

To Superdome

Lafayette

Lafayette Square

Poydras

U.S. Court House

Loyola

Okee

Baronne

Carondelet

St. Charles Ave.

Liberty Extreme

St. Claube

Rampart

Barracks

Esplanade

Gov. Nidholls

Ursuline

St. Philip

Dumaine

St. Ann

Burgundy

Kerelec

Dauphine

Royal

Chartres

Decatur

Latrobe House

Lalaurie House

Gallier House

U.S. Mint

Mardi Gras Museum

N.O. Jazz Collection

Jean Lafitte Blacksmith Shop

Beauregard Keyes-LeCarpenter House

St.Mary's Italian Church

Old Ursuline Convent

Voodoo Museum

Cornstalk Fence

Quadroom Ballroom

Mittenberger Houses

Old Farmers Market

Gardette Le Pretre

Madame John's Legacy

Languille House

Madison

Preservation Hall

Camponel House

Jean Lafitte Nat. Park

Zach Taylor's House

Pontalba Apartments

Dumaine Street Wharf

The Historic New Orleans Collection

Lemonnier Bldg.

Jackson Sq. Museum

French Market

Maison Seignouret

Brennan's

St.Louis Cathedral

Tourist Ctr.

Moon Walk

Degas' House

Café du Monde

Court Bldg.

Napoleon House

Toulouse Street Wharf

Police Station Alley

Blenville

Jax Brewery Mall

Mississippi River

Decatur

Blenville Street Wharf

Custom House

Wells

Canal Place

Canal St. Ferry
To Mardi Gras World

Woldenberg Park

Tchoupitoulas

Aquarium of The Americas

International Trade Center

Natchez, Cajun and Creole Queen

Rivergate Exhib. Center

Poydras Street Wharf

Girod

Water

Riverwalk Mall

who absolutely idolized the "Napolster." When they got the news that the French didn't share their adulation for the man (although they were crazy about the pastry), they constructed what they hoped would be the big N's home away from home. The house unfortunately was not up to Napoleonic code and was turned into a simply swell bar and grill (see restaurants page 140).

Bourbon Street, by far the most fabled street of the **French Quarter** doesn't seem to be a part of the Quarter at all. It looks as if it were transported from the Planet Tawdry. The bars spill onto its littered sidewalks and party animals sometimes behave as the name implies as they down their "go-cups" filled with the local libations (the Hurricane is the drink of choice for those who are seeking their own private **Mardi Gras**). **Bourbon Street** should be swallowed in small sips with long draughts of the rest of the **French Quarter** in-between. I think **Bourbon** after dark is at its best. That's when the really good musicians appear and the whole street resounds with a sweet cacophony of every imaginable form of jazz. Cajun clubs mingle with blues joints up and down the most melodic seven blocks in the world.

Preservation Hall is the most legendary jazz club in the city.

The most renowned of all the jazz temples on or around **Bourbon Street** is of course **Preservation Hall** *at 726 S. Peters Street* (off Bourbon). All the "greats" have made music here (see sights page 28). A very different kind of music is made at **Lafitte's Blacksmith Shop**, mostly the sound of clinking glasses, but back in the late 1700s it was said to be a pirates' den complete with booty that was being "laundered" by that "Sweetie of the Seas" Jean Lafitte. Even if the rumors are slightly over-the-top, the age of this earliest of Creole cottages dates to 1770. Today it's just a bar that makes a mean Hurricane, with nary a parrot in sight, but go anyway—it's a landmark.

Dumaine Street goes from the sublime to the spooky. **Madame John's Legacy at No. 632** is thought to be the oldest building still standing on the **Mississippi** (which at the time, it was built, in 1726, was on its doorstep.) There has been an ongoing dispute with the **Old Ursuline Convent**. They also claim that distinction. Who knows? However, the "back story" that remains to this day is "juicy." A famous New Orleans writer, George Washington Cable wrote the story of Zalli, an exquisite quadroon (1/4 black ancestry) whose white "friend" John, left her the house as a token of his love when he died. (Judith Kranz, are you listening?).

To recover from the sadness of lost loves, you can stroll over to the **New Orleans Historic Voodoo Museum at 724 Dumain** where they drum up trade for lost souls. This is (thank God) the only private museum dedicated to voodoo, anywhere. Voodoo rites and wrongs including a petrified dead cat, can be explored there as well as other artifacts of what was a major (if secret) religion in the old days of the Quarter. Exhibitions of rituals can be arranged but don't be misled, they're really kid stuff and bear little resemblance to voodoo worship in its truest sense.

AGENDA BOO-TIQUE

When the award for the best High Priestess of 1823 was handed out at the "Zoombies," Marie Laveau was the winner. She started as a hairdresser (mine must have gone to the same school) but soon became the witch of the moment in New Orleans in the 1820s. Even today her tomb is covered with symbols and charms by Voodoophiles of note.

Decatur Street, once known only for its seedy dives and flea-bag hotels, has undergone a substantial sprucing. Its length, running from **Jackson Square** to **Esplanade Avenue** (almost the entire boundary of the Quarter) overlooks the **Mississippi** and is the gateway to the historic **French Market**. Along the way there are lots of things to keep the tourists happy including souvenir shops, the most famous **Muffaletta sandwiches** in all New Orleans (see Best Bites page 74) and on upper Decatur there are some great funky antique shops and curio stores. The **French Market** (see Top Sights page 21) is the big draw on **Decatur Street** every

Fielding **NEW ORLEANS**

FRENCH QUARTER TOUR

VIEUX CARRE
(French Quarter)

New Orleans

Mississippi River

Audubon House

505 Dauphine Street
John James Audubon lived here from 1821-1822 while he worked on his *Birds of America* series.

**VIEUX CARRE
(French Quarter)**

ORLEANS

ST. PETER

N. RAMPART ST.

BURGUNDY ST.

IBERVILLE

BIENVILLE

DAUPHINE

TOULOUSE

CANAL

ROYAL

Cabildo

Jackson Square
This Spanish Colonial building dating from 1799 served as city hall, the supreme court and now houses three floors of multicultural exhibits on Louisiana history.

CONTI

ST. LOUIS

DECATUR

World Trade Center

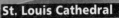

St. Louis Cathedral

615 Pere Antoine Alley
Located in the heart of Jackson Square, this is the oldest active cathedral in the United States. The current building dates from 1794. In 1964 it was awarded minor basilica status.

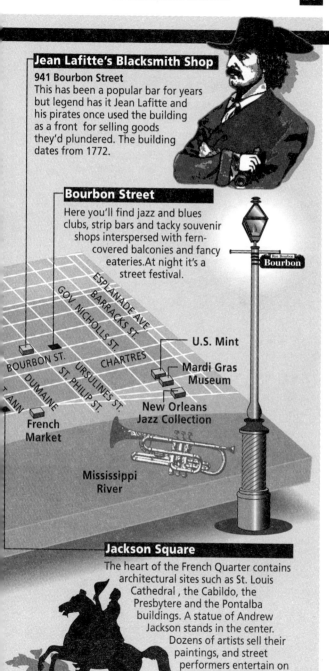

Jean Lafitte's Blacksmith Shop

941 Bourbon Street
This has been a popular bar for years but legend has it Jean Lafitte and his pirates once used the building as a front for selling goods they'd plundered. The building dates from 1772.

Bourbon Street

Here you'll find jazz and blues clubs, strip bars and tacky souvenir shops interspersed with fern-covered balconies and fancy eateries. At night it's a street festival.

ESPLANADE AVE.

GOV. NICHOLLS ST.

BARRACKS ST.

BOURBON ST.

CHARTRES

URSULINES ST.

ST. PHILIP ST.

DUMAINE

ANN

French Market

U.S. Mint

Mardi Gras Museum

New Orleans Jazz Collection

Mississippi River

Bourbon

Jackson Square

The heart of the French Quarter contains architectural sites such as St. Louis Cathedral, the Cabildo, the Presbytere and the Pontalba buildings. A statue of Andrew Jackson stands in the center. Dozens of artists sell their paintings, and street performers entertain on the pedestrian mall.

NEW ORLEANS BY DISTRICT

Fielding   NEW ORLEANS

FRENCH QUARTER TOUR

Hermann-Grima Historic House

820 St. Louis Street
Built in 1831, this National Historic Landmark has been restored to depict the Creole lifestyle from 1930-1960. Tours include the mansion, stable, courtyard and kitchen.

Musee Conti Wax Museum

917 Conti Street
Only a block from Bourbon St, tour 300 years of history, myths and romances depicted in wax.

Louis Armstrong Park

ORLEANS
ST. PETER
TOULOUSE
N. RAMPART ST.

Pat O'Brien's

718 St. Peter Street
This is the place to go in New Orleans to sip a hurricane and take home a souvenir glass. Hordes of tourists and locals cram into the main bar, patio bar and piano lounge to hear nightly entertainers.

ROYAL
CHARTRES
ST. LOUIS
CONTI
BIENVILLE
DECATUR
IBERVILLE
CANAL

World Trade Center

Mississippi River

Preservation Hall

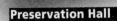

726 St. Peter Street
Jazz has been an institution at this landmark building since the 1920's. The setting is rustic but you'll get to see and hear the city's best musicians.

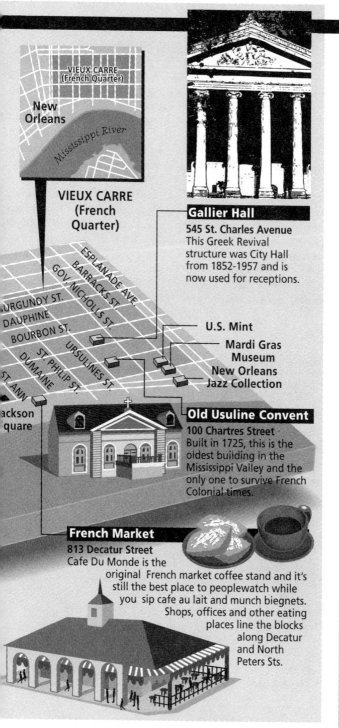

VIEUX CARRE
(French Quarter)

New Orleans

Mississippi River

**VIEUX CARRE
(French
Quarter)**

ESPLANADE AVE
BARRACKS ST.
GOV. NICHOLLS ST.
URGUNDY ST.
DAUPHINE
BOURBON ST.
URSULINES ST.
ST. PHILIP ST.
DUMAINE
ST ANN
ackson
quare

Gallier Hall

545 St. Charles Avenue
This Greek Revival
structure was City Hall
from 1852-1957 and is
now used for receptions.

U.S. Mint

**Mardi Gras
Museum
New Orleans
Jazz Collection**

Old Usuline Convent

100 Chartres Street
Built in 1725, this is the
oldest building in the
Mississippi Valley and the
only one to survive French
Colonial times.

French Market

813 Decatur Street
Cafe Du Monde is the
original French market coffee stand and it's
still the best place to peoplewatch while
you sip cafe au lait and munch biegnets.
Shops, offices and other eating
places line the blocks
along Decatur
and North
Peters Sts.

**NEW ORLEANS BY
DISTRICT**

day but especially on Saturday and Sunday when even the locals come down to pick through the trash and treasures laid out at the back of the market. After making a few of your own Louisiana purchases you can hop on the **Riverfront Streetcar** (its bright red cars are referred to as Red Ladies) or ride up to the **CBD** or the **Warehouse District**, or nearby to the **Jackson Brewery Complex** with over 70 shops and eateries. It also houses the **New Orleans School of Cooking**, for crash courses in jumbo gumbos, and a complete **Acadian Village** located on the Brewery's third floor, where crafts are sold. The very best time to **Moonwalk** is in (hold on to your jalapenos) the moonlight. **The Moonwalk** is the **Mississippi's** promenade. The view of the mighty M just keeps rollin along but under the stars it's particularly beautiful. You can reach the **Moonwalk** entrance at the side of the **French Market**. You are also just a short distance from the small ferry that crosses the river to **Algiers Point** (Algiers, right across the river is one of New Orleans' oldest communities). It's only a 20-minute ride but from its deck you can see the curve of the river making the crescent that inspired New Orleans other alias "The Crescent City." Don't decide to venture very far from the Algiers landing point, unfortunately this area is not one of the safest in the city.

Agenda Shopping/The French Quarter

Bourbon French Parfams

525 St. Ann Street; ☎ *(504) 522-4480, 9 a.m.–5 p.m., daily.*
The perfume that wafts through the air in the **French Quarter** is not always chicory. This very romantic shop has been making delicious scents since 1843. They will, if asked, do custom blending.

Oh Susannah

518 St. Peter Street; ☎ *(504) 586-8701, 9:30 a.m.–5:30 p.m., Mon.–Sat.; 11 a.m.–5 p.m., Sun.*
Doll collectors come from all over because of the museum quality of some of their little darlings. They also have the plain Jane variety for everyday tea parties.

Private Connection

1116 Decatur Street; ☎ *(504) 593-9526, 9 a.m.–6 p.m., Mon.–Sat.*
Exotic bric-a-brac and all manor of things from Thailand including silver and batiks. If you're fit to be "Thaied" you'll love it here.

Librairie Bookshop

823 Chartres Street; ☎ *(504) 525-4837, 10 a.m.–8 p.m., daily.*
Just musty enough to have a fine collection of old books on the area's history and folklore. The maps are particularly tempting.

Faulkner House Books

624 Pirate's Alley; ☎ *(504) 524-2940, 10 a.m.–6 p.m., daily.*

A Bibliophile's paradise. In the very place that Faulkner lived and worked, what more appropriate use of the space? Guess whose books are featured here?

Crafty Louisianians'

813 Royal Street; ☎ *(504) 528-3094, 10 a.m.–5:30 p.m., daily.*
Kitschy nick-nacks made by the crafty set. Mississippi Mud Dolls and Houma Indian Art are both a specialty here.

Dashka Roth

332 Chartres Street; ☎ *(504) 523-0805, 10 a.m.–6 p.m., Mon.–Sat.; 11 a.m.–5 p.m., Sun.*
Original and sophisticated jewelry collection done by artisans from all over the world. Both gold and precious stones make up Dashka's collection.

Mardi Gras Center

831 Chartres Street; ☎ *(504) 524-4384, 10 a.m.–8 p.m., daily.*
This place is just about perfect for the "hard-core" Mardi Gras participant. Its walls are lined with enough masks to keep the Phantom of the Opera busy for years. Also endless swags of beads, glitterdust and costumes.

Centuries

517 St. Louis Street; ☎ *(504) 568-9491, 10:30 a.m.–6 p.m., daily.*
The best collection of antique maps in the Quarter. They have lovely prints and engravings as well. It's a browser's bonanza.

Trade

828 Chartres Street; ☎ *(504) 596-6827, 11 a.m.–7 p.m., daily.*
Not just for the carriage trade either, they have crafts from New Orleans artisans and a large collection of "Day of the Dead" folk art from Mexico.

Texas Body Hangings

835 Decatur Street; ☎ *(504) 524-9856, 10 a.m.–6 p.m., daily.*
Not since the Caped Crusader went shopping have I seen such an array of swinging cape styles. There are romantic little numbers with cowl hoods and plaid throws for walking the moors. They even have capelets for kidlets. It's a true swirling dervish.

Angel Wings

710 St. Louis Street; ☎ *(504) 524-6880, 10 a.m.–10 p.m., Mon.–Sat.; 10 a.m.–6 p.m., Sun.*
Tiny but ethereal to the max. Jewelry, sculpture, accessories, all making a heavenly collection. Great for fans of *It's a Wonderful Life.*

Le Petit Soldier Shop

528 Royal Street; ☎ *(504) 523-7741, 10 a.m.–4 p.m., Mon.–Sat.*
Military miniatures from armies dating all the way back to the Greeks. The shop is a magnet for soldiers with fortunes willing to part with them. Some of the tiny armed forces are collectors' items as well as the commemorative objects from the Royals in England.

Sami Lott

728 St. Louis Street; ☎ *(504) 525-7550, Random hours—call.*
An absolutely one-of-a-kind designer dress shop with the garments all handmade from antique linens. The most delicate of lacy tablecloths and bed linen have been turned into delectable creations done up by

Ms. Lott and her staff. Not since the Great Gatsby has garden-party attire been so romantic. These also translate into unique wedding gowns for unique brides.

Hové Parfumeur, Ltd.

824 Royal Street; ☎ *(504) 525-7827, 10 a.m.–5 p.m., Mon.–Sat.*
They are the oldest perfume manufacturers in New Orleans, having been founded in 1931. They specialize in their own essential oils which they produce in perfumes, candles, talc and my personal choice, solid perfume, that can go out when you do.

Old Children's Books

734 Royal Street; ☎ *(504) 525-3655, 10 a.m.–1 p.m., Mon.–Sat.*
A magical selection of rare, some almost priceless, children's books including a first edition of the Oz series (Judy would be so proud of them). The illustrations are charming, dating back to the early 19th century.

Gallery I/O

829 Royal Street; ☎ *(504) 523-5041, 11 a.m.–6 p.m., daily.*
Great tabletop and jewelry designs. Gifts that are just a little bit off-center for people who thrive on "different."

Barrister's Gallery

526 Royal Street; ☎ *(504) 525-2767, 10 a.m.–5 p.m., Mon.–Sat.*
This wonderful gallery is not for the timid, or someone who thinks of Bloomingdale's as an "archeological dig," but if you love to burrow through fetishes from Zaire, tribal art of Oceana, beaded figures from the Cameroon and assorted tchotkies from other sub-Saharan destinations, just roll up your sleeves and dig into one of the most exciting galleries I've ever been in.

Joan Good Antiques

809 Royal Street; ☎ *(504) 525-1705, 10 a.m.–5 p.m., daily.*
Estate jewelry left for sale as well as other exquisite antique pieces. Good is particularly known for her Garnets.

Gothic Shop

830 Royal Street; ☎ *(504) 558-0175, 10 a.m.–6 p.m., Mon.–Sat.; 11 a.m.–5 p.m., Sun.*
The perfect accessories for an Anne Rice novel. Gargoyles galore as well as angels and architectural accents. Thank God they ship since everything is very affordable but exceedingly heavy.

Wehmeier's

719 Toulouse Street; ☎ *(504) 525-2758, 10 a.m.–6 p.m., daily.*
Known best for their exotic leathers, including alligator and snake (hopefully no one you met on your swamp tour) that are fashioned into trés chic shoes, bags and incredibly expensive boots. Beauty here is definitely skin-deep.

Umbrella Lady

1107 Decatur Street; ☎ *(504) 523-7791, 10 a.m.–6 p.m., daily.*
Don't just drop in, the umbrella lady might be out getting more lace for her one-of-a-kind parasols. You could be "Scarlett for a Day" with one of her creations. She makes regular Mary Poppins specials but the elaborate parasols are irresistible.

Leah's Candy Kitchen

714 St. Louis Street; ☎ *(504) 523-5662,10 a.m.–8 p.m., daily.*
Pralines to the right of me, pralines to the left of me, but I always
return to Leah's for her buttery confections. She does other goodies
as well, but get real! You're in praline heaven. Go for the gold!

Rodrique Gallery

721 Royal Street; ☎ *(504) 581-4244, 10 a.m.–6 p.m., daily.*
The home of that dog of another color, George Rodrique's "Blue
Dog." Get ready to see the blue menace all over the city. He's
become New Orleans' very unofficial mascot. "Am I Blue" must be
Rodrique's favorite song.

Lucullus

610 Chartres Street; ☎ *(504) 528-9620, 9:30 a.m.–5 p.m., Mon.–Sat.*
This antique shop is particularly of interest to cooks, chefs and gourmets because of their delicious collection of culinary antiques dating
back to the 17th century.

Lillian Shon Gallery

533 St. Louis Street; ☎ *(504) 525-5564, 10 a.m.–6 p.m., Mon.–Sat.*
Fine art housed in an old bank. And you'll be called upon to make a
major deposit if you intend to take one of the excellent canvases with
you. This is a top gallery in New Orleans.

M. S. Rau Antiques

630 Royal Street; ☎ *(504) 523-5660, 9 a.m.–5:15 p.m., Mon.–Sat.*
Displaying American antiques of excellent quality since 1912, this is
an internationally known collection.

Moss Antiques

411 Royal Street; ☎ *(504) 522-3981, 9 a.m.–5 p.m., Mon.–Sat.*
Outstanding French and English furniture. Even if you're not in the
market for a settee, one of the sparklers from their estate jewel collection is very packable.

Whisnant Gallerie

222 Chartres Street; ☎ *(504) 524-9766, 9:30 a.m.–5:30 p.m., Mon.–Sat.*
An everything treasure trove from everywhere in the world. The store
is a fascinating mixture of collectibles from Ethiopia, Morocco, Rus-
sia, South America and of course early southern from around the
region.

Diane Genre Oriental Art

233 Royal Street; ☎ *(504) 525-7270, 10 a.m.–5 p.m., Mon.–Sat.*
Chinese and Japanese art and furnishings through the 19th century
prove to be inscrutably beautiful.

Dixon & Dixon of Royal

237 and 318 Royal Street; ☎ *(504) 524-0282, 9 a.m.–5:30 p.m., daily.*
Another knockout in "Antiques Row," on Royal. Both of their shops
have fine antiques, rugs and crystal. They also carry fabulous estate
jewelry which usually does not remain under their roof for very long.

Waldhorn Company

343 Royal Street; ☎ *(504) 581-6379, 10 a.m.–5:30 p.m., daily.*
Four generations of Waldhorns have contributed to the antiques business of Royal Street; in fact they are the oldest having been established
in 1880.

Le Garage

1234 Decatur; ☎ *(504) 522-6639, noon–6 p.m., daily.*
The kitchen sink type "junque shop" which is thoroughly captivating.

Zombies House of Voodoo

723 St. Peter Street; ☎ *(504) 4-Voodoo, 10 a.m.–11 p.m., Mon.–Fri.; 10 a.m.–1 a.m., Sat.–Sun.*
Take it from me, this place is great fun. Plastic skulls, voodoo potions and rude ties. Gifts for Aunt Googie and the kids!

La Belle Gallerie

309 Chartres Street; ☎ *(504) 529-3080, 10 a.m.–7 p.m., daily.*
An entire gallery devoted to the art of the African American culture. Everything from African primitive to racy posters of the great Josephine Baker. They feature the work of African American regional artists as well.

Agenda Best Bites/The French Quarter

Coffee Pot Restaurant $

714 St. Peter Street; ☎ *(504) 524-3500.*
Cuisine: American. Avg. $10–$20.
Hours: 8 a.m.–midnight, daily.
Much more than just a quick cup of Jo, their special French Quarter breakfast fare includes a Creole rice cake called a "Cala." Crisp and crusty on the outside, the inside is buttery and fragrant with cinnamon. For added cholesterol they're accompanied by grits, syrup and a dusting of powdered sugar. Credit Cards: All Major.

Lucky Cheng's $$$

720 St. Louis Street; ☎ *(504) 529-2045.*
Cuisine: Asian. Avg. $40–$60.
Lunch: 11:30 a.m.–3 p.m., daily.
Dinner: 6–11 p.m., daily.
Don't believe everything you *see*. That beautiful blonde serving your egg foo young is more likely to be named Robert than Roberta. Heaping portions of camp and drag, along with "OK" Chinese or Thai specialties. The decor is elegantly decadent enough for your average voyeur. Credit Cards: All Major.

Central Grocery Co. $

923 Decatur Street; ☎ *(504) 523-1620.*
Cuisine: Italian. Avg. $10–$20.
Hours: 8 a.m.–5:30 p.m., daily.
The sandwich that ate the city. Big enough for Godzilla's lunch, the muffaletta (whole round loaf of Italian bread stuffed with layers of deli meats, cheese, peppers and olive salad—burp!) is the national sandwich of New Orleans. Central Grocery, open for lunch only, is renowned for these blockbusters. Don't even think of ordering a whole one unless you're part of an army. You can ask for a half or a quarter if you're alone. The counter seating arrangements don't make

lingering over your muffaletta a possibility which is just as well since brisk movement after ingestion is vital. Credit Cards: Not Accepted.

Tujague's $$

823 Decatur Street; ☎ (504) 525-8676.
Cuisine: French/Southern. Avg. $20–$40.
Lunch: 11 a.m.–3 p.m., daily.
Dinner: 5–10:30 p.m., daily.

Two-Jacks in this case means a full house, right across from the French Market. It started as a breakfast spot for the butchers of the market back in 1856. Today the food at lunch and dinner is straightforward good solid briskets and shrimp remoulade. Credit Cards: All Major.

Acme Oyster House $$$

724 Iberville Street; ☎ (504) 522-5973.
Cuisine: Fish house. Avg. $5–$10.
Hours: 11 a.m.–10 p.m., Mon.–Sat.; noon–7 p.m., Sun.

One of the contenders for the best oyster Po-Boy sandwich in town, Acme is packed with crustacean cravers from the minute it opens. They're usually served on thick French bread and washed down with cold beer. If you take your oyster "au natural," then shucks, all you have to do is belly up to Acme's oyster bar. Credit Cards: All Major.

Croissant d'Or $

615-17 Ursulines Street; ☎ (504) 524-4663.
Cuisine: Coffee house. Avg. $5–$10.
Hours: 7 a.m.–5 p.m., daily.

The best kept secret by the locals so that they can have breakfast in peace. Every morning they sit over their steaming café-au-laits and quiches or pastry, with the paper spread out before them. The art-deco room is near perfect for lingering. Credit Cards: Not Accepted.

Rib Room $$$

621 St. Louis Street (Royal Orleans Hotel); ☎ (504) 529-7045.
Cuisine: Steak house. Avg. $30–$60.
Lunch: 11:30-2:30 p.m., daily.
Dinner: 6–10 p.m., daily.

The judges who lunch here, since it's so near the Court, have sentenced themselves to thick aged steaks, terrific potatoes and triple (that's what I said) martinis served in brandy snifters. Most lawyers in town try to have their cases heard in the afternoon. Credit Cards: All Major.

Café Maspero $

601 Decatur Street; ☎ (504) 523-6250.
Cuisine: Deli. Avg. $10–$20.
Hours: 11 a.m.–11 p.m. daily.

Some of the most sought-after sandwiches in the French Quarter. People line up down the street for their deli delights. Credit Cards: Not Accepted.

Louisiana Pizza Kitchen $

95 French Market Pl; ☎ (504) 522-9500.
Cuisine: Italian. Avg. $10–$20.
Hours: 11 a.m.–10 p.m., Sun.–Thurs.; 11 a.m.–11 p.m., Fri. & Sat.

Who goes to New Orleans for pizza? Just follow the Orleanians to the "hottest" pizza oven in town. Some are designer varieties with smoked salmon, caviar and pesto. Others are just good old Neapolitan favorites. Credit Cards: All Major.

Gumbo Shop $$

630 St. Peter Street; ☎ *(504) 525-1486.*
Cuisine: Cajun. Avg. $15–$30.
Hours: 11 a.m.–11 p.m., daily.
Gumbo 101 is the name of the game here. Don't expect wonders but as a first exposure it's terrific. Sit in the garden if it's not too incendiary outside. Credit Cards: All Major.

Café Sbisa $$$

1011 Decatur Street; ☎ *(504) 522-5565.*
Cuisine: French. Avg. $40–$60.
Dinner: 5:30–10 p.m., daily.
This trendy, atmospheric bistro is a gorgeous spot to have a plate of garlicky mussels if you are near the French Market. The garden is luscious and the inside dining rooms are old New Orleans perfection. If you're up to it, the specialty of the house is turtle soup. Credit Cards: All Major.

La Marquise $

625 Chartres Street; ☎ *(504) 524-0420.*
Cuisine: Coffee house. Avg. $10–$20.
Hours: 7 a.m.–5 p.m., daily.
Their pastries are every bit as good as the ones at Croissant D'Or, on **Ursuline Street** because the same baker creates the goodies for both coffee houses. Credit Cards: Not Accepted.

Central Business District (CBD)

Even though the glittering jewel in New Orleans' crown is the **French Quarter**, all is not lost when you cross mighty **Canal Street**, the dividing line between the **Vieux Carré** and the "real world." In the early days **Canal Street** was considered a neutral zone with the elegant, worldly and sophisticated Creole gentry on the **French Quarter** side and those scruffy uncivilized and totally lacking in social graces, Yankee settlers on the other side of the **Canal Street** tracks. Well, today the CBD is hardly the wrong side of the tracks although most of the culture and Old World charm is still in the **French Quarter**. The world of trade, finance and of course that super sports center, the **Superdome**, are all alive and well on the "other side of the tracks." The only loose screw in the CBD's wheel of fortune was the gazillion dollar casino that was to be built at the end of Canal Street. Unfortunately it "crapped-out" before it was even open. The last time I was in town the city fathers were brainstorming furiously to think up a new use for their bankrupt beauty.

The beginning of today's **CBD** is at the point that **Canal Street** meets the **Mississippi**. The street itself is of heroic proportion, its width is over 170 feet, more like a lavish European boulevard than Main Street USA. At the moment, Canal is a bit rundown and filled with discount shops, schlock emporiums and fly-by-night merchants. On its flip side, Canal sports high rise convention hotels, the venerable old department stores of New Orleans and **Canal Place**, a glitzy mall decked out with Saks, Gucci and the deluxe Weston Canal Place Hotel. No matter how depressed some of **Canal Street** looks most of the time during the Mardi Gras all of the major parades show themselves off on **Fat Tuesday** by "floating" down its wide expanse, which is the city's primary parade route.

The rest of the **CBD** is really booming. **Woldenberg Riverfront Park**, which was brand new as of 1989, includes the **Aquarium of the Americas** (see Top Sights page 23), begins way up at the **Moonwalk** in the **French Quarter** and extends down to the **Canal Street Ferry** landing. The entrance to **Riverwalk**, a mall that connects the **Hilton** with the **Convention Center** is right next door. The park itself is over 13 acres of flowering magnolia trees, crepe myrtles and live oaks. It's a wonderful spot to just sit and gaze at the **Mississippi**. Don't miss the exciting kinetic sculpture by native New Orleanian John Scott. He named it Ocean Song and it rises to 16 feet, all made of stainless steel. **The World Trade Center** is also a part of the Park Complex and soars to the splendid height of 33 stories. Used for consulates and foreign trade missions there are occasional art shows in the lobby, so if you're passing take a peek. Most people visit the **Trade Center** for the glorious view from its revolving cocktail lounge on (see Bars, page 178) the top floor, **Top of the Mart**, or a couple of floors below on the observation deck.

The **Morial Convention Center** (*900 Convention Center Boulevard*) will probably never win a prize for avant garde architecture, but it is $88 million worth of floor space that makes it the third largest exhibition space in the country. It was named after Ernest Morial, New Orleans' first black mayor. It has been enlarged twice and now covers more than 1 million square feet. One of the best things about the **Convention Center** is **Riverwalk** which connects it to the **Hilton** or the **Warehouse District** in a mercifully climate-controlled atmosphere. The mall itself is identical to any other mall on the planet with the exception of its lovely outside terrace that overlooks "Ole Man River." A perfect spot to reflect upon your Haagan Daz or chili dog.

AGENDA'S GAYLORD RAVANOL MEMORIAL

Riverboat gambling has held a romantic place in everyone's hearts since Magnolia waited for Gaylord to deal his last hand. Today, New Orleans' Riverboat Casinos ply the Mississippi without "good old Gay!" They're not quite as romantic but they're lively and well run. The most celebrated of the moment is the Flamingo which runs 24 hours a day. It may not be the Cottonblossom but it's a real experience—you can bet on it!

AGENDA'S GAYLORD RAVANOL MEMORIAL

Poydras Street at the River;

☎ (504) 587-1640.

The most overwhelming of the newer attractions in the Big Easy is unquestionably the **Superdome** (See Top Sights page 21). It's the home of the **Saints**, New Orleans home team. Nearby is the **Civic Center** which houses **City Hall**, the **State Supreme Court**, as well as the **New Orleans Public Library**, which is known for its excellent research collection *(219 Loyola Avenue,* ☎ *(504) 529-7323).*

The fabled **Orpheum Theatre** at *129 University Place* was one of the most famous vaudeville houses in the country. Every big "act" played the Orpheum during the era of the "2-a-day." At the present Orpheum is the home of the **Louisiana Philharmonic**. If the orchestra is in town when you visit it would be a treat to look inside. *(*☎ *(504) 524-3285).*

AGENDA RAISES THE ROOF

The U.S. Customs House which is a massive, city-block square edifice has within its gloomy interior an astonishment called the Marble Hall. Nothing in the rest of this very dull structure prepares you for this amazing space. Located on the third floor is a chamber 54 feet high. The weight of its immense skylight is borne by 14 floor to ceiling marble pillars. Talk about being supportive.

Agenda Shopping/
Central Business District

Meyer the Hatter

120 St. Charles Avenue; ☎ *(504) 525-1048, 10 a.m.–5:45 p.m., Mon.–Sat. Closed Sun.*

He's been keeping a lid on things since 1894 so if you're in the market for a Panama or a Stetson, Meyer is your man.

Mignon Faget

Canal Place (Mall), Level I; ☎ *(504) 524-2973, 10 a.m.–6 p.m., Mon.–Wed.; 10 a.m.–7 p.m., Thurs.–Sat.; noon–6 p.m., Sun.*

A remarkable local jewelry designer with excitingly unique pieces. She works not only in 14K gold and sterling but also in "bronze d'oré."

RHINO

Canal Place (Mall) Level I; ☎ *(504) 523-7945, 10 a.m.–6 p.m., Mon.–Wed.; 10 a.m.–7 p.m., Thurs.–Sat.; noon–6 p.m., Sun.*

Talk about cooperation, 80 artists have formed one of the most glamorous nonprofit cooperatives to be seen anywhere. Their gallery is filled with showstoppers. Glass, furniture designs, sculpture, ceramics and textiles are all represented in an ultramodern shop.

Brooks Brothers

365 Canal Street; ☎ *(504) 522-4200, 10 a.m.–7 p.m., Mon.–Wed; 10 a.m.–7 p.m., Thurs.–Sat.; noon–6 p.m., Sun.*
Just in case you drip jambalaya on your favorite B.B. blazer, there are hundreds more where it comes from!

Wild Wings Gallery

Riverwalk #1 (Mall); ☎ *(504) 522-9464, 10 a.m.–9 p.m., Mon.–Sat.; 11 a.m.–7 p.m., Sun.*
This is not a place where you can get an order of spicy buffalo wings, it's a wildlife publisher's showcase for prints and books as well as fine bronzes and original wildlife art. Just the place to let nature take its course.

Rubenstein Bros.

Canal Street at St. Charles Avenue; ☎ *(504) 581-6666, 10 a.m.–5:45 p.m., Mon.–Sat.*
Armani and Tommy Hilfiger come to New Orleans here along with all the other top men's designers.

Louisiana Potpourri

Canal Place (Mall); ☎ *(504) 524-9023, 10 a.m.–6 p.m., Mon.–Wed.; 10 a.m.–7 p.m., Thurs.–Sat.; 11 a.m.–5 p.m., Sun.*
Gumbo to go in this shop that lets you carry off a taste of the "Big Easy."

Adler & Sons

722 Canal Street; ☎ *(504) 523-5292, 10 a.m.–5:30 p.m., daily.*
A venerable jeweler in the city since 1898, when Mardi Gras jewels were real. The "best" families still shop for engagement sparklers here.

Linens

Canal Place (Mall); ☎ *(504) 586-8148, 10 a.m.–6 p.m., Mon.–Wed.; 10 a.m.–7 p.m., Thurs.–Sat.; 11 a.m.–5 p.m., Sun.*
A very matter-of-fact name for a shop that stocks sumptuous linens and bedding from all over the world. Their collection of christening gowns is especially delicate.

Agenda Best Bites/ Central Business District

Kabby's $$$ ★

New Orleans Hilton, 2 Poydras Street; ☎ *(504) 584-3880.*
Cuisine: American. Avg. $40–$60.
Lunch: 11 a.m.–2:30 p.m., daily.
Dinner: 6–11 p.m., daily.
I have to say in all honesty, don't go for the food, but just as honestly, Kabby's has a dynamite view of the Mississippi. Your best bet would

be brunch here—what can they do to soft-boiled eggs? Credit Cards: All
Major.

Bon Ton Cafe $$$

401 Magazine Street; ☎ *(504) 524-3386.*
Cuisine: Creole. Avg. $40–$60.
Lunch: 11 a.m.–2 p.m., Mon.–Fri.
Dinner: 5–9:30 p.m., Mon.–Fri.
One of the best Creole restaurants in the city, the locals guard its
identity with the same dedication as "Deep Throat." Since it's on
lower Magazine Street, it's near enough to **Canal Street** to stroll over
for a memorable lunch in a not so memorable setting. But don't let
the simple surroundings fool you, the kitchen has been turning out
"serious" cuisine for the past 40 years. The seafood bisques alone are
worth a visit. Credit Cards: All Major.

Hummingbird Grill $

804 St. Charles Avenue; ☎ *(504) 561-9229.*
Cuisine: American. Avg. $10–$20.
Hours: 24 hours, 7 days.
Breakfast devoteés call this place their 24 hour mecca. Aside from
that, it's where the elite love to eat after the ball is over. Rich and
richer meet cops and cabbies over huge plates of grits and eggs or
chops. Credit Cards: Not Accepted.

New City Diner $

828 Gravier Street; ☎ *(504) 522-8198.*
Cuisine: Diner. Avg. $10–$20.
Hours: 7 a.m.–2 p.m., Mon.–Fri.
A wonderful, wholesome cafeteria type place with fine American cui-
sine. By the look of it you'd never guess that the locals regard it a very
"in" place for lunch. They also specialize in the best of salads. Credit
Cards: Not Accepted.

El Liborio Cuban Restaurant $$

322 Magazine Street; ☎ *(504) 581-9680.*
Cuisine: Cuban. Avg. $20–$35.
Lunch: 11 a.m.–2 p.m.
Dinner: 6–9 p.m.
A Cuban beat in New Orleans. Of course, it blends perfectly with all
the other beats around town not to mention adding Cuban soul food
to the landscape. Credit Cards: All Major.

Pearl $

119 St. Charles Avenue; ☎ *(504) 525-2901.*
Cuisine: Oyster house. Avg. $10–$20.
Hours: 10 a.m.–9 p.m. daily.
Not the best of the oyster "temples" but the **St. Charles Avenue
Streetcar** stops right outside so it's just too convenient to pass up.
Try their signature pastrami sandwich.

Garden District

Who would have thought that the same "frosty" reception
some Parisians give "Les Americans" when they try to get a table
in a top restaurant, or ask directions on the Champs-Elyseés is

the very reason the **Garden District** of New Orleans came about. The Americans who started to show up in New Orleans in the early 1800s, soon found that the Creoles were intent on carrying chauvinism, heavily laced with snobbery to new heights. They strongly suggested that the uncouth, uncivilized upstarts form their own colony across **Canal Street**, not even within sniffing distance of a decent bowl of onion soup. What's a settler from the wrong side of the tracks to do? One solution was to get rich as soon as possible which is exactly what they did. In retaliation for the rapid success of "those barbarians," the Creoles blocked the recognition of English as the official language of the city, built their own public square in the **Vieux Carré** and most importantly made sure that all significant civic improvements were first done for them (translation: plumbing and street paving). Not satisfied with making as much trouble as possible for the Americans, the Creoles continued to complain very vocally about the courts having favored the "dirty-fingernail set" with rulings that made it even easier for their financial lot to improve. The **Louisiana Purchase** was an item the Creoles wished in their hearts the Americans would decide to return.

The Garden District boasts many architectural gems.

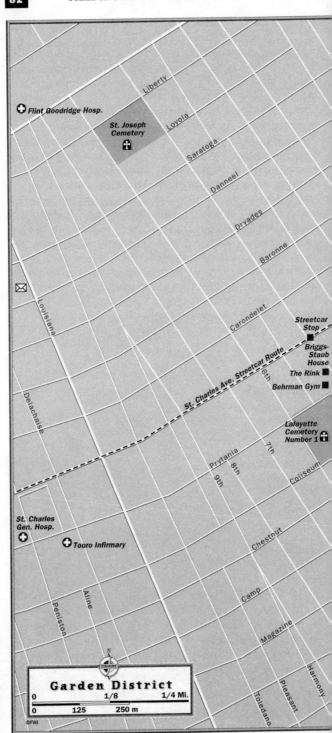

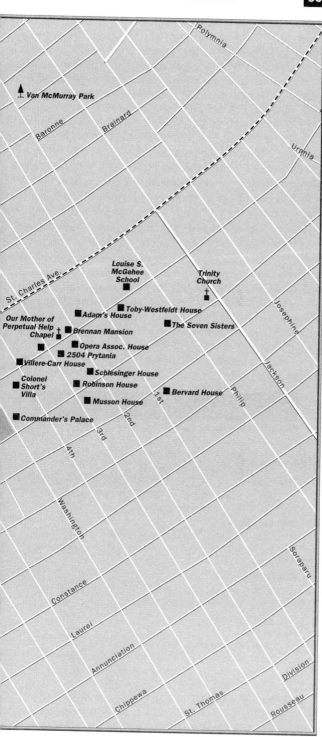

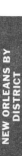

Back on the other side of **Canal Street** huge fortunes were being made by the Yankee interlopers who excelled in both merchandising and commerce. They began to build their homes further and further from Canal until their very own District stretched uptown as far as the tiny town of **Carrollton**. They named their new town **Lafayette City**. The homes that were built by the nouveau riche Yankees became more and more extravagant, with styles that ranged from Greek Revival, to Victorian, to Antebellum Plantation house. Sometimes all three came together to display a new romanticism. Eventually all of the separate areas of the city were joined together in a united New Orleans. **Lafayette City** became known as the **Garden District** since most of the mansions had magnificent gardens that only enhanced their architectural extravagance.

Today the **Garden District** is somewhat more a state of mind than its botanical name would imply. It is an area of great contrasts. Some of the opulent homes have been preserved with great flair and drama, and some have deteriorated to "haunted house" status, ripe for Anne Rice to use as one of Lestat's accommodations. The trees however are still the magnificent live oaks that were originally planted in the early 1800s. They stretch across the streets to form covered arbors. The flowers in the gardens that do remain are lush bougainvillaea, jasmine, gardenias, sweet olives, camellias, and lavender. In the spring the **Garden District** is alive with color.

REAL ESTATE MR. BLANDINGS WOULD HAVE DIED FOR!

Brevard-Mmahat House
> *1239 First St. (Chestnut), 1857.*
> Today Anne Rice has "interviews" with her very own family here.

Toby's Corner
> *2340 Prytania (First Street), 1838.*
> The oldest house in the District.

Robinson House
> *1415 Third Street (Coliseum Street), 1859.*
> It was built with tobacco money and no expense was spared.

Grima House
> *1604 Fourth Street (St. Charles), 1850.*
> Second Empire in design, it has three magnificent landscaped gardens.

Buckner House
> *1410 Jackson Avenue (Coliseum Street), 1856.*
> White plantation style house with 48 columns and a wraparound gallery. Even though it takes up a spectacular 22,000 sq feet, it's still held as a private residence.

Wedding Cake House, The
> *5809 St. Charles Avenue.*
> The name speaks for itself.

The streets that hold most of the residential gems in the **Garden District** are **Prytania**, **Coliseum**, **Third**, **Fourth**, **Esplanade** and of course **St. Charles Avenue**. Even though the word for most of this area is delightful, there is also a less comforting description and that is "changeable." Within seconds one can go from the sublime to the dangerous. Interspersed within the streets are pockets of run-down, poverty level housing that make walking a careful adventure. By all means tour the streets of the **Garden District** but don't wander off the main routes. And most importantly, do not explore **Lafayette Cemetery** alone, try to join a small tour. This particular cemetery is one of Anne Rice's favorite Lestat hangouts. Maybe you'll get lucky!

The somber, elegant Gothic cathedral, **Christ Church** is at *2919 St. Charles Avenue* and has more than 100 stained-glass windows. It was begun in 1887. Close by, the oddest newly acquired "landmark" in the Garden District is a steel and glass replica of the **Eiffel Tower** that stands forlornly at *2040 St. Charles Avenue*. The entire structure was originally a restaurant within the real Eiffel Tower in you-know-where. It seems that the weight of it was doing real damage to the Eiffel eye-full so it was taken apart, packed-up and shipped off to its New Orleans cousins. However, the moral of the story is never trust a Frenchman bearing towers. The restaurant was a disaster and today is used only for catering.

Lower Magazine Street (see Garden District shopping) is part of the **Garden District**. It's full of junkshops, antique galleries and everything but the kitchen sink. Even if you only have a couple of hours to spare, this part of New Orleans is as fascinating in its own way as the French Quarter. The **Garden District** is truly the Old South come to life before you.

Agenda Shopping/Garden District

Magazine Street from Bottom to Top

Shopping hours are traditionally 11 a.m.–6 p.m., daily, on Magazine Street. However, it is always best to call in advance.

Potsalot
1516 Magazine Street, ☎ *(504) 524-6238.*
Handmade kitchenware, metal and ceramics.

Leon Irwin Antiques
1800 Magazine Street, ☎ *(504) 522-5555.*
Expensive antique furniture.

Magazine Street from Bottom to Top

Jim Smiley Vintage Clothes
2001 Magazine Street, ☎ *(504) 528-9449.*
Exceptional 19th & 20th century wearing apparel and textiles.

Almost New, Inc.
2005 Magazine Street, ☎ *(504) 522-8355.*
Vintage resale, costumes, nostalgia broker.

Hands
2023 Magazine Street, ☎ *(504) 522-2590.*
Pre-Columbian artifacts.

Bep's
2051 Magazine Street, ☎ *(504) 525-7726.*
English and American antiques including small collectibles.

Mona Mia's Antiques
2105 Magazine Street, ☎ *(504) 525-8686.*
A little bit of everything that's fun.

Bush Antiques
2109 Magazine Street, ☎ *(504) 581-3518.*
Antiques and furniture from old New Orleans homes.

Antique Vault
2123 Magazine Street, ☎ *(504) 523-8888.*
A little bit of everything.

Morton Goldberg's Antique Annex
2205 Magazine Street, ☎ *(504) 525-2639.*
A huge collection of furniture and accessories.

Antiques & Things
2855 Magazine Street, ☎ *(504) 897-9466.*
Collectibles Mall, it goes on and on.

Belladonna
2900 Magazine Street, ☎ *(504) 891-4393.*
A mini-spa right in the middle of Magazine Street. They have a gift shop as well.

Aurat Antiques
3009 Magazine Street, ☎ *(504) 897-3210.*
Very special Anglo-Indian as well as Indo-Portuguese colonial furniture. Also antique carpets.

Magazine Arcade Antiques
3017 Magazine Street, ☎ *(504) 895-5451.*
Furniture, Bric-A-Brac, curiosities. Browsers heaven.

Curzon Hall
3105 Magazine Street, ☎ *(504) 899-0078.*
Originally a shop on Portobello Road in London the owner brings English antiques regularly from "Blighty."

Magazine Street from Bottom to Top

George Herget Books

3109 Magazine Street, ☎ *(504) 891-5595.*
Bookworm heaven. Over 20,000 used and rare books to browse. It could take most of your day.

Quest

3118 Magazine Street, ☎ *(504) 891-6434.*
Antique toys, trains, cameras.

Wilkerson Row

3137 Magazine Street, ☎ *(504) 899-3311.*
Architectural artifacts from houses that have been torn down are incorporated into new designs by Shaun Wilkerson. Very special.

Fiesta

3322 Magazine Street, ☎ *(504) 895-7877.*
Vintage clothes and assorted kitsch.

Morgan-West

3326 Magazine Street, ☎ *(504) 895-7976.*
New Orleans artist, Perry Morgan exhibits contemporary furniture and crafts in all media from both local and nationally known artists.

Didier Inc.

3439 Magazine Street, ☎ *(504) 899-7749.*
Very pricey 19th century Americana.

Carmen Llewellyn

3901 Magazine Street, ☎ *(504) 891-5301.*
Contemporary Latin American Art.

Orient Expressed

3905 Magazine Street, ☎ *(504) 899-3060.*
Oriental and Spanish antiques as well as handmade childrens clothes.

Davis Gallery

3964 Magazine Street, ☎ *(504) 897-0780.*
Serious collectors love their African and Pre-Columbian Art.

Talebloo

4130 Magazine Street, ☎ *(504) 899-8114.*
A Persian bazaar of antiques and contemporary rugs.

Magazine Street Books

4222 Magazine Street, ☎ *(504) 899-6905.*
For the comic book collector. Over 250,000 in stock.

Textile Arts

4526 Magazine Street, ☎ *(504) 899-5865.*
Needlepoint, crewel, and crocheting canvases. A huge selection for the needle-person.

La Librairie d'Arcadie

4729 Magazine Street, ☎ *(504) 523-4138.*
Imported French books and prints.

Magazine Street from Bottom to Top

Sixpence, Inc.
4904 Magazine Street, ☎ (504) 895-1267.
Gifts as well as fine antiques.

British Antiques
5415 Magazine Street, ☎ (504) 895-3716.
Fine English and Oriental pieces.

Shoe Outlet
5419 Magazine Street, ☎ (504) 895-5319.
By the time you reach this place you'll need a new pair.
Magazine Street goes on forever. They have major discounts.

Gallery for Fine Photography
5423A Magazine Street, ☎ (504) 891-1002.
19th and 20th century photos, books and posters.

Audubon Antiques
5509 Magazine Street, ☎ (504) 897-1733.
American and English furniture, glass, silver and costume
jewelry at very modest prices.

Wirthmore
5723 Magazine Street, ☎ (504) 897-9727.
Very important 18th and 19th century French antiques.

"But, in the end, you will become bored with that, too."
Drawing by Gahan Wilson; ©1995 The New Yorker Magazine, Inc.

Garden District Books
*2727 Prytania Street; ☎ (504) 895-2266, 10 a.m.–6 p.m., Mon.–Sat.; 11
a.m.–4 p.m., Sun.*

Since this very excellent collection of books is only several blocks from "vampire chronicler" Anne Rice's house, guess who gets shelf space to the max here?

Stan Levy Imports

1028 Louisiana Avenue; ☎ *(504) 899-6384, 9:30 a.m.–5:30 p.m., Mon.–Sat. Closed Sun.*
This is a warehouse setting for 18th, 19th and 20th century antiques. Also rare paintings and bronzes.

Agenda Best Bites/Garden District

Semolina $$

3242 Magazine Street; ☎ *(504) 895-4260.*
Cuisine: Italian. Avg. $20–$30.
Hours: 11 a.m.–10 p.m., Mon.–Thurs.; 11 a.m.–11 p.m., Fri.–Sat.
If you feel like noodling around Magazine Street, Semolina does pasta every which way. The salads are gigantic and the bread drips with garlic butter. Credit Cards: All Major.

Café Atchafalaya $

901 Louisiana Avenue; ☎ *(504) 891-5271.*
Cuisine: Southern. Avg. $10–$20.
Lunch: 11:30 a.m.–2 p.m., daily.
Dinner: 5:30–9 p.m., daily.
Home cooking that the locals in the Garden District simply can't do without. They were making their fried green tomatoes long before they became Hollywood's favorite dish.

Casamento's $$

4330 Magazine Street; ☎ *(504) 895-9761.*
Cuisine: Oyster house. Avg. $20–$40.
Lunch: 11:30 a.m.–1:30 p.m., Tues.–Sun.
Dinner: 5:30–9 p.m., Tues.–Sun.
It's not clear which sparkles the most at this hallowed eatery in the G.D., the walls or the oysters. The place is as white as an operating room and the crusty crustaceans are opened with surgical skill. Credit Cards: Not Accepted.

Pie in the Sky $

1818 Magazine Street; ☎ *(504) 522-6291.*
Cuisine: Italian. Avg. $10–$20.
Hours: 11 a.m.–10 p.m., daily.
Pizza is the pie in question but the answer is obvious. Great pie, great sandwiches and a great funky fringe group of regulars. Credit Cards: All Major.

Joey K $

3001 Magazine Street; ☎ *(504) 891-0997.*
Cuisine: American. Avg. $10–$20.
Hours: 11 a.m.–10 p.m., daily.

Creole to the max with great onion rings thrown in for good measure. Also a superior chicken fried steak if you're on a cholesterol spree. <small>Credit Cards: All Major.</small>

Parasol's $

2533 Constance Street (1st Street); ☎ *(504) 899-2054.*
Cuisine: Southern. Avg. $10–$20.
Hours: 11 a.m.–3 p.m., Mon.–Thurs.; 11 a.m.–6 p.m., Fri.–Sat.
A "good ole boy's" good ole neighborhood bar. Miles of sausage Po-Boys and gallons of ice cold beer. They say you have to eat the delectably drippy sandwiches in a raincoat. <small>Credit Cards: Not Accepted.</small>

Home Furnishings Store Café $

1600 Prytania Street; ☎ *(504) 566-1707.*
Cuisine: Burgers. Avg. $10–$20.
Hours: 11 a.m.–3 p.m., Mon.–Sat.
Yes—it looks like a furniture store, but walk all the way to the back. There's a small self-service cafe that serves one of the best lunches in town. All the basics like terrific burgers, chunky salads, good pasta. What becomes a well-furnished room more? <small>Credit Cards: All Major.</small>

Rue de la Course $

1500 Magazine Street; ☎ *(504) 899-0242.*
Cuisine: Coffee house. Avg. $10–$20.
Hours: 7 a.m.–11 p.m., daily.
Cappuccinos, lattes and desserts served up with chess boards for caffeine overachievers. <small>Credit Cards: Not Accepted.</small>

Caribbean Room $$$

2031 St. Charles Avenue (The Pontchartrain Hotel); ☎ *(504) 524-0581.*
Cuisine: Southern. Avg. $40–$60.
Dinner: 5:30–9:30 p.m., Tues.–Sat.
Very fancy with prices to match but it has its very own legendary "mile-high" ice cream pie, an unbelievable towering testimony to overindulgence. Sauces, colors, flavors, textures and most of all size. Eat at your own risk. <small>Credit Cards: All Major.</small>

Warehouse/Arts District

If Shakespeare were alive today he might well have observed "the gallery's the thing." All the world seems to be sprouting centers for artists, craftspeople, and of course "boutique babies" to gentrify the low rent districts. After all, they are the most hospitable area for the young and the struggling. Taking a leaf from the New York book of trendy triumphs, New Orleans has created its very own SoHo in the **Warehouse District** of town. The big spaces that were once used for coffee and cotton have been transformed into glitzy galleries along with the really charming **Louisiana Children's Museum** (see Museums, page 165). In fact, even if you're not accessorized by a kid or two you'll still have a terrific time trying out all the bells and whistles that make this museum a joy. The gift shop has some of the best goodies in town for the small ones you've left behind.

The building that is at the center of the contemporary arts community in New Orleans is very aptly called **The Contemporary Arts Center**, at *900 Camp Street*. Both Camp and Julia are the streets with the most action in this ever-growing complex dedicated to the newest of New Orleans' talent. The Art Center itself is a huge rambling warehouse that was donated to the cause by an equally huge corporation when it changed locations. So far the 40,000 feet of open space has umpteen galleries, twin theatres and is planning a museum of modern art. The design of the Center itself is a miracle of glass, exposed steel beams and splotches of color (see Museums and Galleries, page 161).

Not only is the art scene percolating furiously in the **Warehouse District**, the real estate and hotel developers have not been totally unaware of the creeping capitalism that has descended on an otherwise seedy blue-collar community. Aside from the artists lofts, there is a booming co-op market for "Y'all yuppies." Cappuccino bars have appeared in the dead of night and you know what that means.

If you're lucky enough to be in The Big Easy on the first Saturday of the month there is a celebration open to the public so that new artists and their exhibitions can be highlighted. Restaurants serve tidbits on the street and viewers are invited to roam the galleries. They are very well-attended events, perhaps because of the party atmosphere. The biggest of these block parties is held on the first Saturday in October. The event is called "Art for Art Sake" and the whole city comes out to give a boost to the new fall season.

A little further up **St. Charles Avenue** and at the end of the Warehouse District is **Lee Circle**. There's a stern statue of old Robert E. and a few depressing benches. This is not a place to have a picnic but it's on the way to **K&B Plaza** which has a wonderful sculpture gallery both inside the lobby and outside in the Plaza. A heroic piece by Isamu Noguchi entitled "The Mississippi" is darkly dramatic. It's definitely worth stopping on your way uptown as you leave the Warehouse District. If you have some time to spare after all that gallery hopping, wander down to **Julia Row** which is in the 600's on **Julia Street**. There are magnificent 19th century houses that line the streets, particularly a stretch known as the **Thirteen Sisters**, 13 row houses of elegant distinction. The **Preservation Resource Center of New Orleans** nearby at *604 Julia Street* sometimes give wonderful tours of the area at no cost. (☎ *(504) 581-7032*).

The Irish immigrants who found they were definitely not wanted in that monument to French Colonialism called the **French Quarter** had the last laugh when they built their own impressively Gothic St. Patrick's Church uptown, on **Camp Street**. Not only was it named for the Patron Saint of Ireland but it was designed by Irish architects. What makes the Cathedral so ap-

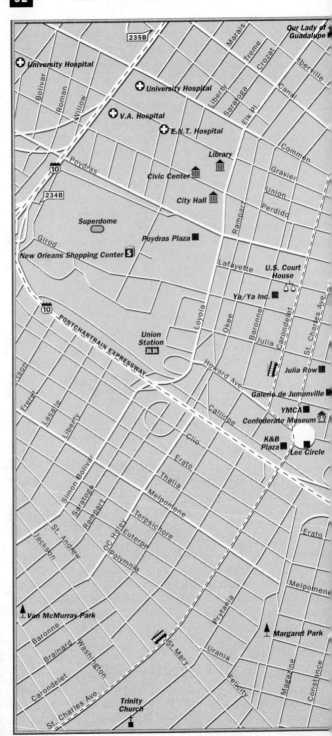

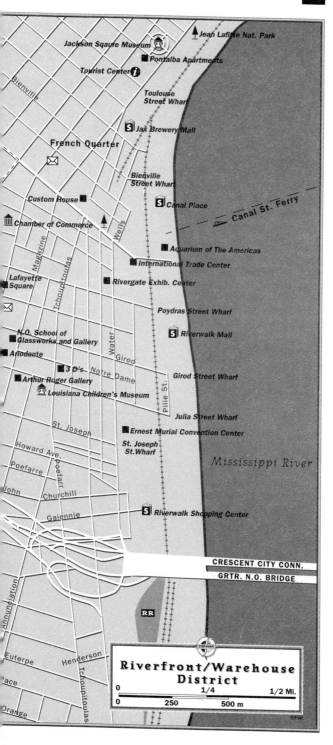

Jean Lafitte Nat. Park

Jackson Sqaure Museum
Pontalba Apartments

Tourist Center

Bienville

Toulouse
Street Wharf

Jax Brewery Mall

French Quarter

Bienville
Street Wharf

Custom House

Canal Place

Canal St. Ferry

Chamber of Commerce

Wells

Aquarium of The Americas

International Trade Center

Lafayette
Square

Magazine

Tchoupitoulas

Rivergate Exhib. Center

Poydras Street Wharf

N.O. School of
Glassworks and Gallery

Water

Riverwalk Mall

Ariodante

Girod

3 D's   Notre Dame

Girod Street Wharf

Pile St.

Arthur Roger Gallery
Louisiana Children's Museum

Julia Street Wharf

St. Joseph

Ernest Murial Convention Center

St. Joseph
St.Wharf

Howard Ave.

Poefarre

Poefarr

Mississippi River

John

Churchill

Gaiennie

Riverwalk Shopping Center

Annunciation

CRESCENT CITY CONN.

GRTR. N.O. BRIDGE

Euterpe

Henderson

RR

Tchoupitoulas

Pace

**Riverfront/Warehouse
District**

Orange

| 0 | | 1/4 | 1/2 Mi. |
| 0 | 250 | 500 m | |

©FW

pealing is its slender elegance. *724 Camp Street,* ☎ *(504) 525-4413.*

Agenda Shopping/Warehouse/ Arts District

Ariodante

535 Julia Street; ☎ *(504) 524-3233, 11 a.m.–5 p.m., Mon.–Sat.*
Snazzy jewelry, accessories and crafts that go just fine with the area.

Christopher Maier

329 Julia Street; ☎ *(504) 586-9079, 9 a.m.–6 p.m., Mon.–Fri; 11 a.m.–4 p.m., Sat. Closed Sun.*
Gilded, hand-carved fantasy furniture—extraordinary!

628 Gallery

628 Barrone Street; ☎ *(504) 529-3306, 10 a.m.–6 p.m., Mon.–Sat.*
Ya/Ya (Young aspirations/Young artists) is a nonprofit organization for inner-city "Picassos" ranging in age from 14 to 26 who display their amazingly professional renderings here. Genius can be bought here at a discount since only 50% goes to the artist. The rest goes back into the trust. These creative young artists have been displayed all over the globe.

Simonne Stern

518 Julia Street; ☎ *(504) 529-1118, 11 a.m.–5 p.m., Mon; 10 a.m.–5 p.m., Tue.–Sat.*
Contemporary artists are showcased at this venerable **New Orleans Gallery**. It moved to the **Arts District** to specialize in abstract including sculpture.

Mimi

400 Julia Street; ☎ *(504) 527-6464, 10 a.m.–5:30 p.m., Mon.–Sat.*
The newest, most artistic make-up and clothes that complement the cutting edge of the area.

New Orleans School of Glassworks & Gallery

727 Magazine (between Julia and Girod); ☎ *(504) 529-7277, 11 a.m.–6 p.m., Mon.–Sat.*
You'll be absolutely shattered by watching the master glassblowing demonstrations. Everything becomes crystal clear as you visit the showroom filled with goblets and other fragile frippery.

Agenda Best Bites/Warehouse/ Arts District

Warehouse Café $

1179 Annunciation Street; ☎ *(504) 586-1282.*

Cuisine: American. Avg. $10–$20.
Hours: 6 p.m.–2 a.m., Mon.–Sat.
Great music that comes from the great bands who rotate here, drawing crowds night after night. Credit Cards: Not Accepted.

Red Bike $

746 Tchoupitoulas Street; ☎ (504) 529-BIKE.
Cuisine: American. Avg. $10–$20.
Hours: 8 a.m.–10 p.m., Tues.–Sat.
Fresh salads and homemade cakes and pastries make this a perfect stop in between galleries. Credit Cards: Not Accepted.

Doug's Place $$

748 Camp Street; ☎ (504) 527-5433.
Cuisine: Steak house. Avg. $20–$40.
Lunch: 11 a.m.–2 p.m., Mon.–Sat.
Dinner: 5–9:30 p.m., Mon.–Sat.
Steak appreciation after some serious art appreciation. Doug's is just right for a steak joint: rough brick walls, beamed ceiling, great burgers and grills. So far so good. Carnivores unite! Credit Cards: All Major.

Vic's Kangaroo Cafe $$

636 Tchoupitoulas Street; ☎ (504) 524-4329.
Cuisine: Australian. Avg. $20–$40.
Hours: 11:30 a.m.–3:30 a.m., 7 days.
The kangaroo in the name should be taken very seriously since they serve Australian pub food. Hopefully the shepherd's pie contains neither kangaroo nor shepherd, in fact it's pretty good. So go and have a "g'day." Credit Cards: All Major.

L'Economie $$$

325 Girod Street; ☎ (504) 524-7405.
Cuisine: French. Avg. $40–$60.
Lunch: 11:30 a.m.–2 p.m., Wed.–Sat.
Dinner: 6–10:30 p.m., Wed.–Sat.
A bistro for all seasons. The artists in the neighborhood love the "trés funky" surroundings. The real scoop here is that exotic creatures such as ostrich appear on the menu from time to time. The upside is that their omelets are enormous. Credit Cards: All Major.

Howlin' Wolf $$

828 St. Peter Street; ☎ (504) 523-2551.
Cuisine: B.B.Q. Avg. $20–$30.
Hours: 8 p.m.–2 a.m., Mon.–Sat.
Open only in the P.M. for great music served up with B.B.Q and Cajun tidbits. Credit Cards: Not Accepted.

Mid-City/Uptown

One of the most endearing eccentricities about New Orleans is its dedication to meaningless and often ambiguous names that it gives to sections of the city. **Mid-City** is not really in the middle of town but includes part of the edge of the **CBD** as well as the fringe of the **Garden District**. Uptown is referred to as Upriver and takes in some of the upper **Garden District** and the community of **Carrollton**. Of course we all know by this time that Downriver is where the French Quarter is located. Blanche DuBois wasn't the only one confused by directions in New Orleans.

The best way to think of **Mid-City** is that it runs the entire length of **Canal Street**. New arrivals who felt safe settling close to Canal at the turn of the century were made even happier by the draining of the muddy swamp land that was part of the area so that they could build further up and down Canal. They spread out to form a neighborhood made up of the core working class in the city. Today it is far more expansive, taking in **City Park** with its notorious area called "Dueling-Oaks" (the scene of the town's most elegant shoot-outs) and **Esplanade Ridge** which is one of the best places to see the Victorian shotgun and camel-back shotgun houses, in New Orleans. They go from front to back, room after room, without a separating hallway. Shotguns got their colorful name when someone remarked you could shoot a bullet right through to the back.

Mid-City is also filled with the small, "down-home" restaurants and bars in which New Orleanians love to party.

Audubon Park features gardens, a riverboat, aquarium and zoo.

AGENDA LEGAL-EAGLE EYE

The Louisiana Criminal District Court is where Jim Garrison conducted his famous "conspiracy" trial. Director Oliver Stone used it to make fact out of fiction in J.F.K.

Aside from the wonderful New Orleans architecture of **Esplanade Ridge**, the leafy serenity of **City Park**, and **St. Louis No. 3**, the rambling cemetery at the end of **Esplanade Avenue**, the most exciting landmark of Mid-City is by far the **New Orleans Museum of Art** (NOMA, see top sights page 26) which is located in the middle of **City Park**. The park itself covers over 1500 acres and dates back to the 1850s. Originally it was a large very wealthy Plantation. Many of the trees that were on the property back then are the very ones that supply the luxurious shade that comes in so handy on one of New Orleans' blistering summer days. There's also an amusement area known as **Carousel Gardens**, the home of New Orleans beloved "Flying Horses." The Carousel was built in 1906 and is in the National Register. This is the niftiest way I know to go around in circles.

The best way to get to the Uptown historic district as well as the most scenic is on the **St. Charles Avenue Streetcar**. Uptown is made up of **Upper St. Charles Avenue**, the very learned University strip, (**Tulane** and **Loyola** are practically back to back. See Top Sights, page 24.), the sweet, albeit rich little community of **Carrollton**, **Audubon Park** with the charming **Audubon Zoo** (see Top Sights, page 22.) and **Riverbend**, a chic little clutch of boutiques and shops. Riverbend is also home to a veritable restaurant legend in New Orleans, the **Camellia Grill**. All of this is packed into one of the priciest neighborhoods in New Orleans. Turn of the century mansions are par for the course Uptown. In fact a very famous as well as macabre example of the "lifestyles of the rich and creepy" is the **Dolls House**, an exact replica of the Tudor mansion it sits in front of. Every detail is so perfect that it has its own address *(7209 St. Charles Avenue)*. Best of all, when you get to **Carrollton Avenue** and **Riverbend** and look to your left you will see a real Levee, as in …. "down on the levee, waitin for the Robert E. Lee." If you climb up the grassy slope you can see Ole Man River. Now you know you're really Down South.

Agenda Shopping/Mid-City/Uptown

Gaetana's

> *7732 Maple Street;* ☎ *(504) 865-9625, 9:30 a.m.–6 p.m., Mon.–Sat.; Noon–5 p.m., Sun.*
> A collection of women's clothes that is right off the rack but looks specific enough to be part of a designer's show. Very individual and sometimes a touch of the exotic from ethnic influences.

Encore

> *7814 Maple Street;* ☎ *(504) 861-9028, 11 a.m.–4 p.m., Tues.–Sat.*

If you're in town and someone asks you to attend one of the "gabillion" events or balls that go on endlessly, you can rent some serious "glam" for the evening.

Uptown architecture

Ballin's Ltd.

721 Dante Street; ☎ *(504) 866-4367, 10 a.m.–6 p.m., Mon.–Sat.*
Very stylish clothes that make the very statement New Orleans' top women want to make. Lots of sleek European imports, as well.

Yvonne La Fleur

8131 Hampson Street; ☎ *(504) 866-9666, 10 a.m.–6 p.m., Mon.–Sat.*
Even Scarlett O'Hara would be impressed by the extravagance of these extraordinary garden-party hats. Calling them hats is indeed an over-simplification, they are fantastic confections of straw, ribbons, flowers, and occasionally an odd cherry or two. Her hats are movie stars in their own right having appeared in *The Great Gatsby* as well as other films. The cost, as you might have guessed, is as extravagant as the creations, running easily into three figures.

Mignon Faget Ltd.

710 Dublin Street; ☎ *(504) 865-1107, 10 a.m.–5:30 p.m., Mon.–Sat.*
Sophisticated and unique jewelry designs that are also in the Faget Shop at the **Canal Place Mall**. Her store at **Riverbend** is more expansive and there are tabletop and gift items that are equally unique.

Sun Shop

7722 Maple Street; ☎ *(504) 861-8338, Noon–5:30 p.m., Mon.–Sat.*
A treasure hunter's dream come true. Even though the sun is the last thing you'll find in this small "Junque" shop. All kinds of North American art-cum-kitsch. I defy you not to find something to buy!

Little Professor Books

1000 S. Carrollton Avenue; ☎ *(504) 866-7646, 9 a.m.–6 p.m., Mon.–Sat.*
Locals who are the literary lights of the community are featured in this personable book shop.

On the Other Hand

8126 Hampson Street; ☎ *(504) 861-0159, 10 a.m.–6 p.m., Mon.–Sat.*
Bargain Hunters Unite! If you are a resale addict (and who isn't), they have the crème de la crème from all over, on consignment. Designer originals yet!

Ricca's White Pillars

8312 Oak Street; ☎ *(504) 861-7113, 10 a.m.–5 p.m., Tues.–Fri.; 10 a.m.–3 p.m., Sat.*
All kinds of memorabilia of the city's past. Architectural trash and treasures together with some fine Victorian antiques. A fun browse.

Agenda Best Bites/Mid-City/Uptown

Genghis Khan $$$

4053 Tulane Avenue; ☎ *(504) 482-4044.*
Cuisine: Asian. Avg. $40–$60.
Dinner: 5:30–11 p.m., Sun.–Tues.
A former member of the New Orleans symphony now makes beautiful music in this Asian boite. He not only owns it but plays with a string quartet almost every night. Credit Cards: All Major.

Palamer's Restaurant $$

135 N. Carrollton Avenue; ☎ *(504) 482-3658.*
Cuisine: Jamaican. Avg. $20–$40.
Hours: 11:30 a.m.–2:30 a.m., Tues.–Sat.
Jamaican Creole in this very simple "island" storefront. This place not only gets your goat but they turn it into some interesting stews and sautées. Try their Bahamian chowder if you are an animal lover, instead. Credit Cards: Not Accepted.

Mandina's $$

3800 Canal Street; ☎ *(504) 482-9179.*
Cuisine: Southern. Avg. $20–$40.
Hours: 11 a.m.–10 p.m., daily.
If you're someone who just can't come out of your shell, you might not want to order the turtle soup here, even though people come from all over the city to scarf it down. They have some of the best down-home comfort food in the city and their fans are legion. Credit Cards: Not Accepted.

Katie's $$

3701 Iberville Street; ☎ *(504) 488-6582.*
Cuisine: Creole. Avg. $20–$40.
Hours: 11 a.m.–10 p.m., Mon.–Sat.

Better at lunch than dinner because the specials go on and on. But in the p.m. count on great Creole-Italian and Katie's famous onion rings. Credit Cards: All Major.

Tavern on the Park $$$

900 City Park Avenue; ☎ *(504) 486-3333.*
Cuisine: Southern. Avg. $40–$60.
Lunch: 11 a.m.–2 p.m., Tues.–Fri.
Dinner: 5–11 p.m., Tues.–Sat.

The building that houses the Tavern dates back to the Civil War. In those days it was a bit naughty. Married men brought their mistresses, or the "swells" would drop in to observe the risqué goings-on. Today the food takes a back seat to the history. The views of the park will help to nourish you even if the menu doesn't. Credit Cards: All Major.

Angelo Brocato Confectionery $

214 N. Carrollton Avenue; ☎ *(504) 486-0078.*
Cuisine: Ice Cream Parlor. Avg. $10–$20.
Hours: 9:30 a.m.–10 p.m., daily.

Spumoni, tortoni, cannoli and all the other delicious "i's" that make up toothsome Italian desserts. The perfect old ice cream parlor that's harder to find than a decent guidebook (how very fortunate you are). Save up all your calories. Credit Cards: All Major.

Clancy's $$$

6100 Annunciation Street; ☎ *(504) 895-1111.*
Cuisine: Continental. Avg. $40–$60.
Lunch: 11:30 a.m.–2 p.m., daily.
Dinner: 5:30–11 p.m., daily.

Class to the Max is the M.O. here. Even though they call themselves a bistro this place has a very serious approach to culinary creativity. Minimalist decor is relegated to the surroundings. Your plate however, is the chef's canvas for oysters with a rich brié, or steak with a bernaise straight from Paris. This place is a "keeper." Credit Cards: All Major.

Bluebird Café $

3625 Prytania Street; ☎ *(504) 895-7166.*
Cuisine: American. Avg. $10–$20.
Hours: 7 a.m.–3 p.m., Mon.–Fri; 8 a.m.–3 p.m., Sat. –Sun.

Be prepared to wait—be prepared to love it. By the time you reach your gargantuan pancakes or super-thick malt waffles you'll be looking forward to your next visit. Slip a piece of pie in your pocket for later. Credit Cards: Not Accepted.

Frankie's Café $$

8132 Hampson Street; ☎ *(504) 866-9555.*
Cuisine: Creole. Avg. $20–$30.
Lunch: 11 a.m.–2 p.m., Mon.–Sat.
Dinner: 5:30–10 p.m., Mon.–Sat.

This is a college type restaurant at its country best. Don't look for valet parking. Just kick back and enjoy some of the very good Creole specials as well as the wonderfully done grills. Credit Cards: All Major.

Zachary's $$

8400 Oak Street; ☎ *(504) 865-1559.*
Cuisine: Southern. Avg. $20–$40.
Lunch: 11 a.m.–2:30 p.m., daily.
Dinner: 5:30–9:30 p.m., daily.
Home cooking in a homey cottage with a homey staff knocking themselves out to make you feel at home. A perfect example of a charming Louisiana cottage is the background for crisp fried catfish, Creole bread pudding, and gumbos galore. Credit Cards: All Major.

La Madeleine Bakery & Cafe $

601 S. Carrollton Avenue; ☎ *(504) 861-8661.*
Cuisine: Coffee house. Avg. $10–$20.
Hours: 7 a.m.–10 p.m., daily.
This is the same French delight that you've probably stopped at in Jackson Square. Their Riverbend outpost is just as good and the perfect place for a tea and pastry break when you get off the St. Charles Streetcar. Credit Cards: All Major.

Pascal's Manale $$$

1838 Napoleon Avenue; ☎ *(504) 895-4877.*
Cuisine: Continental. Avg. $40–$60.
Hours: 11:30 a.m.–10 p.m., Mon.–Fri.; 4–10 p.m., Sat.; 4–9 p.m., Sun.
A New Orleans institution devoted to excess, which of course gets my vote immediately. Henry VIII concoctions such as fried oysters served over grilled ham smothered in a mega-egg hollandaise. Everything also comes dripping in butter and served in huge quantities. Sounds like a place you wouldn't really want your doctor to catch you clogging up the old arteries. However, Manale's is always packed with people who will be only too happy to share your deception, so go for it. Credit Cards: All Major.

Faubourg Marigny

Bernard de Marigny was called the "Last of the Creole Aristocracy." Even though in the early 1800s he was known as a playboy around town, he had an even more colorful claim to fame. Since he could never resist any game of chance, he squandered millions of the family's francs on a new diversion called "Le Crapaud." It got its name "toad" from the fact that people had to play it crouched on the ground, assuming a toadlike position. (Is this all ringing a bell yet?) Le Crapaud was eventually shortened to the all-too-familiar Craps and Monsieur de Marigny spent the rest of his fortune over the years trying desperately to roll sevens instead of snake-eyes. Finally when he had lost the entire Marigny fortune he began to subdivide the family plantation which soon became a whole new neighborhood, downriver from the **Vieux Carré**. Because it was farther out than the rest of the area, they added Faubourg (suburb) to the Marigny name.

A feeling of La Vie de Boheme is everywhere as you walk through this small, intimate community, its streets lined with Creole cottages painted in bright pastels. "The Marigny" most suggests a sleepy Caribbean port city. It is bordered by **Esplanade**

Central Park
Tad Gormley Stadium
Roosevelt Mall
Golf Dr.
Stadium Dr.
Friedrichs Ave.
Parkview Pl.
Botanical Gardens
Victory Ave.
Storyland
Art Museum
Moss
Carousel Gardens
Dreyfous Dr.
Casino
Lelong Dr.
City Park
St. Louis Cemetery III
City Park Ave.
Esplanade
Leda
St. Ann
Moss
Lola's
Orleans Ave.
St. Peter
Tavern on the Park
Moss
Solomon
Bungalow
Delgado
Toulouse
Alard
IDA
Dumaine
Taft Pl.
Wilson
Harding
Harding
Grand
David
Olga
Roosevelt
Desoto
Contl
Pitot House
Helen Pitkin Schertz House
David
Carrollton
Bienville
Pierce
Parkway
Hagan
Scott
Cortez
Rendon
Lopez
Salcedo
Cleveland
Toulouse
Palmyra
Mercy Hosp.
Lafitte
Telemachus
Jefferson Davis
Genois
Clark
Rendon
Lopez
Gayosa
Montelepre Memorial Hospital
Salcedo
Canal
Gayosa
(90)
Dupre
White
Jane Pl.
Broad Ave.

Esplanade Ave. (North)

| 0 | 1/8 | 1/4 Mi. |
| 0 | 62.5 | 125 m |

©FW

Florida Ave.

610

Tensas

Army

Roger Williams

Chalfont

Fortage

Winthrop

Castine

Tunica

Hathaway Pl.

Alden Pl.

Gibson

Dugue

Treasure

e Saix Blvd.

Abundance

Agriculture

Trafalgar

Derby

Saltus

Industry

Nosiere

Serantini

Castiglione

Belfort

Crete

Castiglione

Duels

Bernard Ave.

Gayoso

Castiglione

Republic

**Fairgrounds
Race Track and
Jazz Fest.
Grounds**

Dupre

O'Reilly

Luling Mansion

Genfilly Blvd.

4th

Paul Murphy

Aubry

Maurepas

3330 Esplanade

Rousselin

D'Abadie

Ponce DeLeon

Broad Ave.

Dorgenois

St. John

Lepage

Rochenblave

Onzaga

2936 Esplanade

White

Lahalpe

Lapeyrouse

2809 Esplanade

Columbus

Kerlerec

Dupre

Crete

2623 Esplanade

Tonti

Orchid

Bell

2540 Esplanade

Miro

Galvez

Barracks

2453 Esplanade

Johnson

Bellechasse

Bayou Rd.

Kerlerec

Gov. Nicholls

Ursuline

Esplanade

Dumaine

St. Philip

✉

Cresent City Steakhouse

Dooky Chase

**Ruth Chris
Steakhouse**

St. Ann

St. Peter

Orleans Ave.

St. Louis

Conti

236A

Oak Pl.

Bienville

235A

erville

St. Louis

Lafitte

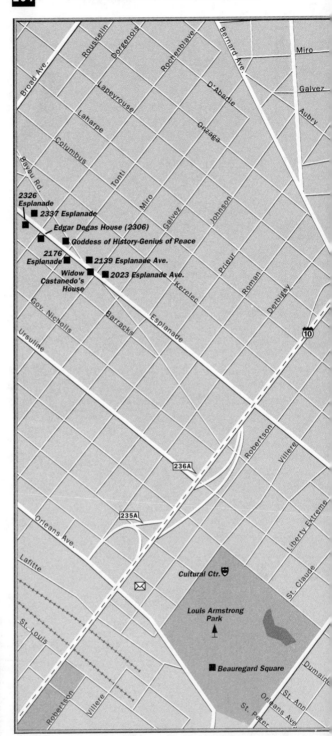

**Esplanade Ave.
(South)**

0   1/4   1/2 Mi.

0   250 m   500 m

©FWI

Miro

Pauger

Touro

Johnson

Prieur

Roman

Anthony

Derbigny

Annette

Claiborne

Pauger

Touro

Frenchmen

Elysian Fields

Franklin

Almonaster

Robertson

236C

39

Villere

Urquahart

Marais

Mc Shane   **46**

Rampart

Kerelec

Burgundy

Rampart

Dauphine

Barracks

Praline Connection ✕ 🛍 **S**   ✕ **Alberto's**

Royal

Gov. Nicholls

LaMothe House ◼

Chartres

New Orleans Guest House

✕ Feeling's Cafe   Decatur

St. Philip

✕ Fiorella's Cafe

✕ Croissant d'or   Old U.S. Mint ◼

Derbigny

Chartres

Decatur   Peters

M **Farmers Market**

86B

6eilly

Avenue and runs down to the **Mississippi River**. It is considered an historic district along with an area known as Treme which in the late 1800s became the site of the bawdy **Storyville**. Named after the city alderman Sidney Story because in a flash of civic efficiency he decided to group the town brothels together. **Storyville** became one of the most fabulous red light districts in the country. Not only were the "fun and games" that could be sampled there the reason for its notoriety but it was also the place Louis Armstrong practiced his "pucker." Some of the greatest jazz musicians of our time such as King Oliver, Jelly Roll Morton and Buddy Bolden, Louis Armstrong's mentor, started in the rollicking bordellos of **Storyville**.

Rampart Street, also in the Treme section of the outer Marigny is today a street to walk very cautiously on, but in the past its houses were often owned by the beautiful Quadroon mistresses of New Orleans best aristocracy. Beautiful and poised Quadroon debutantes were presented in elegant balls that were held at the Quadroon Ballroom once located on **Orleans Street** in the **French Quarter**. In the 1800s this was an openly practiced arrangement for the local male gentry to meet beautiful and "appreciative" women of color who were then set up in glorious homes, given servants and ultimately left rich and often famous when their "gentlemen callers" finally married. The very mention of Rampart Street in those days signified the most titillating of "romances" in New Orleans.

Even more responsible than the fabled **Storyville** for the birth of jazz in the **Big Easy**, was a place called **Congo Square**. Today the area is named for the great "Satchmo," which translates into a more sedate, **Armstrong Park**. However, **Congo Square** in the 1700s was the place to be on a Sunday if you were a slave. The much more liberal and enlightened slave owners of New Orleans gave their slaves one day off to meet, picnic, and make music together. In fact, they were making the sounds and rhythms that would come down over the centuries to become jazz as it's known today. Congo Square was a means of other kinds of relaxation for the slaves, some of them quite illicit. Voodoo rites were a definite no no on the plantations, but in the park under the guise of simply making music, that "Ole Black Magic" had everyone under its spell. The superstar of voodoo hoodoo, Marie Laveau herself, presided over some of the more spiritual ceremonies in the Square. At the sound of a cannon fired in what is now **Jackson Square**, it was time for the spells to be broken and the slaves to return to their quarters. Today **Congo Square** is part of Armstrong Park which spreads over 32 acres. Within is a 12-foot statue of Louis himself. The park has had a rather dismal history since its 1980 opening. A planned casino was abandoned, artificial lagoons that were meant for boating are deserted, and saddest of all is an arch of tiny bulbs at the entrance in a failed ttempt to give the park a Tivoli kind of glitter. I'm told as we go o press that all is not lost, the park just needs some fine tuning. Under no circumstances enter Armstrong Park alone at night. At he present time it has virtually no security. (Located at **North Rampart Street**)

The most exciting street in the Marigny, hands-down, is Frenchman's. Some of the best jazz clubs and down-home res-aurants are found here. The neighborhood may look a little cruffy, but at night it rocks with terrific music and equally ter-ific food.

Agenda Shopping/Faubourg Marigny

American Aquatic Gardens

621 Elysian Fields; ☎ *(504) 944-0410, 9 a.m.–5 p.m., daily.*
For gardeners who like their roots underwater, the American Aquatic people are prepared to quench their thirst. All manner of pond grasses, lily pads, reeds and the stone accessories to go with them can be found here. They ship all over the country, or if you want your cuttings "to go" they'll pack them in misted plastic.

Praline Connection Gift Shop

542 Frenchman Street; ☎ *(504) 943-3934, 11 a.m.–10:30 p.m., daily.*
One of the greats on the restaurant scene (See Restaurants page 140) they have a small shop right next door where you can purchase their amazing sweet potato pie, pralines and other goodies that are featured on the menu. After your lunch or dinner be sure to stop in and take something back to your hotel, even if you think you'll never be hungry again.

Agenda Best Bites/Faubourg Marigny

Snug Harbor $

626 Frenchman Street; ☎ *(504) 949-0696.*
Cuisine: American. Avg. $10–$20.
Dinner: 5–11 p.m., Sun.–Thurs.; 5 p.m.–midnight, Fri.–Sat.
Great hamburgers and great jazz. What could be a better combination? Wynton Marsalis' dad, Ellis, appears weekly to tickle the ivories along with other local "greats." The food is very basic but very very good. This is not just a place to groove. They really drum up some fine grills, fries and thick sandwiches. Credit Cards: All Major.

Alberto's $$

611 Frenchman Street; ☎ *(504) 949-5952.*

Cuisine: Italian. Avg. $20–$30.
Hours: 11:30 a.m.–11 p.m., daily.
Homey Italian, and a great favorite of the locals, especially other restaurateurs. Red sauce covers almost everything, just as if you were in Naples. Don't even think designer pasta here, just good old spaghetti and meatballs. Credit Cards: All Major.

La Peniche $$
1940 Dauphine Street; ☎ *(504) 943-1460.*
Cuisine: American. Avg. $20–$40.
Hours: 24 hours, 6 days. Closed Wed.
If you get the munchies at 2 a.m. La Peniche has a waffle with your name on it. They can beat up a decent omelet or a burger or breakfast, 24 hours a day. Credit Cards: All Major.

Montrel's Creole Cafe $
4116 Marigny Street; ☎ *(504) 288-6374.*
Cuisine: Creole. Avg. $10–$20.
Hours: 11 a.m.–9 p.m., Mon.–Thurs.; 11 a.m.–11 p.m., Fri.–Sat.
Simple po'boys, fried chicken and down-home soul food. Wonderfully cheap and surprisingly good. Credit Cards: Not Accepted.

Feelings Cafe $$$
2600 Chartres Street; ☎ *(504) 945-2222.*
Cuisine: Southern. Avg. $40–$60.
Dinner: 5:30–11 p.m., daily.
One of the most beautiful settings in the city with food that more than holds its own against the gorgeous ambience. Once the carriage house of a plantation, its courtyard is filled with lush trees and its fountain is filled with goldfish. Credit Cards: All Major.

Lake Pontchartrain/Lakeshore Drive

At the end of the day when the setting sun is reflected on the water and looks like a million melted pennies, it is well worth renting a car to see that most beautiful of sights on **Lake Pontchartrain**. The waterfront of the lake stretches over 5-1/2 miles of seawall that surrounds it. The **Lake district** is to the north of the city and aside from the residential communities that overlook the beautiful views, there are great spots for picnics, boating, fishing and an incredibly scenic walk around the seawall to better appreciate the Lake. More than 24 miles at its widest, it is spanned by the world's longest bridge, the **Lake Pontchartrain Causeway**. The bridge makes it possible for New Orleanians to live rather luxuriously on the shores of the Lake while earning their daily beignets, in town.

My advice on car rental would be to wait until the end of your time in New Orleans and save a day or two for **Lakeshore Drive** and perhaps a visit to the great old plantations on **Great River Road**. Since parking rates in the hotel garages are so astronomic, you're better off saving your "road warrior" agenda till then.

The seafood houses at the Lakefront are always jammed from the time the thermometer hits about 55°F. There seems to be perpetual party atmosphere to the area that carries over from the city. But unlike the subtropical steaminess of New Orleans, the breezes blow cool and long at the Lake. Aside from the great seafood restaurants and the host of watersports available here, the **University of New Orleans** takes up 420 acres of Lakefront all by itself. Nearby the University is the **Mardi Gras Fountain** for all the party animals that haven't "OD'd" yet on Mardi Gras "lore." The fountain periodically gets filled with detergent by the same kind of jokesters who have water-pistols and plastic vomit in their repertoire. They delight in watching the bubbles clog the fountain spray. If you need further stimulation after the fountain fantasy, you can always take a chance at the **Star Casino** in **South Shore Harbor** not far away. It's a mini Las Vegas on the lake and it goes nonstop 24 hours a day.

The small fishing village of **Buckstown** which is nestled on the levee of **Lake Pontchartrain** is teeming with tiny fish restaurants and markets. It's lost in its own charming time warp, and well worth exploring if you happen to be in the area.

Agenda Best Bites/
Lake Pontchartrain/Lakeshore Drive

Sid-Mar's   **$$**
1824 Orpheum Avenue; Bucktown; ☎ *(504) 831-9541.*
Cuisine: Seafood. Avg. $20–$40.
Hours: 11 a.m.–10:30 p.m., Tues.–Sun.
Even the "crankiest crabs" in the world will love the ones they serve here. An old sea shanty cum suds joint, beloved by one and all who toss their crab shells off the porch. Credit Cards: All Major.

West End Café   **$$**
8536 Pontchartrain Boulevard; ☎ *(504) 288-0711.*
Cuisine: Seafood. Avg. $20–$40.
Hours: 11 a.m.–10:30 p.m., daily.
The jukebox never stops nor do the "fishy" fantasies coming from the kitchen. If the Electric Chair were in my future I'd order the fried shrimp, fried onion rings and a side of crabmeat au gratin. Credit Cards: All Major.

Deanie's   **$$**
1713 Lake Avenue; Bucktown; ☎ *(504) 834-1225.*
Cuisine: Seafood. Avg. $20–$40.
Hours: 11 a.m.–10 p.m., daily.
They are legendary for their huge portions of fresh fried fish. You'll probably have to wait on line but think of the money you'll save when you give up food for the week. Credit Cards: All Major.

Bozo's   **$$**
3117 21st St. Causeway Boulevard/Lakeshore; ☎ *(504) 831-8666.*
Cuisine: Seafood. Avg. $20–$40.

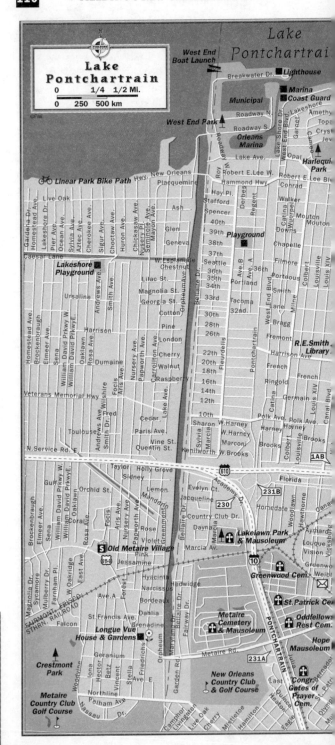

London Outfall Canal

Orleans Outfall Canal

Lake Shore Dr.
Mardi Gras Fountains

Lake Terrace Park

N. Lake Shore Dr.

Swan
Stilt
Ozone

Tweed Cir.

Marconi Blvd.

Gen. Haig

Parkway
Amethyst
Topaz
Crystal
Jewel

Jade
Agate

Snipe
Thrasher
Wren
Willet
Hawk
Finch

Warbler
Swallow
Tern
Rail
Plover

Breeze

Foliage

Zephyr
Oriole
Lark

S
Lake Vista Shop. Ctr.

Flamingo
Spanish

Oriole
Lark
Killdeer
Jay
Frankfort
New York

Oriole
Lark
Killdeer
Jay

Floral

Kilbee
Pratt
Paris Ave.
Bertha Dr.
Caldwell Dr.
Lisbon
N.Y.

Madison Dr.

Tourmaline Park

Emerald

Bluebird
Crane
Dove
Egret

Gill

Aviators
Madrid
Soldiers
Burbank

Hamburg
Paris Ave.

Chatham Dr.
Chamberlain Dr.

Orleans Park

Conrad
Walker

U.S. Reg. Research Lab

Wisner Blvd.

Bayou St. John

St. Bernard

Pressburg
Athis
Prentiss Ave.
Mendez
Rapides
Cabrini
Crescent
Mithra
Filmore Ave.

Bancroft

Gen. Diaz
Argonne Blvd.
General Haig
Orleans Ave.

Marshall Foch
Chapelle

Filmore

Porteous

Lane

Bragg

Marconi Blvd.

Golf Course Club House

▲ **City Park**

Gardena Dr.
Seville Dr.
Rivera Ave.
Granada
Mirabeau Ave.

St. Bernard

Perlita

Wakefield
Westbrook
Paula
Owens Blvd.

Virginia Marie

Mandolin
Harrison
Senate

Caton
Foy

Carter

Croft Way

Park Island Dr.

Wellington
Kennon
Randolf

Dreux
Encampment
Pelopidas
Caton
Milton

Jumonville
Duplessis

Cadillac
Buchanan
Alfred

Gibson
Hamburg

Alfred
Foy
Milton

Harrison Ave.

Magnolia Dr.

Marconi Dr.

Quadraplex Softball Facility

⛳ **Golf Course**

Zachary Taylor Dr.

St. Dennis
Imperial
Sere

2A

Duplessis

Florida Ave.

Kenilworth

Palm Dr.

Roosevelt Mall

Golf Dr.

Marconi Blvd.

Park Pl.
Middle Park

Vavre

Orleans Ave.

Tad Gormley Stadium

Stadium Dr.

Victory Ave.

Friedrichs Ave.

De Saix Blvd.

Parkview

Mariel
Roger Williams
Tunica
Trafalgar
Derby

Tensas

Armant

Chaffon
Fortage
Costine
Seltus
Castiglione

Winthrop
Hathaway Pl.
Aiden Pl.

Gibson

Belfort
Crete

Gayoso
Seraffini
Dugue

Delgado C.C.

⬦ **Botanical Garden**
■ **Carousel**

Art Museum

Lelong Dr.

Dreyfous Dr.

Moss

St. Vincent

Bell

St. Louis Cem.

Leda

Verna

The Casino

Tavern on the Park

City Park Ave.
St. Ann
Orleans Ave.
St. Peter
Toulouse

Solomon
Bungalow
Abard

Dumaine
St. Philip

Delgado Dr.

Mystery
Marie
Verna

Esplanade

Fairgrounds Race Track and Jazz Fest. Grounds

4th
Maurepas
Deleon
Grand St. John

Gentilly Blvd.

Dupre
Paul Murphy
Broad Ave.
Sharpe
Columbus

Gayoso
Rousselin
Reilly

Bell
Kerlerec

Bayou Rd.

Alexander
Mesterville
Conti

Blenville
Banks

David

St. Louis Canal
David

Pierce

Scott

Cortez

Bundalow

Olga

Roosevelt

Taft Pl.
Wilson

Ida

Harding

Mosss

■ **Pitot House**

Helen Pitkin Schertz House

Desoto
Lepage

Ursulines
Duarte
Orchid
White

Hagan
Dumaine
Randolph
Lopez
Salcedo
Gayoso

Bell
Barracks

Bellechasse

Lunch: 11 a.m.–2:15 p.m.
Dinner: 5–10 p.m.
Lines, lines, lines, but the sublime gumbo will give you the courage to hang in. The catfish would make anyone purr and the oysters are the best in the area. Mama Bozo presides over her very own chicken andouille gumbo which is to say the least "boffo." Credit Cards: All Major.

Bruning's   **$$**
1924 West End Pkway; ☎ *(504) 282-9395.*
Cuisine: Seafood. Avg. $20–$40.
Hours: 11 a.m.–9:30 p.m., Mon.–Thurs.; 11 a.m.–10:30 p.m., Fri.–Sat.
Oceans of space to serve their great fish fries and stuffed flounder. The view of the lake competes for attention but it's no contest. This place has been serving extraordinary seafood since 1859 to the adoring generations that still appear with the same dedication as their great-grandparents. Who can argue with that kind of fish story? Credit Cards: All Major.

"Do you want that with or without angioplasty?"

Drawing by P. Steiner; ©1995 The New Yorker Magazine, Inc.

NEW ORLEANS SHOPPING AGENDA

Antique shops are centered around Royal and Chartres.

The Best Around Town

New Orleans is a veritable Persian bazaar bursting with antiques, crafts, Mardi Gras kitsch, clothes designed with tropical flair, Cajun spices, jazz memorabilia, some of the best poster and print art around, and last but not least, the very essence of the

113

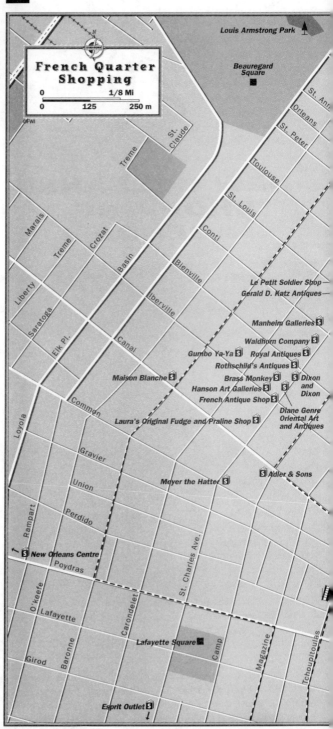

**French Quarter
Shopping**

0 ——————— 1/8 Mi
0 —— 125 —— 250 m

©FWI

Louis Armstrong Park

Beauregard
Square

St. Claude

Treme

St. Ann

Orleans

St. Peter

Toulouse

St. Louis

Conti

Marais

Treme

Crozat

Basin

Blenville

Iberville

Liberty

Saratoga

Elk Pl.

Canal

Le Petit Soldier Shop —
Gerald D. Katz Antiques —

Manheim Galleries 🅂

Waldhorn Company 🅂

Gumbo Ya-Ya 🅂   Royal Antiques 🅂

Rothschild's Antiques 🅂

Brass Monkey 🅂   Dixon
and
Dixon

Maison Blanche 🅂

Hanson Art Galleries 🅂 🅂
French Antique Shop 🅂

Common

Laura's Original Fudge and Praline Shop 🅂

Diane Genre
Oriental Art
and Antiques

Loyola

Gravier

Union

Meyer the Hatter 🅂

🅂 Adler & Sons

Rampart

Perdido

🅂 New Orleans Centre

Poydras

O'keefe

Lafayette

Carondelet

St. Charles Ave.

Baronne

Girod

Lafayette Square ■

Camp

Magazine

Tchoupitoulas

Esprit Outlet 🅂
↓

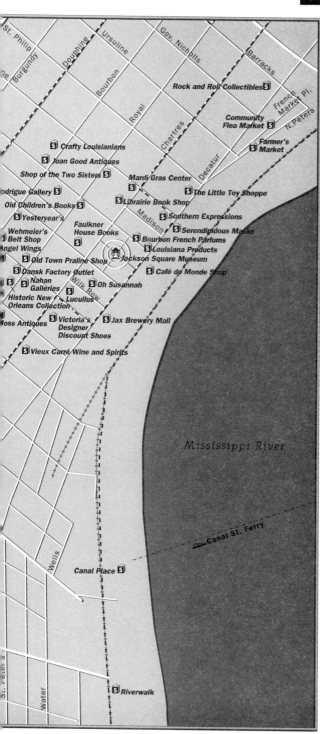

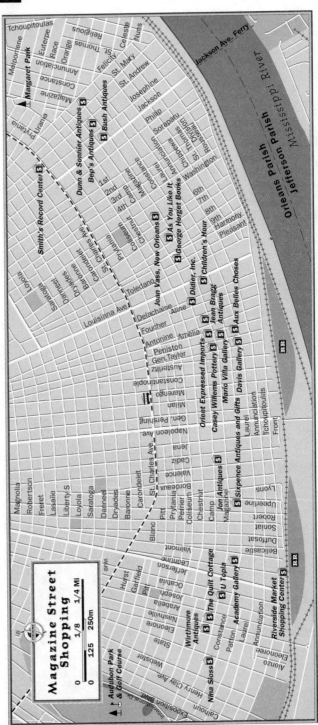

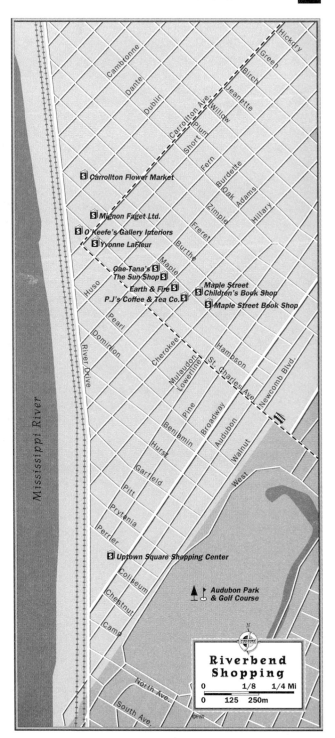

Riverbend
Shopping

0   1/8   1/4 Mi
0   125   250m
©PWI

city, its food. Tasso sausage, pralines, beignets, chili sauces, and over 500 different coffee bean varieties to take away with you. Leaving with a taste of New Orleans in your suitcase makes separation anxiety a snap.

The **French Quarter** has always been the center for treasure since its old pirate days. Jean Lafitte himself contributed to a major part of the **Vieux Carré's** inventory of European goodies. Even today the Quarter has the most exquisite collection of antiques, as well as the work of local master cabinetmakers of the south. Nowhere else can you get antiques that were once part of the great plantations of Louisiana.

The two most important streets in the Quarter for fine domestic and imported antiques are **Royal** and **Chartres**. To go from the sublime to the "Boulevard of Kitsch" you'll have go shop Magazine Street. Talk about something for everyone!

The newest center for contemporary crafts and shopping is, of course, the **Warehouse District**. Artists sell their wares from the galleries that line its streets. Uptown around the **Riverbend** area off **St. Charles Avenue** is a clutch of designer boutiques and artisan ateliers with extravagant, handmade designs. Top fashion is identified with **Riverbend** perhaps because the surrounding community can well afford it.

If you're visiting from overseas (and God knows the U.S. is the best buy on the planet right now) shops that have tax free signs in their windows will give you a voucher to redeem at the airport. The 9% sales tax added to purchases will be refunded up to $100.00 on the spot. If you have spent a tidier sum (over $100.00) then the additional tax will be returned by check to your home.

Antiques

Centuries

517 St. Louis Street; ☎ *(504) 568-9491, 10:30 a.m.–6 p.m., daily.*
The best collection of antique maps in the Quarter. They have lovely prints and engravings as well. It's a browser's bonanza.

Le Petit Soldier Shop

528 Royal Street; ☎ *(504) 523-7741, 10 a.m.–4 p.m., Mon.–Sat.*
Military miniatures from armies dating all the way back to the Greeks. The shop is a magnet for soldiers with fortunes willing to part with them. Some of the tiny armed forces are collectors items as well as the commemorative objects from the Royals in England.

Barrister's Gallery

526 Royal Street; ☎ *(504) 525-2767, 10 a.m.–5 p.m., Mon.–Sat.*
This gallery is not for the timid, or someone who thinks of Bloomingdale's as an "archeological dig," but if you love to burrow through fetishes from Zaire, tribal art of Oceana, beaded figures from the Cameroon's and assorted tchotkies from other sub-Saharan destinations, just roll up your sleeves and dig into one of the most exciting galleries I've ever been in.

Lucullus

610 Chartres Street; ☎ *(504) 528-9620, 9:30 a.m.–5 p.m., Mon.–Sat.*
This antique shop is particularly of interest to cooks, chefs and gourmets because of their delicious collection of culinary antiques dating back to the 17th century.

M. S. Rau Antiques

630 Royal Street; ☎ *(504) 523-5660, 9 a.m.–5:15 p.m., Mon.–Sat.*
Displaying American antiques of excellent quality since 1912 this is an internationally known collection.

Moss Antiques

411 Royal Street; ☎ *(504) 522-3981, 9 a.m.–5 p.m., Mon.–Sat.*
Outstanding French and English furniture. Even if you're not in the market for a settee one of the sparklers from their estate jewel collection is very packable.

Diane Genre Oriental Art

233 Royal Street; ☎ *(504) 525-7270,10 a.m.–5 p.m., Mon.–Sat.*
Chinese and Japanese art and furnishings through the 19th century prove to be inscrutably beautiful.

Dixon & Dixon of Royal

237 and 318 Royal Street; ☎ *(504) 524-0282, 9 a.m.–5:30 p.m., daily.*
Another knockout in "Antiques Row" on Royal. Both of their shops have fine antiques, rugs and crystal. They have fabulous estate jewelry.

Waldhorn Company

343 Royal Street; ☎ *(504) 581-6379, 10 a.m.–5:30 p.m., daily.*
Four generations of Waldhorn have contributed to the antiques business of Royal Street, in fact they are the oldest having been established in 1880.

Le Garage

1234 Decatur; ☎ *(504) 522-6639, 10 a.m.–6 p.m., daily.*
The kitchen sink type "junque shop" which is thoroughly captivating.

Gentique's

25 Riverwalk (Mall); ☎ *(504) 524-5149*
For him only. They feature among their "testosterone treasures" walking sticks, Civil War memorabilia, antique medical accessories and collectibles from the past.

Leon Irwin Antiques

1800 Magazine Street; ☎ *(504) 522-5555 (see Magazine Street, page 85).*
Expensive antique furniture.

Bep's

2051 Magazine Street; ☎ *(504) 525-7726 (see Magazine Street, page 86).*
English and American antiques including small collectibles.

Mama Mia's Antiques

2105 Magazine Street; ☎ *(504) 525-8686 (see Magazine Street, page 86).*
A little bit of everything that's fun.

Bush Antiques

2109-2111 Magazine Street; ☎ *(504) 582-3518 (see Magazine Street, page 86).*

Antiques and furniture from old New Orleans homes.

Antique Vault

2123 Magazine Street; ☎ *(504) 523-8888 (see Magazine Street, page 86).*
A little bit of everything.

Morton Goldberg's Antique Annex

2205 Magazine Street; ☎ *(504) 525-2639 (see Magazine Street, page 86).*
Artists. The displays are ever-changing but always creatively exciting.

Orient Expressed

3905 Magazine Street; ☎ *(504) 899-3060 (see Magazine Street, page 87).*
Oriental and Spanish antiques as well as handmade children's clothes.

Talebloo

4130 Magazine Street; ☎ *(504) 899-8114 (see Magazine Street, page 87).*
A Persian bazaar of antiques and contemporary rugs.

Sixpence, Inc.

4904 Magazine Street; ☎ *(504) 895-1267 (see Magazine Street, page 88).*
Gifts as well as fine antiques.

British Antiques

5415 Magazine Street; ☎ *(504) 895-3716 (see Magazine Street, page 88).*
Fine English and Oriental pieces.

Audubon Antiques

5509 Magazine Street; ☎ *(504) 897-1733 (see Magazine Street, page 88).*
American and English furniture, glass, silver and costume jewelry at very modest prices.

Wirthmore

5723 Magazine Street; ☎ *(504) 897-9727, (see Magazine Street, page 88).*
Very important 18th and 19th century French antiques.

Stan Levy Imports

1028 Louisiana Avenue; ☎ *(504) 899-6384, 9:30 a.m.–5:30 p.m., Mon.–Sat.*
This is a warehouse—big setting for 18th, 19th and 20th century antiques. Also rare paintings and bronzes.

Ricca's White Pillars

8312 Oak Street; ☎ *(504) 861-7113, 10 a.m.–5 p.m. Tues.–Fri; 10 a.m.–3 p.m. Sat.*
All kinds of memorabilia of the city's past. Architectural treasures and trash together with some fine Victorian antiques. A fun browse.

Auction Houses

Morton Goldberg Auction Galleries, Inc.

547 Baronne Street; ☎ *(504) 592-2300.*

Neal Auction Co

4038 Magazine Street; ☎ *(504) 899-5329.*

New Orleans Auction Galleries

801 Magazine Street; ☎ *(504) 566-1849.*

Books

Librarie Bookshop

823 Chartres Street; ☎ *(504) 525-4837, 10 a.m.–5 p.m., daily.*
Just musty enough to have a fine collection of old books on the area's history and folklore. The maps are particularly tempting.

Faulkner House Books

624 Pirate's Alley; ☎ *(504) 524-2940, 10 a.m.–6 p.m., daily.*
A Bibliophile's paradise. In the very place that Faulkner lived and worked what more appropriate use of the space? Guess whose books are featured here?

Old Children's Books

734 Royal Street; ☎ *(504) 525-3655, 10 a.m.–1 p.m., Mon.–Sat.*
A magical selection of rare, some almost priceless children's books including a first edition of the Oz series (Judy would be so proud of them).

Magazine Street Books

4222 Magazine Street; ☎ *(504) 899-6905 (see Magazine Street, page 87).*
For the comic book collector. Over 250,000.

La Librarie d'Arcadie

4729 Magazine Street; ☎ *(504) 523-4138 (see Magazine Street, page 87).*
Imported French books and prints.

Garden District Books

2727 Pyrtania Street; ☎ *(504) 895-2266, 10 a.m.–6 p.m., Mon.–Sat.; 11 a.m.–4 p.m., Sun.*
Since this very excellent collection of books is only several blocks from "Vampire Chronicler" Anne Rice, guess who gets shelf space to the max here?

Little Professor Books

1000 S. Carrollton Avenue; ☎ *(504) 866-7646, 9 a.m.–6 p.m., Mon.–Sat.*
Locals who are the literary lights of the community are featured in this personable book shop.

Bookstar

424 N. Peters Street; ☎ *(504) 523-6411, 9 a.m.–midnight, daily.*
Big superstore of books and magazines. It's the largest in New Orleans so if you need to buy the newest Stephen King, stop in.

Children

Oh Susannah

518 St. Peter Street; ☎ *(504) 586-8701, 9:30 a.m.–5:30 p.m., Mon.–Sat; 11 a.m.–5 p.m. Sun.*
Doll collectors come from all over because of the museum quality of some of the little darlings.

Orient Expressed

3905 Magazine Street; ☎ *(504) 899-3060 (see Magazine Street, page 87).*
Oriental and Spanish antiques as well as handmade children's clothes.

China and Crystal

Private Connection

1116 Decatur Street; ☎ *(504) 593-9526, 9 a.m.–6 p.m., Mon.–Sat.*
Exotic bric-a-brac and all manor of things from Thailand including silver and batiks. If you're fit to be "Thaied" you'll love it here.

Trade

828 Chartres Street; ☎ *(504) 596-9491, 10 a.m.–7 p.m., daily.*
Not just for the carriage trade either, they have crafts from New Orleans artisans and a large collection of Day of the Dead folk art from Mexico.

Gallery I/O

829 Royal Street; ☎ *(504) 523-5041, 11 a.m.–6 p.m., daily.*
Great tabletop and jewelry designs. Gifts that are just a little bit off-center for people who thrive on "different."

Clothing

Texas Body Hangings

835 Decatur Street; ☎ *(504) 524-9856, 10 a.m.–6 p.m., daily.*
Not since the caped crusader went shopping have I seen such an array of swinging styles. There are romantic little numbers with cowl hoods and plaid throws for walking the moors.

Sami Lott

728 St. Louis Street; ☎ *(504) 525-7550, (Random hours—call).*
An absolutely one-of-a-kind designer dress shop with the dress and gowns all handmade from antique linens. The most delicate of lacy tablecloths and bed linen have been turned into delectable creations done up by Ms. Lott and her staff.

Wehmeier's

719 Toulouse Street; ☎ *(504) 525-2758, 10 a.m.–6 p.m., daily.*
Known best for their exotic leathers, including alligator and snake (hopefully no one you met on your swamp tour) that are fashioned into trés chic shoes, bags and incredibly expensive boots. Beauty here is definitely skin-deep.

Umbrella Lady

1107 Decatur Street; ☎ *(504) 523-7791, 10 a.m.–6 p.m., daily.*
Don't just drop in—the umbrella lady might be out getting more lace for her one-of-a-kind parasols. You could be "Scarlett for a day" with one of her creations. She makes regular Mary Poppins specials but her parasols are unique.

Meyer the Hatter

120 St. Charles Avenue; ☎ *(504) 525-1048, 10 a.m.–5:45 p.m., Mon.–Sat.*
He's been keeping a lid on things since 1894 so if you're in the market for a Panama or a Stetson, Meyers is your man.

Brooks Brothers

365 Canal Street; ☎ *(504) 522-4200, 10 a.m.–7 p.m., Mon.–Wed; 10 a.m.–7 p.m., Thurs., Sat.; noon–6 p.m., Sun.*
Just in case you drip jambalaya on your favorite B.B. blazer, there are hundreds more where it comes from!

Rubenstein Bros.

Canal St. at St. Charles Avenue; ☎ *(504) 581-6666, 10 a.m.–5:45 p.m., Mon.–Sat.*
Armani and Tommy Hilfiger come to New Orleans along with all the other top men's designers on the planet.

Jim Smiley Vintage Clothes

2001 Magazine Street; ☎ *(504) 528-9449 (see Magazine Street, page 86).*
Exceptional 19th and 20th century clothes and textiles.

Almost New, Inc.

2005 Magazine Street; ☎ *(504) 522-8355 (see Magazine Street, page 86).*
Vintage resale costumes, nostalgia broker.

Shoe Outlet

5419 Magazine Street; ☎ *(504) 895-5319 (see Magazine Street, page 88).*
By the time you reach this place you'll need a new pair.

Mimi

400 Julia Street; ☎ *(504) 527-6464, 10 a.m.–5:30 p.m., Mon.–Sat.*
The newest most artistic makeup and clothes that compliment the cutting edge of the area.

Gaetana's

7732 Maple Street; ☎ *(504) 865-9625, 9:30 a.m.–6 p.m., Mon.–Sat.; noon–5 p.m., Sun.*
This is a collection of women's clothes that are off the rack but look terrific enough to be part of a designer's show. Very individual and sometimes a touch of the exotic from ethnic influences.

Encore

7814 Maple Street; ☎ *(504) 861-9028, 11 a.m.–4 p.m., Tues.–Sat.*
If you're in town and someone asks you to attend one of the gazillion events and balls that go on endlessly, you can rent some serious "glam" for the evening.

Ballin's Ltd.

721 Dante Street; ☎ *(504) 866-4367, 10 a.m.–6 p.m., Mon.–Sat.*
Very stylish clothes that make the statement that New Orleans' top women want to make. Lots of sleek European imports, as well.

Yvonne La Fleur

8131 Hampson Street; ☎ *(504) 866-9666, 10 a.m.–6 p.m., Mon.–Sat.*
Even Scarlett O'Hara would be impressed by the extravagance of these extraordinary garden-party hats. Calling them hats is indeed an oversimplification. They are fantastic confections of straw, ribbons, flowers, and occasionally an odd cherry or two. The cost, as you might have guessed, is as extravagant as the creations running easily into three figures.

On the Other Hand

8126 Hampson Street; ☎ *(504) 861-0159, 10 a.m.–6 p.m., Mon.–Sat.*
Bargain hunters unite! If you are a resale addict (and who isn't), they have the créme de la créme from all over on consignment. Designer originals yet!

Confections

Leah's Candy Kitchen

714 St. Louis Street; ☎ *(504) 523-5662, 10 a.m.–8 p.m., daily.*
Pralines to the right of me, pralines to the left of me, but I always
return to Leah's for her buttery confections. She does other candies as
well, but get real! You're in praline heaven. Go for the gold!

Praline Connection Gift Shop

542 Frenchman Street; ☎ *(504) 943-3934, 11 a.m.–10:30 p.m., Mon.–
Fri.; 11 a.m.–midnight, Sat & Sun.*
One of the greats on the restaurant scene (see Restaurants page 140)
they have a small shop right next door where you can purchase their
amazing sweet potato pie, pralines and other goodies that are featured
on the menu.

Old Town Praline Shop

627 Royal Street; ☎ *(504) 525-1413,*
Old Town is very old time in feeling, and the quality of the pralines is
excellent. They have other goodies as well.

Aunt Sally's

810 Decatur Street; ☎ *(504) 524-5107, 8 a.m.–8 p.m., daily.*
She has her own little shop in the French Market where she makes
these delectable devils in all flavors. She packs for shipping as well.

Department Stores

Maison Blanche

901 Canal Street; ☎ *(504) 566-1000, 10 a.m.–6 p.m., Mon.–Sat.; 10
a.m.–9 p.m., Thurs.*
Where New Orleans "society" shopped in the old days. It was built in
1909 and is still a Canal Street landmark. It's always been devoted to
service and quality.

Krauss Department Store

1201 Canal Street; ☎ *(504) 523-3311, 10 a.m.–6 p.m., Mon.–Sat.; 10
a.m.–9 p.m., Thurs.*
Not quite as venerable as good old Blanche, but it still has a comforting selection of everything.

Food Shops

Louisiana Potpourri

Canal Place (Mall); ☎ *(504) 524-9023, 9 a.m.–10 p.m., daily.*
Gumbo to go in this shop that lets you carry off a taste of the "Big
Easy."

Cafe du Monde Shop

800 Decatur Street; ☎ *(504) 525-4544, 10 a.m.–6 p.m., daily.*
The very same coffee everybody dunks at some point during their trip
is sold in tins and to go with it a beignet mix. How can you resist?

Gumbo YaYa

219 Bourbon Street; ☎ *(504) 522-7484, 9 a.m.–midnight, Mon.–Thurs.
9 a.m.–1 a.m., Fri.–Sun.*
You can spice up your life here. The real McCoy—Cajun seasonings
and sauces.

Bella Luna Pasta Shoppe

914 N. Peters Street; ☎ *(504) 529-1583, 9 a.m.–5 p.m., daily.*

Not just pastas but great gadgets and gifts. I came away with their chocolate coated demitasse spoons. Really cool!

For the Home

Crafty Louisianians

813 Royal Street; ☎ *(504) 528-3094, 10 a.m.–5:30 p.m., daily.*
Kitschy nick-nacks made by the crafty set. Mississippi Mud Dolls and Houma Indian Art are both a specialty here.

Linens

Canal Place (Mall); ☎ *(504) 586-8148, 10 a.m.–6 p.m., Mon.–Wed; 10 a.m.–7 p.m., Thurs.–Sat.; 11 a.m.–5 p.m., Sun.*
A very matter-of-fact name for a shop that stocks sumptuous linens and bedding from all over the world. Especially delicate and fragile are their selection of christening gowns.

Potsalot

1516 Magazine Street; ☎ *(504) 524-6238 (see Magazine Street, page 85).*
Handmade kitchenware, metal and ceramics.

Christopher Maier

329 Julia Street; ☎ *(504) 586-9079, 9 a.m.–6 p.m., Mon.–Fri.; 11 a.m.–4 p.m., Sat.*
Gilded, hand-carved fantasy furniture—extraordinary!

American Aquatic Gardens

621 Elysian Fields; ☎ *(504) 944-0410, 9 a.m.–5 p.m., daily.*
For gardeners who like their roots underwater, the American Aquatic people will quench their thirst. All manner of pond grasses, lily pads, reeds and the stone accessories to go with them.

Textile Arts

4526 Magazine Street; ☎ *(504) 899-5865 (see Magazine Street, page 87).*
Needlepoint, crewel, and crocheting canvases. A huge selection for the needle-person.

Gifts

Gothic Shop

830 Royal Street; ☎ *(504) 558-0175, 10 a.m.–6 p.m., Mon.–Sat.; 11 a.m.–5 p.m. Sun.*
The perfect accessories for an Anne Rice novel. Gargoyles galore as well as angels and architectural accents. Thank God they ship since everything is very affordable but exceedingly heavy.

Mardi Gras Center

832 Chartres Street; ☎ *(504) 524-4384, 10 a.m.–5 p.m., daily.*
This place is for the "hard-core" Mardi-Gras participant. Its walls are lined with enough masks to keep the Phantom of the Opera busy for years. Also endless swags of beads, glitterdust and costumes.

Jewelry

Dashka Roth

332 Chartres Street; ☎ *(504) 523-0805, 10 a.m.–6 p.m., Mon.–Sat.; 11 a.m.–5 p.m., Sun.*
Original and sophisticated jewelry collection done by artisans from all over the world. Both gold and precious stones make up Dashka's collection.

Angel Wings

710 St. Louis Street; ☎ *(504) 524-6880, 10 a.m.–10 p.m., Mon.–Sat.; 10 a.m.–6 p.m., Sun.*

Tiny but ethereal, this shop is angelic to the max. Jewelry, sculpture, accessories, all making a heavenly collection. Great for fans of *It's a Wonderful Life*.

Joan Good Antiques

809 Royal Street; ☎ *(504) 525-1705, 10 a.m.–5 p.m., daily.*

Estate jewelry left for sale as well as exquisite antique pieces. Good is particularly known for her garnets.

Mignon Faget

Canal Place (Mall), Level I; ☎ *(504) 524-2973, 10 a.m.–6 p.m., Mon.–Wed; 10 a.m.–7 p.m., Thurs.–Sat.; noon–6 p.m., Sun.*

A remarkable local jewelry designer with excitingly unique prices. She works not only in 14K gold and sterling but also in "Bronze d'ore."

Adler & Sons

722 Canal Street; ☎ *(504) 523-5292, 10 a.m.–5:30 p.m., daily.*

A venerable jeweler in the city since 1898, when Mardi-Gras jewels were real. The "best" families still shop for engagement sparklers here.

Ariodante

535 Julia Street; ☎ *(504) 524-3233, 11 a.m.–5 p.m., Mon.–Sat.*

Snazzy jewelry, accessories and crafts that go just fine with the area.

Museum Shops

(For hours see Museums, page 163)

New Orleans Museum of Art

1 Lelong Ave., City Park, ☎ *(504) 488-2631.*

Confederate Museum

828 Camp Street; ☎ *(504) 523-4522.*

Louisiana Children's Museum

428 Julia Street; ☎ *(504) 523-1357.*

Historic New Orleans Collection

533 Royal Street; ☎ *(504) 523-4662.*

Music

Louisiana Music Factory

225 N. Peters Street; ☎ *(504) 586-1094, 10 a.m.–10 p.m., daily.*

Cajun, Jazz, R&B, and everything else you can tap a toe to. They have books as well.

G.H.B. Jazz Foundation

1204 Decatur Street; ☎ *(504) 525-0200, 11 a.m.–6 p.m., Mon.–Sat.*

They publish *Jazzbeat*, a quarterly for jazz buffs. They know everything that's going on and where to buy if you're a collector.

Rock and Roll Collectibles

1214 Decatur Street; ☎ *(504) 561-5683, 10 a.m.–10 p.m., daily.*

Speaks for itself. Records, tapes, CDs for sale or trade.

Perfume

Bourbon French Parfums

525 St. Ann Street; ☎ *(504) 522-4480, 9 a.m.–5 p.m., daily.*

The perfume that wafts through the air in the French Quarter is not always chicory. This very romantic shop has been making perfect blending scents since 1843.

Hové Parfumeur, Ltd.

824 Royal Street; ☎ *(504) 525-7827, 10 a.m.–5 p.m., Mon.–Sat.*
They are the oldest perfume manufacturers in New Orleans, having been founded in 1931. They specialize in their own essential oils which they produce in perfumes, candles, talc and my personal choice, solid perfume, that can go out when you do.

Shopping Centers/Malls

Canal Place at the River

333 Canal Street; ☎ *(504) 522-9200, 10 a.m.–6 p.m., Mon.–Thurs.; 10 a.m.–7 p.m., Fri.–Sun.*
Upscale to the max, housing both Saks and Gucci.

Jackson Brewery

600-620 Decatur Street; ☎ *(504) 566-7245, 10 a.m.–9 p.m., Mon.–Sat.; noon–8 p.m., Sun.*
A huge brewhouse is the anchor for shops and snack bars.

New Orleans Centre

1400 Poydras Street; ☎ *(504) 568-0000, 10 a.m.–8 p.m., Mon.–Sat.; noon–8 p.m., Sun.*
Opposite the Superdome (it connects) so that you can amuse yourself during half-time.

Riverwalk Market Place

1 Poydras Street (at the River); ☎ *(504) 522-1555, 10 a.m.–9 p.m., Mon.–Sat.; 11 a.m.–7 p.m., Sun.*
Most scenic of all the malls, hanging over the Mississippi. They have a vast food court.

"I need a change. Normally, I just wear the faint odor of vague discomfort and unhappiness."

Drawing by Bek; ©1995 The New Yorker Magazine, Inc.

RESTAURANTS

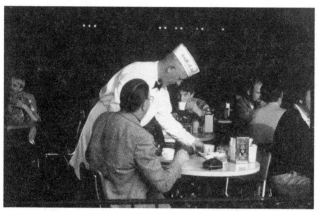

Café du Monde is famous for beignets and café au lait.

The exact meaning of the word food according to the Oxford Dictionary reads: a substance taken into the body to maintain life and growth. In New Orleans one would have to add that food and the profound effect it can have on one's heart and soul is the nourishment that New Orleanians are most interested in. That's the way they interpret the true meaning of maintaining *their* life and *their* growth. In New Orleans eating must be done at pleasurable length and with enormous relish.

All of the many cultures that contribute to the diverse sophistication of the city make the cuisine of New Orleans a glorious patchwork of culinary influences. First and foremost, the elegance of the French when they settled the territory in the 1700s. They brought with them an aristocratic sense of formality of cuisine. Then the Spanish and the natives of the Caribbean added just enough spice and heat to produce a whole new incarnation called Creole cuisine. When the Acadians came down from Canada they settled on farms, out in the country, blending their own French-Canadian signature into what is considered today Cajun, the flip side of Creole food, with not as much heat and a "down-

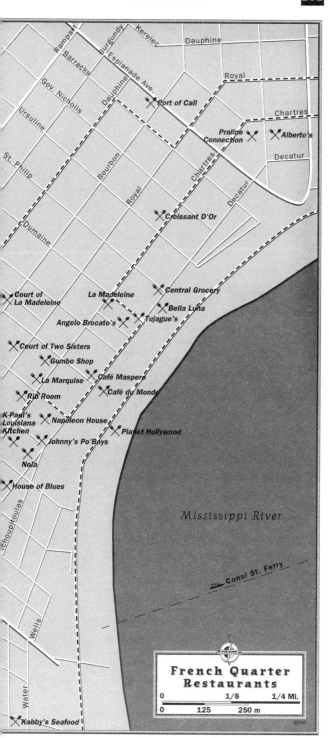

RESTAURANTS

French Quarter
Restaurants

0   1/8   1/4 Mi.
0   125   250 m

©FWI

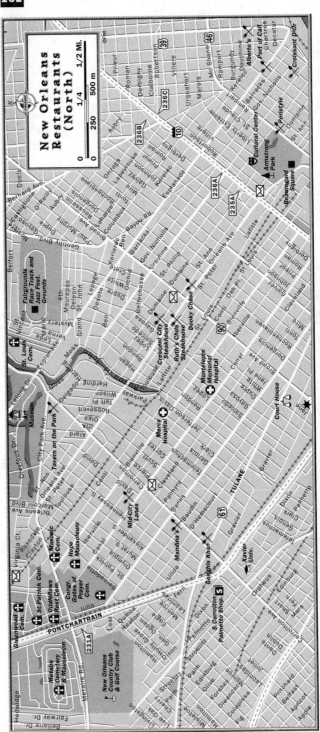

New Orleans Restaurants (North)

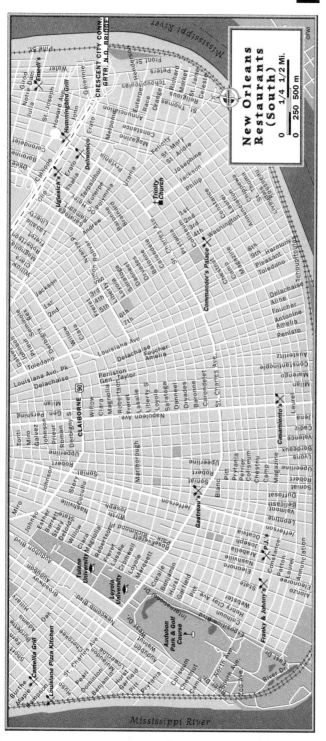

**New Orleans
Restaurants
(South)**

0   1/4   1/2 Mi.

0   250   500 m

home" appeal. Creole is definitely the food of the city while Cajun is laid-back country cooking. However both cuisines have a good deal in common and today they increasingly overlap to produce what most of us think of as "Nouvelle Louisiana."

The restaurants of New Orleans, which to date number over a thousand, run the gamut from the humble po'boy emporium to the "haute-creole" of Commander's Palace and Galatoire's. The sheer concentration of quality restaurants, block after block of them, boggles the mind. New Orleans can more than hold its own in terms of the excellence of its cuisine, with the major capitals of the world, and that includes, dare I say, Paris. That old chestnut "it's hard to get a bad meal in Paris" holds true in all its clichéd glory for New Orleans. Even a simple dish of rice and beans can translate into a fine-dining experience. From the most renowned chefs in the city, to the French Quarter's "down and dirty" oyster bars and gumbo shops, the restaurant scene in The Big Easy is one that you'll find irresistible.

I have profiled restaurants that I regard as quintessential New Orleans; they are synonymous with the excellence, the color and pulse of the city. I hasten to add that these are not the only restaurants in New Orleans that serve good food. Since this book isn't "The Backpacker's Guide to New Orleans," I presume a certain level of sophistication, or at the very least, adventure. I am however, drawing upon my years of experience writing about chefs, restaurants and travel to choose the ones that to me most represent the flavor of New Orleans.

In addition to the restaurants featured, I have made suggestions on where to eat on a more casual, and often less expensive level in each of the districts covered in the book.

BON APPETIT!

Prices

Dining out in New Orleans' finer restaurants can be expensive. There's not much leeway around the $50–$60 per person (exclusive of wine, tax, and tip) figure that keeps cropping up at the "better" restaurants. But there is some: lunches are generally cheaper than dinners, and many of the top restaurants have prix-fixe dinners that are anywhere from one-third to one-half the à la carte menu. Since the object of going to a restaurant is to have a wonderful time, I've never believed in choosing one I couldn't comfortably afford, or afford to splurge on. The good news about dining in the "Big Easy" is enough to make your gumbo runneth over. There are endless choices for moderate or inexpensive meals.

Credit Cards

Unless otherwise noted, all restaurants profiled accept a variety of cards. Do not expect coffee shops or many of the small ethnic restaurants to take credit cards.

New Orleans' Top Restaurants

Antoine's   **$$$**   ★

713 St. Louis Street; ☎ (504) 581-4422.
Cuisine: French. Avg. $40–$60.
Lunch: 11 a.m.–2 p.m., Mon.–Sat.
Dinner: 5:30 p.m.–9 p.m., Mon.–Sat.

If an historic as well as a romantic persona were the makings of the quintessential New Orleans restaurant, Antoine's would be my top choice for "musts" in the city. Unfortunately, cuisine would have to be part of that equation and therefore Antoine's should be evaluated in a separate category devoted to nostalgia. Unfortunately, today it is difficult to see anything other than the most surface signs of its past glory. The physical setting is still historically correct but the heart and soul of a truly great restaurant are missing.

That is not to say that Antoine's, after its 157 years of fame should be avoided like the plague, it simply means that Antoine's should be taken with an oversized grain of salt. No culinary miracles are taking place there today, so a healthy respect for the past should definitely be one of your dinner companions.

The walls are filled with pictures of the greats and the near-greats, all autographed of course. The waiters' eyes seem to stray over to them, perhaps in silent longing for the "good old days." Do not accept a seat in the front room. The very least they can do if not feed you eloquently, is not seat you in their "Siberia." The cuisine of the restaurant is Haute Creole (translation: more French than New Orleans). The signature dishes that are legendary here are Oysters Rockefeller, which are just passable, the creamed spinach, which had it been served hot would have been very good, and the outrageously puffed little pommes soufflés (French fries that are twice fried and magically puffed into tiny crisp, translucent pillows). These were as good as any I've had in Paris. If you could just order the potatoes and a glass of wine you could probably have the best meal on the menu. Credit Cards: All Major.

Camellia Grill   **$**   ★ ★ ★

626 S. Carrollton Avenue; ☎ (504) 866-9573.
Cuisine: Southern. Avg. $15–$30.
Hours: 9 a.m.–1 a.m., Sun.–Thurs.; 9 a.m.–3 a.m., Fri.–Sat.
Twenty-nine stools, count em, and each one of them a ticket to some of the best food in town. The Camellia Grill is a true institution in New Orleans. Everybody goes, everybody waits, and everybody has a simply swell time. After 30 minutes of shifting from foot to foot, eagerly panning the room hoping someone would finish their perfectly done burger, heavenly fries and glorious malted and just move on, a stool became all mine. Let me tell you, I took full advantage of this daunting responsibility by carefully weighing the possibilities of the chili-cheese omelet against the bacon cheeseburger. The clock was ticking, the line at the door was growing, the elegant waiter in his snowy, starched whites stood on the other side of the counter, smiling. Yes, the counter men at the Camellia grill smile. Naturally, the

only way to deal with such a dilemma is to over order: the burger, a side of chili, fries, a black and white ice-cream soda, pecan pie and coffee. This all done in the interest of research, proved that the granddaddy of the "American luncheonette" was alive and well in new Orleans. Just ask Harry Connick, Jr. who was finishing up his coffee freeze, on the stool next to mine. He's a regular, I was just a novice, so I guess my research must continue at length the next time I'm in town. Credit Cards: Not Accepted.

Galatoire's   **$$$**   ★★★

209 Bourbon Street; ☎ *(504) 525-2021.*
Cuisine: French. Avg. $40–$60.
Hours: 11:30 a.m.–9 p.m., Mon.–Sat.; noon–9 p.m., Sun.
Not since "Fiddler on the Roof" has the word "tradition" been taken so seriously. The mirrored walls at Galatoire's reflect a timeless, club-like atmosphere that is dedicated to its past which began in 1905, the golden age of the Creole bistro. Every Sunday is "regulars" day at Galatoire's and the regulars dress elegantly for their weekly pilgrimage. This landmark is a haven for the créme de la créme of New Orleans society. The wonderful thing about Galatoire's is that the food is rated as high as the society. There is hardly a false note on the menu. The oysters are brilliant whether done à la Rockefeller or en brochette. The heavenly shrimp remoulade is in a rich red broth fragrant with olive oil and tangy with cayenne. The bouillabaisse is done in the Creole manner here with shellfish outweighing everything else in the hearty spicy stew. The stock is superb. Trout Marguery is another standard on the menu, served topped with shrimp. Dessert at Galatoire's is as mired in its fanatical traditions as everything else, so when in "Rome" order the crepes maison. That's what the regulars have. Credit Cards: All Major.

Petunia's   **$$**   ★★

817 St. Louis Street; ☎ *(504) 522-6440.*
Cuisine: Southern. Avg. $20–$40.
Hours: 8 a.m.–11 p.m., daily.
They're known for their gargantuan stuffed crepes as well they should be. These babies can measure up to 14 inches and be filled with anything from chicken with hollandaise, to crab ratatouille to bananas foster flambeéd (vanilla ice cream, bananas, brown sugar, rum). They also do a great plate of ribs if your sweet tooth is out for repair.

Petunia's is a homey little Creole townhouse that's been divided into separate cozy dining rooms, each one a parlor done in retro-splendor. They say their ceiling fans were the first ones to be used in the city. They still blow the gentlest of breezes that can only enhance the pleasure you get from the peanut pie. Credit Cards: All Major.

Irene's Cuisine   **$$$**   ★★★

539 St. Phillips; ☎ *(504) 529-8811.*
Cuisine: Italian. Avg. $40–$60.
Dinner: 5:30–10:30 p.m., Mon.–Thurs.; 5:30–11:30 p.m., Fri.–Sat.
More like a tiny Neapolitan trattoria than a French Quarter restaurant, Irene's is just wonderful. It's always packed with people celebrating birthdays, anniversaries, and "affairs" of the moment, because Irene's is just that kind of place. Nowhere is the welcome more gen-

uine or the food more comforting. Irene herself, when she takes a breather from the kitchen, or her adoring husband, Tommy Andrade, bustle around the tables meeting, greeting and urging everyone to "mangia!" Not at all a chore here because the menu is bursting with the best of Southern Italy. The marinara sauce that blankets the mussels is hearty with basil and garlic. Irene, in her infinite wisdom has permitted a hint of Creole to melt into the menu. Her Duck St. Philip, crisp as new money, is served over spinach tossed with dijon mustard and bacon. Back to Sicily for her homemade sausages and sweet roasted peppers dripping in virgin olive oil. For dessert a pyrotechnical extravaganza, Baked Alaska by way of Italy and flamed with an incendiary Grappa Liquor. Goodnight Irene! Credit Cards: All Major.

Port Of Call $ ★★

838 Esplanade Avenue; ☎ *(504) 523-0120.*
Cuisine: Hamburgers. Avg. $15–$30.
Hours: 11 a.m.–1 a.m., Sun.–Thurs.; 11 a.m.–3 a.m., Fri.–Sat.
Dark, smokey, slightly disreputable looking, Port of Call makes about the best hamburger I've ever had. I'm not the only one willing to make such an outrageous claim either. The locals worship at their very "meaty" altar as often as they get the chance.

The "pirate ship chic" of the funky decor and down-at-the-heels atmosphere only seems to heighten the appeal of their big, beautiful burgers. The other standout on their "bar and grill" menu is the show-stopper baked potato that comes with "everything". When anybody asks "Where's the beef?" in the French Quarter the answer is obvious. Credit Cards: All Major.

Arnaud's $$$ ★★★

813 Bienville Street; ☎ *(504) 523-0611.*
Cuisine: French. Avg. $40–$60.
Lunch: 11:30 a.m.–2:30 p.m., daily.
Dinner: 6–10 p.m., daily.
Going to Arnaud's is more like visiting a chateaux with endless rooms and a staff to match. The Chatelaine of the Chateaux is gone now but her presence is all around, from the legends that have grown up since her death to the small museum room upstairs that commemorates her life. Germaine Wells, the daughter of the original founder of Arnaud's, almost totally eclipses the restaurant and its colorful past. She reigned as the queen of 22 carnivals from 1937–1968. All of her fabulously expensive costumes and memorabilia are displayed in the museum above the restaurant. Diners are encouraged to visit after dinner. Downstairs, in the 16 dining rooms, leaded windows, etched glass, great heroic chandeliers and wood-paneled walls covered with painting and mementos.

Kevin Davis, Arnaud's newest chef has put his own spin on their most venerable specialties. Since he's the first American chef to preside over their French-Creole kitchen, he's kept an American eagle eye on the famous shrimp Arnaud (their personal version of sauce remoulade) while slipping in pompano David, done with fresh herbs as well as spicy rack of lamb diablo that melts on the tongue. Do not even think of paying the check without at least a fork full of the chocolate terrine with its velvety layers of hazelnut and dark chocolate. Most of the locals end a dinner at Arnaud's with their version of Café Brulot (bourbon-based coffee) made with great ceremony, at table. Credit Cards: All Major.

Bizou $$$ ★★★

701 St. Charles Avenue; ☎ *(504) 524-4114.*
Cuisine: Creole/Southern. Avg. $40–$60.
Lunch: 11 a.m.–4 p.m., Mon.–Sat.
Dinner: 6–10 p.m., Mon.–Sat.

It's new, it's chic and best of all its chef has a flare for the original. Forget Creole, Cajun, French and think "Nouvelle New Orleans." And why not? The Louisiana Purchase has proven to be a great buy, now it's time to move on to what's new and hot in the other 49 states. Chef Devlin Roussel is doing his delicious best to introduce us to his own spin on elegant bistro cuisine. The clean, sparse room is designed to let the food take center stage, not the decorator.

The way to start is tucking into the crawfish beignets that have been deep fried to a bone-dry, crisp perfection and served with a sweet and sour tomato glaze. Or, a mile-high tomato Napoleon (they really love that little guy in N.O.) stuffed with goat cheese and splashed with a black pepper vinaigrette. On to a slab of peanut-crusted grilled tuna with a cilantro coulis. We're talking inventive here! Jumbo soft shell crab comes with a Lo Mein salad and citrus soy dipping sauce. By now you have the whole dazzling picture except for dessert, if you dare. I ended with Bizou's frozen créme anglaise partnered with a lemon curd parfait. "Bizutiful." Credit Cards: All Major.

Mother's $ ★★

401 Poydras Street; ☎ *(504) 523-9656.*
Cuisine: Southern. Avg. $10–$20.
Hours: 5 a.m.–10 p.m., Mon.–Sat.; 7 a.m.–10 p.m., Sun.

Be prepared for cafeteria-style service, long lines, pushing and shoving to get an uncomfortable chair at an often sticky, gummy table. Also be prepared for one of the best down-home breakfasts or lunches in town. Mother's is an institution devoted to the concept of comfort food as the meaning of life. Grits are ladled out in mountainous portions and topped with enough butter to require an instant triple-bypass. Eggs dripping in butter are served with melting ham biscuits dripping in butter. Breakfast at Mother's takes longer than a mini-series but I promise you it is time well spent. The usual, that the locals start their day with and occasionally end their lives with is as follows: two eggs, any style, grits, homemade biscuits, fried ham and coffee. Lunch is a Godzilla-sized po'boy stuffed with "Debris" (the meat that falls to the bottom of the pan and browns in the fat) or any of their roasts, and then soaked with gravy. Just writing about Mother's is dangerous for my cholesterol profile. If this sounds just too threatening for you, remember, everybody in N.O. goes to Mother's, they just don't admit it. Credit Cards: Not Accepted.

Uglesich's $$ ★★★

1238 Baronne Street; ☎ *(504) 523-8571.*
Cuisine: Oyster house. Avg. $20–$40.
Hours: 9:30 a.m.–4 p.m., Mon.–Fri.

RESTAURANTS

You may have to travel to Uglesich's by armored tank but let me assure you this is a small price to pay for the great food that will be put before you. True, the neighborhood runs a close second to South Central LA, but when you see the limos lined up out in front you'll feel instantly more secure. What do they all come for? They line up for Uggie's deep fried oysters which are easily the best to be found in a city that has a mega-surplus of fried oyster "joints." And you can take "joint" in its most serious sense at Uglesich's. It's run-down, seedy, borderline messy, and packed every single day. Grab a chair, start with the oysters, go on to the super shrimp plate doused with hot chili paste, add a side of fries and a bottle of ice cold beer. You will have entered Uglesich heaven. You'll have to make do with lunch since they put the oysters to bed at about 4 p.m. Uglesich's is a closely guarded secret everybody seems to know about. Credit Cards: Not Accepted.

Dooky Chase   **$$**   ★★★

2301 Orleans Avenue; ☎ *(504) 821-0600.*
Cuisine: Creole. Avg. $20–$40.
Hours: 11:30 a.m.–midnight, daily.
Soul food, Creole style. Everything that's on Dooky's menu seems familiar and even a bit passé until you taste it to realize it's never been so good before. That's because the great chef of down-home Creole cooking, Leah Chase, is in the kitchen here. Her filé gumbo is the darkest, richest gumbo in town. Her fried chicken is an astonishment, the crawfish etouffée is buried in sweet tomatoes and peppers. Grillades (thin slices of veal) are served with Chef Chase's incomparable Creole sauce. There is an elegance and refinement to everything that comes out of the kitchen in this deceptively simple local spot. The art on the walls by local black artists continues the Chase's dedication to the community. Credit Cards: All Major.

Cafe Du Monde   **$**   ★★★

800 Decatur Street; ☎ *(504) 525-4544.*
Cuisine: French. Coffee house. Avg. $10–$15.
Hours: 24 hours, daily.
A supreme dining experience in New Orleans doesn't have to translate into white table cloths and crystal wine goblets. Neither does it have to provide umpteen courses of "super-chef" driven cuisine. There is one spot above all others that personifies the very essence of the Big Easy and all you can hope to order there are doughnuts, coffee and a large helping of history. But what doughnuts and what coffee!

Since the 1860s when it was a simple coffee stand that served the workers of the French Market 24 hours a day, Cafe du Monde has been the place to start the morning and end the evening. In the early hours before dawn, what could be a better way to finish off a fabulous party or Masked Ball than with a crisp, warm, airy beignet smothered in confectioners' sugar? With it, a steaming cup of chicory-flavored café au lait. Revelers in formal attire and market workers sat shoulder to shoulder inhaling the luxurious aroma of the beignets as they came from the fryer. Today not much has changed. Perhaps there are fewer ball gowns (except during Mardi Gras) and more tourists but the beignets are just as heavenly. If at all possible sit outside under the festive green and white awning and watch New Orleans stroll by. Credit Cards: Not Accepted.

Praline Connection $$ ★★★

524 Frenchman Street; ☎ *(504) 943-3934.*
Cuisine: Creole/Southern. Avg. $15–$30.
Hours: 11 a.m.–10:30 p.m., Mon.–Thurs.; 11 a.m.–midnight, Fri.–Sat.

From the outside it looks like nothing more than a tearoom but from the inside, as you watch the ribs being scarfed down by men in three piece suits you know you've reached Soul Food Central. The waiters wear rakish black fedoras, snow-white shirts and have a healthy respect for what comes out of the kitchen. So do most of the diners who can't seem to get enough of the collards or fried chicken or the smothered pork chops. The meatloaf platter could feed a family of four and the crawfish etouffée is ambrosial. Whatever you decide on, start off with the fried chicken livers which are served with a mahogany dark gravy. Naturally, everything is accompanied by warm cornbread dripping in butter. If the waiter catches you trying to leave without a slice of sweet potato pie, he'll be inconsolable. Credit Cards: All Major.

Gabrielle $$$ ★★★

3201 Esplanade Avenue; ☎ *(504) 948-6233.*
Cuisine: Nouvelle Cajun. Avg. $20–$40.
Dinner: 6–10:30 p.m., Mon.–Sat.

Chef Greg Sonnier has the restaurant of the moment in New Orleans. It has garnered praise from nearly everyone of note in the restaurant scene here. And, for a change, everybody's absolutely right. The dedication of Chef Sonnier and his equally dedicated wife, Mary, shows itself best in the innovative, unique menu people come from all over the city to sample. Mary Sonnier, the meeter and greeter at Gabrielle handles the front of the house with grace and warmth, which goes a long way in making this tiniest of spaces appealing. The room is not much bigger than a small diner, so the wait for reservations can stretch over a week. But you won't regret it once you've tucked your fork into the sauteed veal with baked linguine served in a basil wine reduction, or the loin of lamb in a pool of blackberry sauce.

It's hard to know how to characterize this blend of Creole, Cajun, Latin and Soul. The Sonniers call it New American perhaps because it breaks all the rules in the most disarming of ways. Mary is responsible for dessert and she brings the house down with her sensational homemade pies and ice creams. J.J.'s lemon cheese pie, chocolate pecan pie, peppermint patti, or all of the above will make you forget you've ever heard of fat free yogurt forever! Credit Cards: All Major.

Napoleon House $ ★★

500 Chartres Street; ☎ *(504) 522-4152.*
Cuisine: French. Avg. $10–$25.
Hours: 11 a.m.–1 a.m., daily.

This was supposed to be Napoleon's home away from exile but the "tiny one" never made it. What to do, what to do? Well, when you don't know what to do with an empty space, you can always open a restaurant. That is exactly what they did more than 80 years ago and it's been a landmark in the French Quarter ever since. Everybody goes to Napoleon House, not just people passing through town. It's a gathering place for artists, writers and the locals who love the musty, dark, mystery of the place. You can cut the atmosphere with a carving knife. Local art is hung haphazardly on the wall, and tiny, naked, orange light bulbs throw an eerie glow. The biggest surprise at Napoleon House is that despite it being such a great hangout, the muffalettas that are served up are really great. The drink to go along with them is the house's Pimms Cup. The French doors that lead to the street are almost always open making the French Quarter strollers outside part of the scene. Credit Cards: All Major.

Pelican Club   **$$$**   ★★

312 Exchange Alley; ☎ (504) 523-1504
Cuisine: Creole/Southern. Avg. $40–$60.
Dinner: 5 p.m.–midnight, daily.
What a beautiful bistro this is. The room stretches out amid palms and marble floors, and comfortable black leather banquettes which are well-spaced, permitting some privacy. The ceiling fans whir gently through the hum of happy diners. Chef Richard Hughes has filled his eclectic menu with "fusion cuisine" that marries Oriental with Creole as well as cajun. The result is wedded bliss.

Creamy white bean and crawfish bisque is a blend of French and Cajun sensibilities, the beef and shrimp pot stickers are delectably juicy even without their dipping sauce of chili and ginger. The most engaging thing on the menu (and that is no small accomplishment at the Pelican Club) is the St. Louis Baby Ribs with a Thai peanut sauce. They come lolling on a banana leaf filled with Oriental sticky rice. A coconut curried slaw turns down the heat of the chili-laced peanut sauce. The "house" bread pudding comes in a two-tone version. End with white and dark chocolate in a healthy shot of rum for a tropic spin. Credit Cards: All Major.

La Crepe Nanou   **$$**   ★★

1410 Robert Street; ☎ (504) 899-2670.
Cuisine: French. Avg. $20–$40.
Dinner: 6–10 p.m., Mon.–Thurs.; 6–11 p.m., Fri.–Sat.
This is Paris, not New Orleans. Make no mistake, Crepe Nanou is beloved by the locals because it is their absolute French Bistro, with an unmistakable connection to the "Motherland." When they speak about Nanou they usually preface it with "don't tell anyone." They hadn't counted on my selfless dedication to my hungry readers. Don't leave Nanou without a bowl of their superb onion soup or, of course, one of their glorious crepes which are served both savory and sweet. Nanou makes the crepes himself so you can watch each miracle happen right before your eyes. If you find you simply don't want the evening to end, you can order a big bowl of Nanou's garlicky mussels, served with enough French bread to dip your way through for hours. Credit Cards: All Major.

Upperline   **$$$**   ★★★

1413 Upperline Street; ☎ (504) 891-9822.
Cuisine: American/Creole. Avg. $40–$60.
Dinner: 5:30–9:30 p.m., Mon.–Sun. Closed Tuesday.

Upperline is the kind of restaurant you wish you could visit at least once a week. You know by the warm welcome you receive as a stranger, how terrific it would be to join the bonafide regulars. Jo Ann Clevenger is Upperline's keeper of the flame. She lives, breathes and delights in her restaurant's unique artistry. Art is as important as cuisine here judging by the walls, which are covered with the works of Martin Laborde. His most famous subject is a sad looking mysterious little clown who looks down on the diners from most of the canvases in the room. The menu is as artistic and original as the decor. Sautéed duck livers coupled with a sweet garlic dressing over creamy polenta. Crisp fried green tomatoes are smothered in a shrimp remoulade. Creole pot pie has chicken under a tender buttery crust, bathed in a spicy wine and mushroom sauce. End with the warm pecan pie à la mode for an exhilarating exit. If you're lucky enough to visit Upperline during the summer Ms. Clevenger celebrates garlic with its own festival. She features it every which way on the menu. One of her most popular desserts is the vanilla ice cream with honey poached garlic sauce. We know where "Lestat" will *not* be having his dinner during July and August. Credit Cards: All Major.

Brennan's $$ ★ ★
417 Royal Street; ☎ *(504) 525-9711.*
Cuisine: French. Avg. $20–$40.
Lunch: 8 a.m.–2:30 p.m., daily.
Dinner: 6–10 p.m., daily.

You simply cannot visit New Orleans without having breakfast at Brennan's. Maybe one of the reasons people crowd into the Brennan's 200-year old landmark on **Royal Street** in the French Quarter, is that they recommend breaking your fast with a stiff brandy-milk punch. The most celebrated element of Brennan's lavish spread is the egg course which usually starts off the festivities. I counted no fewer than eleven different ways to prepare an egg and that's no "eggs-ageration." If only Humpty Dumpty had lived to see them all! You can start with eggs sardon (poached with artichokes, creamed spinach and Hollandaise), eggs benedict (poached with Canadian bacon and Hollandaise), eggs hussarde (poached with bacon and wine sauce), eggs bayou (poached with cajun sausage and Hollandaise). Are you beginning to see a pattern here. Eggsactly! The traditional finish to all of this is bananas foster which requires bananas, brown sugar, banana liquor, rum and a very long match. At the very end, either steaming cups of café au lait or an ambulance, whichever comes first. Remember, dinner at Antoine's is an option but breakfast at Brennan's is a must. Credit Cards: All Major.

Peristyle $$ ★ ★
1041 Dumaiane Street; ☎ *(504) 593-9535.*
Cuisine: Creole/French. Avg. $20–$40.
Dinner: 6–10 p.m., Tues.–Sat.

When its beloved chef-owner John Neal died suddenly it was thought this marvelous little bistro would wither away. They needn't have worried. Ann Kearney, who worked with Neal for years made the kitchen very much her own. The room itself is cleverly done with mirrors and brass trim to set the stage for an intimate, dining experience.

People come to Peristyle to linger over their last glass of wine and the wonderful afterglow of Ann Kearney's stylish food—cornmeal crusted oysters lazing on a bed of roasted corn and white beans, or grilled lamb, perfectly pink partnered with an orzo risotto. A rare filet comes dressed with a rich coat of roquefort cheese and herbs. For dessert a dense, moist, butterscotch Genoise or a paper-thin raspberry tart that tastes just like summer. Credit Cards: All Major.

Gautreau $$$ ★ ★ ★

1728 Soniat Street; ☎ *(504) 899-7397.*
Cuisine: French. Avg. $40–$60.
Dinner: 6–10 p.m., Mon.–Sat.
Take one old pharmacy, add smart 90s decor, fill it with young trendy movers and shakers, top it all off with great bistro food and you get a prescription for some very fine dining. And that's just what takes place at Gautreau's. It's tucked into a green leafy residential neighborhood but the calm is broken by the limos that are lined up in front. Everything at Gautreau's is very much on the front burner.

Gautreau's regulars come back week after week to soak up the atmosphere and the modern French Creole cuisine that is superbly served to them. The crab cakes alone are worth a trip here. Their game is considered the *only* game in town. Seared venison comes with a velvety chestnut puree and a sauce made with dried cherries and ruby port. Quail sits atop a mascarpone risotto and wears a blueberry glaze. Desserts are no less elegant. A brilliantly done orange créme brulée with the thinnest of caramel crusts crackles as the spoon breaks through. The apricot-pistachio bread pudding is as light as a fallen soufflé. Credit Cards: All Major.

Bayona $$$ ★ ★ ★

430 Dauphine Street; ☎ *(504) 525-4455.*
Cuisine: American. Avg. $40–$60.
Lunch: 11:30 a.m.–3 p.m., Mon.–Thurs.
Dinner: 6–9:30 p.m., Mon.–Thurs.; 10 a.m.–11 p.m., Fri.–Sat.
World class chef, Susan Spicer, is known in New Orleans for her dedication to elegant as well as innovative cuisine. No painted plates, no culinary "hocus-pocus." She traveled to Provence and Greece to form her own philosophy of Mediterranean cuisine and translates it into an endless series of provocative combinations. Spicer is very definitely an original.

Her intimate restaurant is set in a romantic 19th century Creole cottage made up of cozy rooms, some that look out into a tiny tropic courtyard. In the evenings the rooms are softly lit by candlelight. Cream of garlic soup is one of Spicer's best Mediterranean inspirations. It's on the menu year round because of its lusty flavor, a complement to any season. The grilled hoisin tuna with sesame guacamole proves that China and Mexico are made for each other. Dark, smoky flavored duck is soothed by a creamy cashew butter. A tiny pepper jelly "sandwich" is served alongside. The grape-leaf-wrapped salmon sitting on a mound of couscous is made even sunnier with a drizzle of olive vinaigrette. A grilled pork chop nestles next to a jewel-like fruit chutney. After all of those exquisitely rendered, civilized and thoroughly satisfying examples of the "Spicer Touch" the good news is

RESTAURANTS

that it is impossible to resist dessert. I found that the pecan torte layered with cream cheese and lavished with brandied peaches brought me back to the Old South in the sweetest of ways. Credit Cards: All Major

K-Paul's Louisiana Kitchen $$$ ★★
416 Chartres Street; ☎ *(504) 596-2531.*
Cuisine: Cajun/Creole. Avg. $40–$60.
Lunch: 11:30 a.m.–2:30 p.m., Mon.–Fri.
Dinner: 5:30–10 p.m., Tues.–Sat.
Paul Prudhomme is the man who first taught us about the food of Louisiana long before we ever got there. He became one of the most important chefs in the U.S. when his Cajun cooking took the country by storm. We learned to pronounce *andouille* (cajun sausage) we recognized *etouffée* (smothered) on the menu and most deliciously of all his blackened redfish caused a true "foodie" frenzy. Blackened no longer meant burnt, it meant New Orleans, Chef Prudhomme's home. Many pages have fallen off the calendar since then but Paul Prudhomme is still the chef we think of when we think of spicy, rustic, Cajun cooking.

Since Cajun is down-home, country food, K-Paul's won't remind anyone of "Tailliavant." It's rough and tumble, long communal tables with not a hint of a private tete-a-tete in sight. In fact, public humiliation (a gold star slapped on your cheek if you clean your plate) can be the order of the day here. Cajuns love to laugh almost as much as they love to blacken things. Noel Coward would not be a happy camper at K-Paul's. Another caveat to worshipping before the Great Gumbo is the line you have to join on the sidewalk, just to get in. However, when all is said and done K-Paul can load up the table with some mighty good grub. Credit Cards: All Major.

Christian's $$$ ★★
3835 Iberville Street; ☎ *(504) 482-4924.*
Cuisine: French. Avg. $40–$60.
Lunch: 11:30 a.m.–2 p.m., Mon.–Sat.
Dinner: 5:30–10 p.m., Mon.–Sat.
Dining at Christian's is more like a religious experience, not only because of the food but because its physical setting is a converted church. The atmosphere is nothing short of beatific. Cushioned banquettes are in reality pews from the church and the stained glass Gothic windows complete the picture. Of course, as you might have guessed, Christian's has a cathedral ceiling. For over 25 years Christian's has served a classical French menu to their diners who come up the 2-1/2 miles from **Canal Street** to worship in this house of haute cuisine.

To start, the wild mushrooms delicately flavored with madeira come wrapped in crackling phyllo and drizzled with a dark mushroom glaze. The bouillabaisse here is a spectacular rendition with a stock rich as Croeses and an endless assortment of gastronomic sea creatures. Christian's is known for its "tres" classical Coq au Vin which is so authentic it could have been prepared in the Shadow of La Tour Eiffel. Dessert just has to be "Skip." The name may sound like a warning rather than an inducement but its childlike pairing of cookies and ice cream is guaranteed to bring out the kid in you. Credit Cards: All Major.

Emeril's $$$ ★★★

800 Tchoupitoulas Street; ☎ (504) 528-9393.
Cuisine: Cajun/Creole. Avg. $40–$60.
Lunch: 11:30 a.m.–2 p.m.
Dinner: 6–10 p.m., Mon.–Sat.

He's been called "The Engagin' Cajun," which sounds suspiciously like a P.R. label to me. Emeril Lagasse is a fabulous, creative, hands-on chef of amazing talent who captures the very essence of the ingredients and makes them together, infinitely better than they were alone. He can read the changing tastes of the young and restless and interpret them into his own signature cuisine. He is the one chef in New Orleans that has learned to read the palates of his customers with a sharp accuracy. His sprawling, color-splashed, restaurant located in the new Warehouse District echoes the off-center, the avant garde of the neighborhood and adds its own culinary artistry to the galleries that people are flocking to.

The choices that confront one at Emeril's are across-the-board fabulous! It would take five or six visits just to scratch the surface of his extravagant menu. What a delightful problem to have to cope with. Try a wedge of smoked salmon cheesecake iced with cream cheese and Louisiana caviar or smoked trout dumplings served in a potato boat with truffle sauce and onion marmalade. The immense skillet veal chop is poached in a pecan gravy, served over grits with melted cheese and fried parsnip slivers. Coconut cream pie is tall enough to scrape the ceiling. At its side is fresh pineapple ice cream in a pool of thick caramel. No one will ever accuse Emeril Lagasse of serving spa cuisine! Credit Cards: All Major.

Louis XVI $$$ ★★

732 Rue Bienville; ☎ (504) 581-7000.
Cuisine: French. Avg. $40–$60.
Dinner: 6–11 p.m., daily.

As opulently decorated as one of the king's very own dining rooms, Louis XVI would have felt right at home in his namesake. It's royally classic and festive enough for a celebration. Louis' is one of the few restaurants in New Orleans that still has "European" tableside preparation. Pomp and circumstance make the menu come to life right in front of you.

Coquilles St. Jacque Morney presents scallops at their most succulent, covered in a triple-rich sauce mornay. The turtle soup has a briny taste of the sea which only adds to the perfume of the fine sherry that gives the turtle its voice. Duck breast is perfectly roasted to a ruby rare and served in a puddle of raspberry sauce. A salmon roulade is so gossamer in texture that its caviar beurre blanc seems to hold it down on the plate. If you order the Baked Alaska for dessert (it keeps appearing all over town) be prepared for the pyrotechnics to occur close enough to require fire insurance. Credit Cards: All Major.

Brigston's $$$ ★★★

723 Dante Street; ☎ (504) 861-7610.
Cuisine: Creole/Cajun. Avg. $40–$60.

Dinner: 5:30–10 p.m., Tues.–Sat.

Located in the artsy-craftsy little community of Riverbend, Brigston's is a "split personality" winner. Half Cajun, half Creole and the whole is the personal triumph of its guiding light, Frank Brigston. Chef Brigston's small Creole cottage is always packed to its rafters with people who know great Cajun when they meet it. Little wonder, since Brigston learned at the "Iron Skillet" of the master, Paul Prudhomme. The menu changes daily here to add to the excitement, so you will always see a new Brigston brainstorm on his endlessly inventive menu of showstoppers. Mrs. Brigston, Marva, is the meeter, greeter and crowd controller, which is no small task. The tiny rooms of the cottage are always filled with people having a wonderful time. What can anyone say that is better, about a restaurant?

The enticing menu makes any attempt at a decision very difficult. The butternut shrimp bisque is thick with butter and cream not to mention those tasty little guys that melt on the tongue. Rabbit tenderloin lazes on a spicy bed of parmesan grits and tasso, alongside spinach in a sweet mustard sauce. Brigston is totally original in his combinations and his fans are grateful, to say the least. He cooks to a very different drummer. One of the constants on the menu is crisply roasted duck served on "dirty rice," a Cajun classic, but Brigston pushes the envelope with a honey pecan gravy. The best dessert on the menu is the fresh banana ice cream, however you could twist my arm if Chef Brigston's bread pudding appeared suddenly. Don't tell Oprah! Credit Cards: All Major.

Mike's On The Avenue $$$ ★★

628 St. Charles Avenue; ☎ (504) 523-1709
Expensive. American. Avg. $40–$60.
Lunch: 11:30 a.m.–2 p.m., daily.
Dinner: 6–10 p.m., daily.

Chef Mike Fennelly has decided that with a little help from his very eclectic kitchen his customers can take a trip around the world without leaving their tables. We all know, if we are card carrying "Gastronauts," that fusion fever is at the root of Mike's globe-trotting menu. Obviously, Mike never met a cuisine he didn't like or one he couldn't adapt brilliantly to his own style. And style is the operative word in Mike's two dining rooms. They divided the restaurant into two spaces with a tiny elegant hotel lobby separating them. Perhaps one is for right brain gourmets and one for left.

The menu is a travelogue with edible chapters. The shrimp dumplings are plumped with spinach and ginger, to be dipped in a jet-black tahini. The black bean quesadilla is a holdover from Mike's Santa-Fe days. He fills it with Shiitake mushrooms and smoked poblano goat cheese. The honey soy-glazed duck is perfumed with Chinese spices and sauced with a sweet Hoisin. Crawfish and scallop cakes are Mike's spin on the Louisiana crab cakes "obsession." These could become obsessive as well. Crème brulée or brioche bread pudding ends your "around the world in 80 mouthfuls" odyssey with a bang. Credit Cards: All Major.

Graham's $$$ ★★

200 Magazine Street; ☎ (504) 524-9678.
Cuisine: American. Avg. $40–$60.

Lunch: 11:30 a.m.–3 p.m., daily.
Dinner: 6–11 p.m., daily.

Kevin Graham, a Brit originally from Cheshire, was the superstar chef who potted around the kitchens of the Windsor Court Hotel. His private domain was the Grill Room where he introduced his imaginative dishes that are still served there today. But that was then and Graham's is now. When Kevin set up Graham's he decided to give it a cutting edge so sharp you gasp at its minimalist chic and off-the-wall humor. Graham's is definitely a prime example of "attitude." Modern to the point of sterility in everything but the food turns out to old fashioned yummy.

Ebony granite tables show off the colorfully eclectic "Grammys" that cover the china. Take it from the top, with crisp cheese and crab beignets brought to life with a jalapeno remoulade. Then go on to Tagliatelle with foie gras quenelles, or rare duck lacquered with coffee and oranges. The dessert that is talked about endlessly and still served at the Windsor Court is Graham's Chocolate Breathless, which is exactly what you will be after consuming the chocolate mousse covered with chocolate meringue. There is simply no way back from Graham's caloric abyss. Credit Cards: All Major.

Commander's Palace $$$ ★ ★ ★

1403 Washington Avenue; ☎ (504) 899-8221.
Cuisine: Creole/Southern. Avg. $40–$60.
Lunch: 11:30 a.m.–2 p.m., daily.
Dinner: 6–10 p.m., daily.

This is the restaurant that launched a thousand chefs and the restaurant against which all other temples of haute cuisine in New Orleans are measured. This is still the most important restaurant in the city! Commander's Palace is the jewel in the Brennan family's crown. It was founded in 1880 by Emil Commander and as the story goes had a very romantic if slightly checkered past. Known as a rendezvous for riverboat captains who used the rooms upstairs for some very private functions, the Brennan family took it over in the early 70s, and completely redesigned it into a number of elegantly formal dining rooms. Outside, Commander's is a picture-perfect, Disney type, Victorian mansion done in white with turquoise accents. Most of the finest chefs in the city started their careers at Commander's, most notably Paul Prudhomme, Emeril Lagasse and Frank Brigston.

The dining rooms have nothing but space so you can sit back like a mogul, with nary a hint of conversation from your neighbors. Expect to linger, Commander's is an experience to be savored. The most auspicious of starters is a triple threat on the menu called Soup 1-1-1, a trio of gumbo, turtle, and soup du jour served in tiny cups. The butcher's plate is a celebration of choucouterie—an assortment of patés and terrines that could keep even an alligator busy for months. For a bit of the exotic, the Texas boar chops, grilled with hickory and sprawled on a bed of wild mushrooms prove to be anything but boring. Commander's also has quite a sense of humor about their sandwiches: escargot sandwich bordelaise or a caviar and gravlax club. Dessert is without a doubt, Creole bread pudding soufflé. It's reputation is mythic around town. Credit Cards: All Major.

Nola   **$$$**   ★ ★ ★

534 Rue St. Louis; ☎ *(504) 522-6652.*
Cuisine: Cajun. Avg. $40–$60.
Lunch: 11:30 a.m.–2 p.m., Mon.–Sat.
Dinner: 6–10 p.m., Sun.–Thurs.; 6 p.m.–midnight, Fri.–Sat.

Trendy, trendy, trendy! A magnet for all the "Suppies" (southern yuppies) in the city. But who cares! Nola is simply marvelous as is everything Chef Emeril Lagasse seems to be a part of. Emeril is a mega-chef, a cookbook author and a T.V. star. Most of all he's a very nice person. Over the years this bundle of Cajun dynamite has opened two world-class restaurants in New Orleans. Of the two, Nola is techier and more "happening" than the ever-exciting Emeril's which pre-dates it. Located in the middle of the French Quarter it's as satisfying to drop in for one of Nola's paper-thin pizzas as it is to take time for a whole meal amid the roar of the crowd.

The menu can be all things to all people. But as for this person, I had to try the layered Creole tomato napoleon with Italian ham, white cheddar and moistened with a basil pesto. It was a tough decision so I had a bite or two of the homemade boudin sausage stewed in beer, cane syrup and served on a grilled sweet potato bread crouton slathered in creole mustard. Sauteed veal is served with crabmeat ravioli in a red pepper cream sauce.

Peanut butter pie drizzled with dark chocolate is something that will come back to you in your dreams, but if you're an apple pie worshipper, Emeril's flat, crisp, fried apple pie is an out-of-body experience as well. Credit Cards: All Major.

New Orleans balconies are an invitation to dine alfresco.

Rooms With A View

WHEN IS A RESTAURANT NOT A RESTAURANT?

I have a number of favorite restaurants in New Orleans I always suggest to visitors that go far beyond the question of food. Not that some of those listed wouldn't rate inclusion on any "best restaurant" list, but their locations are extraordinary enough to warrant being highlighted in a special category.

Bella Luna $$$ ★ ★ ★

914 N. Peters Street; ☎ (504) 529-1583.
Cuisine: Italian. Avg. $40–$60.
Dinner: 6–10:30 p.m., daily.
With the Mighty Mississippi right at its door, it is surprising that New Orleans boasts so few "rooms with a view." One of the most scenic of those that do exist is Bella Luna. The river just keeps rollin' along past its windows in majestic splendor. There is quite a bit of splendor inside as well. Bella Luna is done with the elegance of an Italian villa complete with moonlight, if you're lucky. If the moon is a no-show you can console yourself with a menu that's stylishly conceived and executed. Using familiar Italian elements the chef has continued on to the rest of the world for his inspirations. Steamed lobster is tossed with calamari-pink fettuccini, basil and a saffron flavored aioli. Pork chops are crusted with pecans in an Abita beer reduction. Quail is boned and stuffed with a peppery tomatillo salsa. Italian food with a Cajun spin is a true adventure. For dessert the warm fig strudel with cinnamon honey ice cream is a voluptuous ending. Credit Cards: All Major.

Tavern on the Park $$$ ★

900 City Park Avenue; ☎ (504) 486-3333.
Cuisine: Continental. Avg. $40–$60.
Dinner: 6–11 p.m., Mon.–Sat.
The building that the Tavern is in dates back to the Civil War. In those days it was a bit naughty. Married men brought their mistresses, or the "uptown swells" dropped in to observe the risqué goings-on. Today the food takes a back seat to history. The views of the park will help to nourish you if the menu doesn't. Drop in for a bite. Credit Cards: All Major.

Kabby's $$$ ★

New Orleans Hilton, 2 Poydras Street; ☎ (504) 584-3880.
Cuisine: American. Avg. $40–$60.
Lunch: 11 a.m.–3 p.m., daily.
Dinner: 6–11 p.m., daily.

I have to say honestly, don't go for the food, but just as honestly, Kabby's has a dynamite view of the Mississippi. Your best bet would be brunch here—what can they do to soft-boiled eggs? Credit Cards: All Major.

Chart House $$$ ★

801 Chartres Street; ☎ *(504) 523-2015.*
Cuisine: Steak house. Avg. $40–$60.
Dinner: 6 p.m.–midnight, daily.
From its splendid balcony, all of Jackson Square is spread out before you. It is possible to get a decent grill and the steaks are fine but really, the view's the thing at Chart House. If you're saving yourself for one of the great dining experiences on your agenda you can stop in for a drink. The bar is very popular with the locals who don't want to miss any of the action taking place below. Try to go at twilight when you can see the flicker of the gaslamps. Credit Cards: All Major.

Le Jardin $$$ ★

Weston Canal Place, 100 Iberville Street; ☎ *(504) 566-7006.*
Expensive. French/Creole. Avg. $40–$60.
Lunch: 11:30 a.m.–2:30 p.m., daily.
Dinner: 6–10:30 p.m., daily.
The Creole menu here may be somewhat lacking but the view surely isn't. Only 11 floors above the madding crowd, but that's high enough to see out over the Mississippi in a sweep of panoramic views. Very plush, which is what you would expect from a high-rise, luxury hotel with a staff that really cares. The only regret is a somewhat mediocre kitchen that is no match for Ole Man River. Come to think of it, what is? Credit Cards: All Major.

Creole Queen $$ ★★★

Canal St. Wharf; ☎ *(504) 524-0814/800-445-4109.*
Cuisine: Creole. Avg. $20–$40.
Call for sailing information.
The most enchanting view that you will have in New Orleans at dinner would have to be from the deck of the Creole Queen. The old fashioned paddlewheeler departs almost every night (call ahead) to cruise the Mississippi just as its ancestors did in the 1800s. There is a surprisingly good Creole dinner which is in the form of a lavish buffet complete with jazz and dancing. The all-inclusive price is about $40 and you'll feel just like Gaylord and Magnolia on their first date. Credit Cards: All Major.

Agenda/Best Hotel Dining Rooms

New Orleans, as one of the top restaurant cities in the world, continues that distinction in its hotel dining rooms. In most other cities the hotel dining room is to be avoided like a bad case of the shingles, but that certainly does not apply to The Big Easy, which has some of the best cuisine around tucked away in its luxury hotels.

Grill Room $$$ ★★★

The Windsor Court Hotel, 300 Gravier Street; ☎ *(504) 522-1992.*
Cuisine: American. Avg. $40–$60.
Lunch: 11 a.m.–2 p.m., daily.
Dinner: 6–10 p.m., daily.

Like Commander's Palace, The Grill Room serves some of the most distinguished cuisine in New Orleans. The dining room itself is a 24-carat classic that draws its diners from some of the most powerful movers and shakers in New Orleans. First under the dazzling showmanship of Kevin Graham, now under the equally creative direction of Chef Jeff Tunks, The Grill Room continues to serve the kind of food that is lauded all over a city where culinary praise has to be measured against restaurants that are legends in themselves.

The room is more French Chateau than Tara, with beautiful tapestries, thick plush rugs and richly brocaded drapes. This in no way prepares you for the crosscultural, adventuresome menu that has great humor and sophistication. Crisp duck is lacquered with coffee, moist and sweet grouper is wrapped in a crackle of phyllo and set atop a mountain of strawberries and mango. A napoleon is layered with shrimp remoulade and fried Mirliton covered in a Tabasco® butter. The shrimp bisque is richer than some of the people who dote upon it and the Chinese smoked lobster shares a plate with French-fried spinach. Dessert here can only be Chocolate Breathless, a beloved holdover from the Graham regime. If it doesn't leave you in the same condition, I will finish it for you! Credit Cards: All Major.

Bistro $$$ ★★★

Maison de Ville, 727 Rue Toulouse; ☎ *(504) 528-9206.*
Cuisine: French. Avg. $40–$60.
Lunch: 11 a.m.–2 p.m., daily.
Dinner: 6–10 p.m., daily.

A tiny jewel of a restaurant attached to a tiny jewel of a hotel makes for a many faceted menu. The Bistro looks just as intimate and warm as its name implies, but the food is anything but simple Bistro fare. The kitchen here turns out some splendid and original presentations—creations such as a velvety mushroom cheesecake for a new taste sensation. The chicken gumbo is dark, rich and thick with homemade Andouille. Comfort food to the max. A crackling crunch to the duck comes from a maple cure and its glaze is of mustard-laced calvados. The color of the duck matches the dark wood paneled walls. Dessert should be The Bistro's chocolate bread pudding, the sexiest in town. Credit Cards: All Major.

Sazerac $$$ ★★

Fairmont Hotel, 123 Baronne Street; ☎ *(504) 529-4733.*
Cuisine: Continental. Avg. $40–$60.
Lunch: 11 a.m.–2:30 p.m., daily.
Dinner: 6–11 p.m., daily.

A grand old dining room in the European tradition of lush decor and glittering chandeliers. Starched white tablecloths look absolutely florescent against the ruby velvet banquettes. This is a room that has history as well as a reputation.

The regulars start dinner with the most famous cocktail in New Orleans The Sazerac, made with cognac, absinthe and bitters. If you're able to go on after that, you'll be rewarded with a fine lobster bisque, or thick smoky gumbo with chunks of moist duck. The steak tartare is especially good with just the right balance of mustard and Tabasco®. The "Grand Dame" hotel dining room standards such as Steak Diane (who is she anyway) or rack of lamb for two are brought off with great aplomb. Desserts seem always to be ignited, like it or not, so lean back and bask in the glow. Credit Cards: All Major.

"With any entrée, you get unlimited access to the trough."
Drawing by S. Harris; ©1995 The New Yorker Magazine, Inc.

Agenda/Best Teas in the City

AGENDA TEA-FORMATION

Tea is served from 3 p.m. to 6 p.m. There are usually no reservations required. Some of the tea choices on my agenda serve a full English tea (sandwiches, scones, clotted cream, and pastries). I find that tea before theater or concerts replaces dinner and doesn't cost anywhere as much. It also leaves a window of opportunity for a snack aprés the show.

Le Salon   **$$$**   ★★★
Windsor Court Hotel, 300 Gravier Street; ☎ *(504) 523-6000. Avg. $36 for 2.*

An oasis of civilization in the midst of this very grand, Grand Hotel. The very place to sink back after a hard day in the French Quarter. Le Salon serves a full tea complete with those tiny "killer" sandwiches of smoked salmon and paté. Then scones with thick clotted cream and to top it off, superb little pastries.

Bottom of the Cup Tearoom $$ ★★

732 Royal Street; ☎ *(504) 524-1997.*
Avg. $10–$15.
This is a quirky, little place that's half curio shop, half tearoom. But that's not all. They read the tea leaves that are in (you got it) the bottom of your cup. They actually have hot and cold running psychics who will, at the flash of coin-of-the-realm, chart horoscopes, do palms, analyze handwriting and read Tarot cards. Tea without any of the above is discouraged but what you lose in petit-fours you gain in future developments.

La Madeleine $ ★★

547 St. Ann Street; ☎ *(504) 568-9950.*
Avg. $5–$10.
Even though this is a chain, it still produces wonderful French pastry for an afternoon sit-down. There are usually fresh croissants or several different kinds of quiches that pair off beautifully with a cup of tea.

P.J.'s Coffee & Tea Co. $ ★

5432 Magazine Street; ☎ *(504) 895-0273.*
Avg. $5–$10.
Eighteen different varieties of tea to smooth the savage shopper in you. After all those antique stores what you need is a strong "cuppa" and an outrageous piece of pastry.

La Marquise $ ★★

625 Chartres Street; ☎ *(504) 524-0420.*
Avg. $5–$10.
Some of the most luxurious pastries and creamiest quiche in town. The eclairs would make a strong "person" cry. There is a small patio in the back so no one will see you.

Croissant d'Or $ ★★★

615-17 Ursulines Street; ☎ *(504) 524-4663.*
Avg. $5–$10.
The locals spend part of their day in this charming little tea room reading and lazing and generally living in the slow lane while enjoying the self-indulgent pastries and tea (if you ask nicely). Croissant d'Or is truly like something out of a Capote short story. It's definitely the flip side of Anne Rice's New Orleans.

The Jazz Brunch Experience

New Orleans jazz brunches are a weekend tradition.

New Orleans in its typically unique way of life elevates the brunch scene from a purely social experience to a "rhythmic rite," and adds Le Jazz Hot to the orange juice cold. The following are some of the swingingest brunches in town.

Palace Cafe $$ ★★★

605 Canal Street; ☎ *(504) 523-1661 (Held on Weekend).*
Cuisine: Southern. Avg. $20–$40.
Brunch: 10:30 a.m.–2:30 p.m., Sun.

Ti Martin, who's the smile behind the Palace Cafe, has made it into the closest thing to a Paris brasserie that one would hope to find on this side of the Atlantic. She's the daughter of Ellen Brennan of the restaurant Brennan's and she's inherited the welcoming gene from her mother. The most dramatic element of the cafe is its wide wrought-iron staircase that winds heroically up to the second floor. But it's much more exciting purpose is as a backdrop for the jazz musicians who heat up the room even more than the chiles in the Creole sauce. The Palace is the youngest of the Brennan endeavors but you wouldn't know that from the crowds, the fun or the amazing things that arrive at your table. The kitchen is the only place The Blues have been banished by Chef Robert Bruce. The way to start is with a brandy milk punch and the only way to end is with the white chocolate bread pudding. In-between there are more hits than Gershwin ever dreamed up. Credit Cards: All Major.

Court of the Two Sisters　　　　**$$**　　　　　　　★ ★

613 Royal Street; (Held daily) ☎ *(504) 522-7261.*
Cuisine: Southern/Creole. Avg. $20–$40.
Brunch: 9 a.m.–3 p.m., daily.
The jazziest of brunches in a tropic setting if the weather is mild. Even inside the musicians make the sedate room rock to the rafters. This all comes with a buffet that spreads out over 50 Louisiana specialties that make beautiful music all by themselves.

House of Blues　　　　　　　**$$**　　　　　　★ ★ ★

225 Decatur Street; (Sunday) ☎ *(504) 529-BLUE.*
Cuisine: American. Avg. $20–$40.
Brunch: 10 a.m.–2:30 p.m., Sat.–Sun.
A state of the art jazz club opened originally by Dan Aykroyd. It has a stage big enough to attract the hottest headliners in the music business. There is also a restaurant that shouldn't be taken too seriously with the exception of the great jazz and gospel sounds that are heard on Sundays. A big "down home" buffet goes with it. Credit Cards: All Major.

Praline Connection Gospel
and Blues Hall　　　　　　**$$**　　　　　　★ ★ ★

907 S.Peters Street; (Sunday) ☎ *(504) 523-3973.*
Cuisine: Southern/Creole. Avg. $20–$40.
Brunch: 11 a.m.–1 p.m.; 2–4 p.m., Sunday.
This is the same praline connection that appears in the restaurant section but this branch is located in the Warehouse District. All you have to do is add a great Gospel Brunch to the great food and chances are you'll have a great time. Credit Cards: All Major.

Commander's Palace　　　　　**$$$**　　　　　　★ ★

1403 Washington Avenue; (Weekend) ☎ *(504) 899-8221.*
Brunch: 11 a.m.–12:30 p.m., Sat.; 10 a.m.–12:30 p.m., Sun.
Avg. $40–$60.
A very spirited jazz celebration is added to Brennan's hundreds of brunch concoctions including their endless catalogue of egg specialties. What could be bad? Credit Cards: All Major.

Menu Speak

New Orleans, even when speaking the "Mother Tongue" speaks it just a little differently than the rest of us. This is most apparent in their use of French and Cajun culinary specialties that appear on their menus. Below are some of the terms you'll see again and again as you eat your way around the city.

Andouille　　　　　　*Country sausage, usually spicy, used with red beans and in gumbos.*

Boudin	Ground pork sausage mixed with onions.
Boudin Rouge	Blood sausage.
Étouffée	Thick sauce made with tomatoes, shrimp or crawfish is usually added.
Gumbo	Thick country soup with vegetables or meat or sausage. Almost a meal.
Dirty Rice	Rice sauteed with giblets that eventually takes on a dark color.
Filé	Seasoning made of ground sassafras leaves.
Grits	Ground hominy grain that when boiled becomes creamy. Served with breakfast.
Beignet	Sweet, crisp doughnut, usually square, served with powdered sugar.
Café au Lait	Half coffee, half steamed milk poured in equal amounts.
Crawfish	Tiny lobsterlike shellfish. Cajuns call them mudbugs. They are not to be confused with an insect.
Grillades	Broiled pieces of beef or veal.
Dressed	You are requesting that your sandwich come with all the extras (lettuce, tomatoes, mayonnaise, etc.)
Jambalaya	Much like a paella with a rice base and then any combination of meat and shellfish, ham, peppers, etc.
Mirliton	Vegetable in the squash family.
Tasso	Cajun pepper ham.
Rémoulade	Bright red mayonnaiselike mixture flavored with cayenne and paprika.
Créme Bruleé	Rich cream custard with a thin crust of caramelized sugar.
Po'Boy	Huge sandwich on French bread usually stuffed with oysters, shrimp or meat.
Chicory	Root that is roasted and ground and then added to coffee for a unique flavor.
Muffuletta	Whole round Italian bread stuffed with meats, cheeses, spices, and a spicy olive salad. Then it is sliced into wedges.

Wine "Speak"

Grudgingly, restaurateurs are willing to admit that their fellow countrymen have come to understand some of the complexities of haute cuisine. But breathes a sommelier who believes an average diner knows the first thing about wine?

The first giant step toward "wine-lib" is to understand the enemy. The sommelier is your wine waiter. However, behind the scenes he's known as "Supergrape," the resident wine expert who stocks and maintains the wine cellar. The sommelier's role is steeped in tradition and that's where your trouble begins.

Wine is the only part of your meal to arrive *a table* in its store-bought clothes. It is the sommelier's prime responsibility to do nothing to the wine other than store and serve it perfectly. Rely on him to heighten the enjoyment of an outrageously-priced meal. Confess what you've ordered. Ask what he thinks you should drink.

The only unbreakable rule in town, if the wine he suggests is from the most expensive half of the list DO NOT TAKE HIS ADVICE. Unless he offers at least one enthusiastic suggestion from the least expensive half, he's surely trying to help pay off the new microwave in the kitchen. Worse still, should he confide that none of the cheaper wines are worthwhile, he's trying to back you into an expensive corner.

Assuming your sommelier has suggested a 1929 Latour as the perfect accompaniment for your jambalaya, and you can't quite agree, don't overreact.

Wine is the one area in which a little knowledge is not only dangerous but worse—it's boring. I've never understood why people who are civil enough when ordering a lamb chop become so pompous when confronted with a wine list. Buying a bottle to drink with your bird is not like laying down a cellar for your heirs. You don't have to be a neurosurgeon to buy an aspirin.

Here's all you really need to know: white wines are delicate and complement fish and white meats. Reds are heartier and stand up better to the more robust red meats and game. Never order a white over five years old. Never (except for a Beaujolais) order a red under five years old. Don't try to play the numbers game with vintages. Stay away from the cheapest and stay away from the most expensive. If your accent is sad enough to make your lapels wilt, order by number or ask for the house wine!

RESTAURANTS

AGENDA
ENTERTAINMENT

Legendary jazz artists got their start in The Big Easy.

Restaurants and music are the two most important agendas for entertainment in New Orleans. Of course, there are museums and theatre and opera going on all year round but what really makes "Les Bons Temps Rouler" is high calorie, spirited fun. Going out, for a New Orleanian has to feed the soul as well as the body and that means jazz! There are two themes that translate into an evening on the town here: Food, glorious food and jazz, glorious jazz.

New York is usually referred to as "the city that never sleeps" but New Orleans has to be a close second in its round-the-clock appreciation of a good time. Jazz clubs vibrate with the newest, hottest sound till dawn. And then it's usually off to a coffee house for a prebreakfast beignet and some conversation. These people are insatiable "entertainaholics." Not only is their addiction widespread, it's also highly contagious.

Meals in The Big Easy go on forever, so don't even plan to get to a club before 11 or so. Since no one ever seems to need any sleep in New Orleans, that's about the time everyone is just getting a second wind. Heavy drinking is also a part of New Orleans action, and in that respect it may be better to observe the natives with some long distance perspective. Yes, you may see almost everyone on Bourbon Street carrying a plastic "go-cup" brimming with one of the local lethal liquids, but keep in mind they've been doing it longer and they don't have the heavy duty sightseeing of a visitor, to accomplish in the morning.

Here are the things you'll have to think about to fine-tune your entertainment agenda. If you're as neurotic as I am about buttoning down most of your agenda before you leave home, you'll try to get a copy of the *Times Picayune*, the paper of record in New Orleans. Out of state newspapers are sold in most cities. Then you can make up your "wish list" in advance.

When you arrive in town pick up a copy of *Where*, or *Gambit* or *Offbeat*. These are weekly guides that have very good entertainment listings as well as reviews. The magazines can be bought at any newsstand. You can charge tickets for all cultural events from Ticketmaster. ☎ *(504) 522-5555.*

The Jazz Heritage Festival is always a sellout.

AGENDA "JIVE" ON JAZZ FEST

If you plan to attend the New Orleans Jazz Heritage Festival which takes place the last weekend in April and the first weekend in May, you should be reaching for the phone even as you read this. If you can't reserve your tickets before February of that year, you can plan on watching it on the six o'clock news from your hotel room. The tickets usually disappear faster than an ice cube in August.

AGENDA "JIVE" ON JAZZ FEST

With the exception of Mardi Gras, this is New Orleans' most popular and "exhaustively" attended event. More than 4000 musicians descend upon the city to perform jazz, gospel, folk, zydeco and rock'n roll for the acres of fans who gather at the New Orleans Fair Grounds. You never know who's going to be tapping their toes in the audience. There are just as many celebs who are jazz-o-holics as the rest of us. Aside from the music going on at the Fair Grounds there are special events going on all week long around the city. The place really rocks. Music is not enough to feed the savage jazz fanatic either so the very best chefs in the city have their own booths at the Fair Grounds to play the pots and pans. The ground rules are only regional specialties (no pastrami sandwiches).

Jazz Fest is a multifaceted jewel that New Orleans carefully polishes all year as a gift to her music heritage and the rest of the world as well. If you can manage to come and join the fun then contact the Jazz & Heritage Festival, P.O. Box 53407, New Orleans, LA 70153; ☎ (504) 522-4786. For advance tickets–Ticketmaster, ☎ (800) 488-5252.

Theatre

Even though most of the other performing arts tend to take a backseat to music in New Orleans, it is interesting to note that the first theatre, in what is now the city, was founded in 1792 by the Henry brothers of Paris. Ever since, theatre has continued to thrive, with some of its most respected productions being mounted by the theatre department of Tulane and Loyola Universities. Experimental theatre is coming to the fore around town with fine productions taking place at the Contemporary Arts Center in the Warehouse District. How could theatre not be exciting in the city that gave us Lillian Hellman and Truman Capote, and of course Tennessee Williams who left the poignant memory of Blanche Du Bois behind?

Contemporary Arts Center

900 Camp Street; ☎ (504) 523-1216.

Two theatres operating year round. They present new playwrights and experimental productions.

Le Petit Théâtre

616 St. Peter Street; ☎ (504) 522-2081.

(See French Quarter, page 161.)

La Maison des Beaux Arts

1140 St. Charles Avenue; ☎ (504) 524-4278.

Only open since 1992 they are fast becoming the theatre for New Orleans contemporary mainstream playwrights.

Saenger Theatre

143 N. Rampart Street; ☎ *(504) 525-1052.*
The Saenger is New Orleans' most "Broadway" of old houses. Restored recently, it truly is a showplace. They use it for the big touring musicals that come down from New York. If you're lucky maybe "Sunset Boulevard" will be playing.

Theatre Marigny

616 Frenchman Street; ☎ *(504) 944-2653.*
The avant-garde works it presents go very well with this "Vie de Boheme" neighborhood.

Southern Repertory Theatre

333 Canal Street; ☎ *(504) 861-8163.*
It focuses on mostly southern playwrights, especially in the summer when their new plays are showcased.

N.O.R.D. Theatre

☎ *(504) 483-2536.*
They are an umbrella group who are sponsored by New Orleans Recreation. They have information on what's on stage around town as well as their own productions.

Tulane University

☎ *(504) 865-5361.*
They don't always have a production going on but if you happen to be in town when they do, the level is consistently high and the choice of plays provocative.

Concert Halls, Opera and the Dance

Not everything in New Orleans is about all that jazz. The rest of the musical life in the city is as active and vigorous as its multicultural heritage.

Louisiana Philharmonic Symphony

☎ *(504) 523-6530.*
Their season runs from fall to spring. In the summer they give a series of pop concerts (☎ *(504) 525-7677).*

New Orleans Opera Association

☎ *(504) 529-2278.*
They perform several times a year and also play host to touring companies such as the Metropolitan Opera.

Xavier University

☎ *(504) 486-7411.*
Very professional random productions overseen by the Opera Department.

New Orleans Ballet Association

☎ *(504) 522-0996.*

Performances are held in season at the New Orleans Theatre of the Performing Arts.

Film

Art and foreign films as well as revivals are very popular with the locals. In fact Loyola University screens films during the regular school year. They draw people from all over the area so not only is it a film experience but also a wonderful opportunity to meet some fellow "buffs."

Film Buffs Institute

Loyola University; ☎ *(504) 865-2152.*

They publish a schedule of the films for the year. If you call in advance they'll mail it to you.

Prytania

5339 Pyrtania Street; ☎ *(504) 895-4513.*

Art films and revivals.

Movie Pitchers

3941 Bienville Avenue; ☎ *(504) 488-8881.*

Foreign films as well as avant-garde. The New Orleans Video and Film Society holds its yearly festival here in the Fall *(☎ (504) 523-3818).*

Museums

New Orleans is fiercely proud of its history, its traditions, both good and bad and its customs which are carefully preserved. Nowhere is it more obvious than the many museums that deal with its rich past. New Orleans has one of the most fascinating groups of museums anywhere. Aside from the city's Art Museum (NOMA) the rest of them have invaluable insights into New Orleans' exotic history.

New Orleans Museum of Art

1 Collins Diboll Circle (Lelong Avenue); ☎ *(504) 488-2631.*
(See top sights, page 26.)

Confederate Museum

929 Camp Street; ☎ *(504) 523-4522, 10 a.m.–4 p.m., Mon.–Sat. Admission $4 adults, $2 children.*

Memorabilia of the Civil War. It's considered the oldest museum in the state and dates to 1891. There are flags and weapons and for some reason Jefferson Davis' evening clothes (Maybe one too many parties gave the North a certain edge.)

The Louisiana State Museum is one of the finest historical museums in the United States.

New Orleans Historic Voodoo Museum

724 Dumaine Street; ☎ *(504) 523-7685.10 a.m.–6 p.m., daily. Admission $5 adults, $4 children.*

Wonderfully spooky and more informative than its name might suggest. It makes understanding the Catholic-influenced African rites more than a refresher course on Zombies (not the kind you drink, either). It puts into perspective a serious religion that is still practiced today. Even Martha Stewart would applaud their brilliant variation on the "pin cushion." Admission.

New Orleans Pharmacy Museum

514 Chartres Street; ☎ *(504) 565-8027, 10 a.m.–5 p.m., Tues.–Sun. Admission $2.*

This absolutely authentic pharmacy was opened in 1823 by the first licensed pharmacist in the U.S. In those days it was called an apothecary. It's been restored handsomely and is really a delightful stop. Admission.

Jackson Barracks Military Museum

6400 St. Claude Avenue; ☎ *(504) 278-8242, 7:30 a.m.–4 p.m., Mon.–Fri, by appointment. Admission by donation.*

The Barracks were built to house troops in the 1820s. Today it houses the National Guard as well as exhibits of military memorabilia from the state's history up through Operation Desert Storm. It's perfect for an armchair General. Free.

Louisiana Toy Train Museum

519 Williams Boulevard; ☎ *(504) 468-7223, 9 a.m.–5 p.m., Tues.–Sat. Admission $3 adults, $2 children.*

Chugging through the seven miniature train displays complete with a toy carousel is a real trip. Children are allowed to touch the exhibits, as well as view slide shows. Grown-ups love the "choo choos" just as much. Admission.

Irish Louisiana Museum

508 Toulouse Street; ☎ *(504) 529-1317, Noon–11 p.m., daily. Admission free.*

Artifacts depicting the long hard struggle of the Irish community in New Orleans, which began in the early 1800s. Perhaps it is fitting that it should be housed in O'Flaherty's Irish Channel, a pub in the French Quarter. Admission.

Louisiana Wildlife and Fisheries Museum

Rivertown, 303 Williams Boulevard; ☎ *(504) 468-7232. 9 a.m.–5 p.m., Tues.–Sat. Admission $3 adults, $2 children.*

This museum is located in a complex called Rivertown U.S.A. consisting of six different small museums, the most important of which is the Fisheries Museum. It's run by the Louisiana Nature and Science Center to display all of the state's species. Admission.

Blaine Kern's Mardi Gras World

233 Newton Street, Algiers; ☎ *(504) 361-7821, 9:30 a.m.–4:30 p.m., daily. (Closed 14 days before Mardi Gras) Admission $5.50 adults, $3.25 children.*

To get to this uproarious place you have first to take a scenic ferry ride out to a bus that drops you off at Mardi Gras World. Of course it's commercial and a blatant advertorial for Mardi Gras! It's also a lot of fun to see the floats actually being made. Sculptors, painters, carpenters, all engrossed in the creation of absolute magic. Don't pass it up because it sounds impossibly hokey. It is but don't miss it. Admission.

Musée Conti Wax Museum

917 Conti Street; ☎ *(504) 525-2605, 10 a.m.–5 p.m., daily. Admission $5.75 adults, $3.75 children.*

Definite waxy build-up here with all of the famous figures in New Orleans' past. If you feel a historical meltdown is imminent, the outrageous costumes of the famous Mardi Gras Indians will raise your spirits. Admission.

Historic New Orleans Collection

533 Royal Street; ☎ *(504) 523-4662,10 a.m.–4:45 p.m., Tues.–Sat. Admission free.*

The Williams' residence is a 19th century townhouse in a complex of historic buildings in the French Quarter including Merieult House dating from 1792. The contents of the houses and the galleries make up the collection. Free

Louisiana Children's Museum

420 Julia Street; ☎ *(504) 523-1357, 9:30 a.m.–4:30 p.m., Mon.–Sat. Admission $5.*

Lots of bells and whistles for the small set to explore, even a super, supermarket for playing "cashier for a day." (Maybe you won't need that College Fund, after all.) This is one of the most creative children's museums in the county. Don't miss it, even if you're full grown. Admission.

Ursuline Museum

2635 State Street; ☎ *(504) 866-1472, noon–4:30 p.m., Sun. By appointment. Admission free.*

Even though this very special collection is by appointment only, if you have the time it is more than worth it. Priceless historic documents and religious artifacts have been preserved there. The most compelling are letters written by Thomas Jefferson.

Galleries

Royal Street offers several notable art galleries.

Gallery hours and days change frequently—call in advance for schedules.

American Indian Art

824 Chartres Street; ☎ *(504) 586-0479.*
Antique and modern Native American art.

Ariodante

535 Julia Street; ☎ *(504) 524-3233.*
Snazzy jewelry, accessories and crafts that go just fine with the area.

Wyndy Morehead Fine Arts

603 Julia Street; ☎ *(504) 568-9754.*
Paintings, sculpture, prints.

Hall-Barnett Gallery

320 Exchange Alley; ☎ *(504) 525-5656.*
Regional artists.

628 Gallery

628 Baronne Street; ☎ *(504) 529-3306.*
See Warehouse District, page 94.

Marguerite Oestreicher

626 Julia Street; ☎ *(504) 581-9253.*
Contemporary painting and prints.

Loyola Downtown

440 Julia Street; ☎ *(504) 523-3285.*
New and emerging artists.

New Orleans School of Glassworks

727 Magazine Street; ☎ *(504) 529-7277.*
See Warehouse District, page 94.

Le Mieux Galleries

332 Julia Street; ☎ *(504) 522-5988.*
Louisiana and Third Coast artists.

Estudio

630 Barrone Street; ☎ *(504) 524-7982.*
Contemporary artists.

Kurt E. Schon Ltd.

510 St. Louis Street; ☎ *(504) 524-5462.*
18th and 19th century French and British art.

Gasperi

854 S. Peters Street; ☎ *(504) 524-9373.*
Folk artists.

Davis Gallery

3964 Magazine Street; ☎ *(504) 897-0780.*
African art, contemporary and antique.

Rodrique Gallery

721 Royal Street; ☎ *(504) 581-4244.*
See French Quarter, page 73.

Lillian Shon Gallery

533 St. Louis Street; ☎ *(504) 525-5564.*
Fine art housed in an old bank. You'll be called upon to make a major
deposit if you intend to take one of the excellent canvases with you.
This is a top gallery in New Orleans.

La Belle Gallerie

309 Chartres Street; ☎ *(504) 529-3080.*
An entire huge gallery devoted to the art of the African-American culture. Everything from African primitive to racy posters of the great
Josephine Baker. They feature the work of African-American regional
artists as well. It is quite moving to have all this richness of culture
under one roof.

Simone Stern

> *518 Julia Street;* ☎ *(504) 529-1118.*
> Contemporary artists are displayed at this venerable New Orleans Gallery. It moved to the Arts District to specialize in abstract including sculpture.

Diane Genre Oriental Art

> *233 Royal Street;* ☎ *(504) 525-7270.*
> See French Quarter, page 73.

The New Orleans Club Scene

Le Jazz Hot is hotter in New Orleans than anywhere else in the world. Jazz is the mother tongue of the city and it's spoken in the endless dialects that accompany this multicultural paradise. Even more importantly, the birth of the blues took place right here over a hundred years ago. Today traditional jazz has been joined by a host of new musical developments that took the original form and embellished it to fit New Orleans' diverse society. The greats, the legendary Louis Armstrong, King Oliver and Jelly Roll Morton put traditional jazz on the international map. To this day it is still the most exciting of all jazz forms. Rhythm and blues came as late as the '50s when Fats Domino and Dave Bartholomew were developing this new sound for the rest of the country. Then, gospel music, when jazz and the blues met religion head-on to add a passionate celebration of God. Aretha Franklin and Whitney Houston both started their careers in their church choirs, praising the Lord. In the '60s rock and roll was introduced in New Orleans clubs when Elvis could no longer be ignored by the "purists." Some of the most spirited music to be heard around town is Cajun and its counterpart Zydeco. Both have evolved from the Acadian folk traditions brought down from Canada to the Louisiana Bayous. Zydeco is the blending of Cajun and Creole. Most of the original instruments were homemade, some still are.

The music scene in New Orleans is spread through the town. All you have to do is make a club agenda that includes a sampling of the musical menu of the city. After all, in the "Big Easy" "the beat goes on, and on" and on!

(Since the clubs that follow are all over town, be sure to take a cab to and from. The neighborhoods change very quickly within the city. *Prices and cover charges as well as hours change frequently; call to make sure of both.*)

Jazz & Blues

Preservation Hall, 726 St. Peter Street.
(See Top Sights, page 28.)

House of Blues

225 Decatur Street; ☎ *(504) 529-BLUE.*
Owned by Dan Aykroyd this is a great big complex including a restaurant. Headliners from all over do gigs here. Seven million dollars were spent to see that the stage was acoustically A-OK for the likes of Natalie Cole, Eric Clapton and Bob Dylan. Very high-tech blues heaven. Be prepared to stand in line.

Maple Leaf Bar

8316 Oak Street; ☎ *(504) 866-9358.*
A tin ceiling sets the scene for real downhome music. Maple Leaf runs the gamut from R&B to Cajun played by a local band.

Pete Fountain's

2 Poydras Street; ☎ *(504) 523-4374.*
Pete Fountain is the code name for Dixieland in New Orleans. His continually packed room at the Hilton is one of the best places to watch the saints go marchin' in. Pete himself is all over the world doing club dates but his musicmakers mind the store in the liveliest of ways.

Jimmy Buffet's Margaritaville

1104 Decatur Street; ☎ *(504) 592-2565.*
All kinds of music to accompany a whole wardrobe of margaritas and some pretty decent cheeseburgers. Sometimes Jimmy sits in on a few sets himself.

Howlin' Wolf

1104 Decatur Street/828 S. Peters Street; ☎ *(504) 523-2551.*
A Warehouse district favorite with nightly shows featuring alternative and progressive Jazz.

Funky Butt

714 N. Rampart Street; ☎ *(504) 558-0872.*
No I'm not even going to try to explain the name. It's enough to know they have new, hot, jazz done by local "biggies."

Donna's

800 N. Rampart Street; ☎ *(504) 596-6914.*
Donna's is called the home of the brass band. This is not a place to go for conversation but it certainly is the brassiest place in town.

Check Point Charlie's

501 Esplanade Avenue; ☎ *(504) 947-0979.*
A combination laundromat, pool room and library with live alternative and progressive music. Wall to wall entertainment if you supply the fabric softener. Ring around the collar has never been so much fun.

Funky Pirate

727 Bourbon Street; ☎ *(504) 523-1960.*
If that's the way you like your pirates then you're in luck. Blues are played nightly by their resident "Blues Boy," Al Carson.

Fritzel's Jazz Pub

733 Bourbon Street; ☎ *(504) 561-0432.*

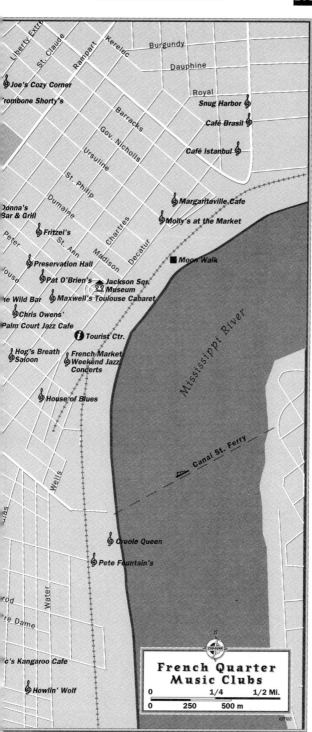

Joe's Cozy Corner
Trombone Shorty's

Snug Harbor
Café Brasil
Café Istanbul

Margaritaville Cafe
Molly's at the Market

Donna's Bar & Grill
Fritzel's

Moon Walk

Preservation Hall
Pat O'Brien's
Jackson Sqr. Museum
The Wild Bar
Maxwell's Toulouse Cabaret
Chris Owens'
Palm Court Jazz Cafe

Tourist Ctr.

Hog's Breath Saloon
French Market Weekend Jazz Concerts

House of Blues

Canal St. Ferry

Mississippi River

Creole Queen
Pete Fountain's

's Kangaroo Cafe

Howlin' Wolf

French Quarter Music Clubs

0   1/4   1/2 Mi.

0   250   500 m

©FWI

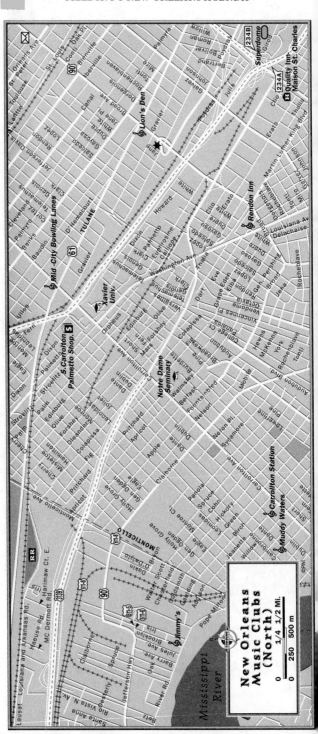

New Orleans Music Clubs (North)

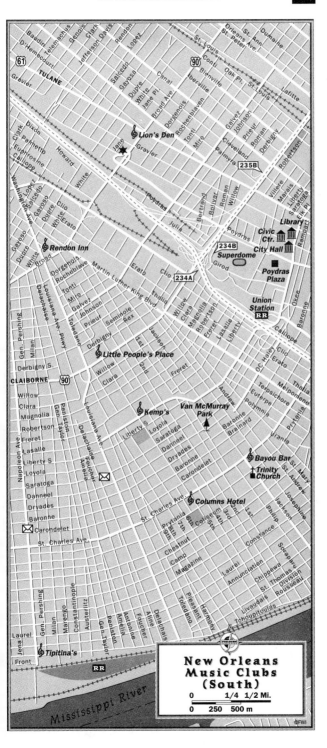

**New Orleans
Music Clubs
(South)**

0   1/4   1/2 Mi.

0   250   500 m

As its name implies, it's more beer garden than jazz club but in fact, they get all the progressive jazz musicians straight from Germany.

Chris Owens Club

500 Bourbon Street; ☎ *(504) 523-6400.*

She's a true institution in the city, their own combination Ethel Merman, Mae West showgirl of the 40s who has just gone on and on. She can still belt out country-western with the best of them. There's jazz as well which will give your eyes a rest from too much "sequin exposure."

Tipitina's

501 Napoleon Avenue; ☎ *(504) 895-8477.*

A mixed bag here of everything: blues, zydeco, cajun, rock 'n roll, jazz. This place is one stop shopping.

Mint

504 Esplanade Avenue; ☎ *(504) 525-2000.*

A club that covers more territory than just jazz. They have comedy as well as some "drag" acts. It's very in, in New Orleans.

Jelly Roll's/Al's Place

501 Bourbon Street; ☎ *(504) 568-0501.*

The great Al Hurt is back in his home town and you can hear him several times a week here. It's absolutely essential to call in advance since he's very "loose" about his schedules, but with a little luck you'll get to hear the best trumpet since Satchmo.

Dragon's Den

435 Esplanade Avenue; ☎ *(504) 949-1750.*

A true avant-garde adventure. Pillows on the floor, poets on the pillows, Thai food for a Zen touch and very cutting-edge jazz. Could definitely be mind-altering.

Snug Harbor

626 Frenchmen Street; ☎ *(504) 949-0696.*

The home of the Marsalis clan because Ellis Marsalis, father of Wynton and Bradford is the legendary pianist here. When the kids visit you can imagine the excitement around town. Snug Harbor is one of New Orleans' most important jazz clubs not only because of Ellis but because he attracts some of the most powerful performers in jazz today.

Mulate's

201 Julia Street; ☎ *(504) 522-1492.*

Wall to wall Cajun in a vast hall seating more than 400 fans of this wonderful sound. There is also a dance floor for a chance to Fais-do-do (Cajun for a dance party) with the locals.

Mid-City Bowling Lanes

4133 S. Carrollton Street; ☎ *(504) 482-3133.*

Bowl and rock'n roll. It's one of those mixed media palaces the Big Easy is so fond of. There's a local band, dancing and free lessons in the art of wonderful Cajun Fais-do-do. Life in the fast lanes.

Muddy Waters

8301 Oak Street; ☎ *(504) 866-7174.*

A college hangout that's popular enough for the uptown crowd. Local and national bands.

Famous Door

339 Bourbon Street; ☎ *(504) 522-7626.*
Around since 1934. Live entertainment till early in the a.m. and
between sets music videos. Very much a "tourist" spot, still it can be
fun.

Cafe Brasil

2100 Chartres Street; ☎ *(504) 947-9386.*
Packed all the time with jazz fans who come to hear salsa, Cajun,
country, even Klezmer bands. There is dancing, if you can find the
room.

Vic's Kangaroo Cafe

636 Tchoupitoulas Street; ☎ *(504) 524-4329.*
Do kangaroos like jazz? Obviously the Australians know more than
they're telling about the "springy" ones. Blues start here every
evening after 10 p.m. The food is fine too.

Old Absinthe House Bar

400 Bourbon Street; ☎ *(504) 525-8108.*
Not to be confused with the restaurant at 240 Bourbon. Rhythm and
blues and progressive jazz rock the rafters night after night, sometimes till dawn.

The Best Bars in New Orleans

The bar scene in the Big Easy is somewhat subdued since the
jazz clubs are the primary focus for relaxation. But there are
some places that serve a daiquiri or a hurricane or even a glass of
wine. But the king of cocktails for any New Orleanian is the sazerac which will always commemorate the romantic 18th century
history of the city. Hours are usually from 4 in the afternoon till
the wee-hours. Since everyone is so relaxed in New Orleans,
scheduling is casual to say the least.

Sazerac Bar/The Fairmont Hotel

123 Baronne Street; ☎ *(504) 529-7111.*
The only place in town to have the original, authentic, 24-carat sazerac is in the bar of the same name. The bar is credited with not only
inventing the sazarec (cognac, absinthe and a dash of bitters) but even
more importantly with inventing at the same time the world's first
cocktail. However they never got around to inventing the cocktail
frank, thank God!

Napoleon House

500 Chartres Street; ☎ *(504) 524-9752.*
Both the literary and artistic intelligencia gather around the bar at
Napoleon House to discuss the human condition and watch the pass-

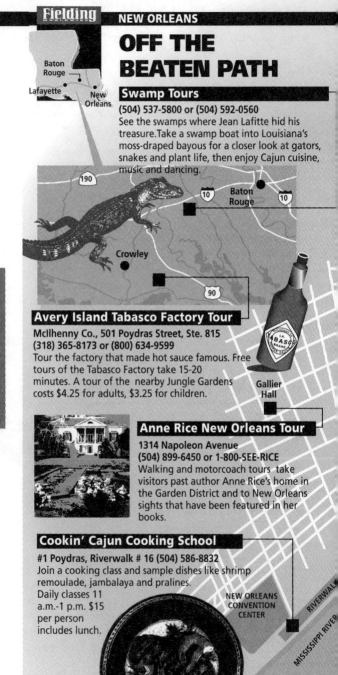

Fielding NEW ORLEANS

OFF THE BEATEN PATH

Baton Rouge
Lafayette
New Orleans

Swamp Tours

(504) 537-5800 or (504) 592-0560
See the swamps where Jean Lafitte hid his treasure. Take a swamp boat into Louisiana's moss-draped bayous for a closer look at gators, snakes and plant life, then enjoy Cajun cuisine, music and dancing.

190

10 Baton Rouge 10

Crowley

90

Avery Island Tabasco Factory Tour

McIlhenny Co., 501 Poydras Street, Ste. 815
(318) 365-8173 or (800) 634-9599
Tour the factory that made hot sauce famous. Free tours of the Tabasco Factory take 15-20 minutes. A tour of the nearby Jungle Gardens costs $4.25 for adults, $3.25 for children.

Gallier Hall

Anne Rice New Orleans Tour

1314 Napoleon Avenue
(504) 899-6450 or 1-800-SEE-RICE
Walking and motorcoach tours take visitors past author Anne Rice's home in the Garden District and to New Orleans sights that have been featured in her books.

Cookin' Cajun Cooking School

#1 Poydras, Riverwalk # 16 (504) 586-8832
Join a cooking class and sample dishes like shrimp remoulade, jambalaya and pralines.
Daily classes 11 a.m.-1 p.m. $15 per person includes lunch.

NEW ORLEANS CONVENTION CENTER

RIVERWALK

MISSISSIPPI RIVER

Cemeteries

St. Louis # 1, outside the French Quarter, **St. Louis #2,** Claiborne Avenue, **St. Louis # 3,** Esplanade (504) 588-9357
New Orleans' above-ground cemeteries, St. Louis #1 and #2 are often called "Cities of the Dead." Voodoo queen Marie Laveau is buried in St. Louis #2. The famous cemetery scene in *Easy Rider* was filmed at St. Louis # 1. Although fascinating, the cemeteries can be dangerous. Go in a group but not alone.

St. Louis Cemetery Number Two

Bourbon French Parfums

**525 St. Ann Street,
(504) 522-4480**
Choose your favorite scents and create your own perfume. Located near Jackson Square, this perfumery has been hand blending fragrances for over 150 years using imported oils and natural ingredients.

St. Louis Cemetery Number One

N. RAMPART

DAUPHINE

VIEUX CARRE
(French Quarter)

BOURBON ST.

ROYAL

CANAL
BERVILLE
BIENVILLE
CONTI
ST. LOUIS
TOULOUSE
ST. PETER
ORLEANS
ST. ANN
DUMAINE

CHARTRES
DECATUR

FRENCH
MARKET

Voodoo Museum

**724 Dumaine
(504) 522-5223**
Learn the history of voodoo and view artifacts from the voodoo culture. A fascinating blend of past and present voodoo rites and rituals.

Haunted New Orleans

635 Toulouse Street (504) 522-0045
Join a trained paranormal guide for a two hour tour of the French Quarter's haunted buildings. "Hauntings" have been featured on TV shows including "Unsolved Mysteries" and in such publications as *TV Guide* and *The Wall Street Journal.* Each expedition is unique and tours depart daily at 2 p.m. and 8 p.m.

Mardi Gras World

233 Newton Street (504) 361-7821
Get a close look at the colorful floats, costumes and masks that make Mardi Gras come alive each year. This massive warehouse is filled with parade and costume ball memorabilia. Take the ferry at Canal Street to the free shuttle.

ing French Quarter parade. The drink du jour is always a frosty Pimms Cup complete with cucumber swizzle stick.

Victorian Lounge/Columns Hotel

3811 St. Charles Avenue; ☎ *(504) 899-9308.*
The perfect place for an "interview" with a vampire.

Pat O'Brien's is home of the "Hurricane."

Pat O'Brien's

718 St. Peter Street; ☎ *(504) 525-4823.*
The home of the hurricane. This is not a weather report but a drink that has almost the same effect. It is served in a glass the size of the Empire State Building, made with lots of rum and a splash of fruit juice. O'Brien's makes them extra lethal so watch out.

Lafitte's Blacksmith Shop

941 Bourbon Street; ☎ *(504) 523-0066.*
See French Quarter, page 65.

Top of the Mart

2 Canal Street; ☎ *(504) 522-9795.*
See Top Sights, World Trade Center, page 24.

Daiquiri Shoppe

409 Decatur Street; ☎ *(504) 341-3722.*
This chain that has 12 other shoppes all around Louisiana serves more than 60 different types of daiquiris. Some are made with alcohol, some are not. All are delicious fun.

Crescent City Brewhouse

527 Decatur Street; ☎ *(504) 522-0571.*
They make four different brews in this pleasant airy new pub in the Quarter. Their Red Stallion and Black Forest on tap are very popular with the locals.

SPORTS

The Superdome has hosted eight Super Bowls.

Sports are almost as big a deal in New Orleans as Mardi Gras, particularly when the Super Bowl rolls around. The same qualities that make The Big Easy a perfect convention, leisure and festival town make it a great sports town, too. A balmy climate, an accessible downtown area and all major attractions within easy walking or riding distance, and a host of hotels and venues come together to attract sports fans in droves.

In recent years the city has hosted eight Super Bowls, three NCAA Men's Final Four championships, the 1992 Olympic Track and Field trials, the SEC Basketball Tournament and the AAU Junior Olympics. Apparently the city that loves a parade, also loves athletic competition. The Louisiana State Legislature in 1993 allocated a $215 million shot of adrenaline for sports development and improvement that included $84 million for a new sports arena behind the Superdome to accommodate professional hockey, basketball, boxing and concerts. The Superdome itself has undergone $20.5 million in renovations and $6 million has gone into a new training facility for the New Orleans Saints. Another $20 million has gone into a 15,000 seat stadium to be the home of the Zephyrs minor league baseball team. Last but not least, $7 million has gone to an Olympic Volleyball Training Center at Bayou Segnette State Park.

Participant Sports

Bicycling

Crescent City Cyclists
> *Information via their hotline* ☎ *(504) 486-3683.*

Boating

Tim Murray Boats for Hire
> *Lake Ponchartrain, 402 Roadway;* ☎ *(504) 283-2507.*

Canoeing

Canoeing at City Park
> *Dreyfous Drive;* ☎ *(504) 483-9871.*

Canoeing at Jean Lafitte National Park
> *Lafitte, Louisiana;* ☎ *(504) 689-2002.*

Fishing at City Park
> *Dreyfous Drive;* ☎ *(504) 483-9371.*

Fishing

Captain Nick's Fishing Charters
> ☎ *(504) 361-3004.*

Golf

Audubon Park
> *473 Walnut Street;* ☎ *(504) 865-8260.*

City Park
> *1040 Filmore Street;* ☎ *(504) 483-9396.*

Joe Bartholomew Golf Course
> *6514 Congress Drive;* ☎ *(504) 288-0928.*

Royal Golf Club
> *201 Royal Drive, Slidell, LA;* ☎ *(504) 643-3000.*

Tennis

Audubon Park
> ☎ *(504) 895-1042.*

City Park
> *Dreyfous Drive;* ☎ *(504) 483-9383.*

In-Line Skating

Park Skate
> *6108 Magazine Street;* ☎ *(504) 891-7055.*

Jogging

Audubon Park
> *City Park, River Levee Walk at Riverbend.*

Horseback Riding

Cascade Stables
> *6500 Magazine Street;* ☎ *(504) 891-2246.*

Spectator Sports

Baseball

New Orleans Zephyrs
☎ *(504) 282-6777.*

Ticketmaster
☎ *(504) 522-5555.*

Basketball

Superdome
☎ *(504) 522-2600.*

Football

New Orleans Saints
Superdome; ☎ *(504) 522-2600.*

Horse Racing

Season Runs from Nov. to April; ☎ *(504) 944-5515.*

SPORTS

EXCURSIONS

A steamboat cruise on the Natchez *is perfect for getting into the "Nawlins" frame of mind.*

Historic and exciting though New Orleans may be, the fact is that it is also near some of the most exotic and diversely fascinating attractions in the United States. That makes it a bit easier to try to persuade you to use some of your admittedly precious travel time to leave it for a day or so. Traveling just a short distance from the city can put you in touch with the Old South, the primitive bayous and best of all the Cajun experience which is a world unto itself. I'm suggesting several trips I feel would enrich your visit to New Orleans without going too far afield. Check at the hotel desk for car rental agencies or call:

National

☎ *(504) 466-4335/(800) 227-7368.*

Budget

☎ *(504) 467-2277/(800) 527-0700.*

Alamo

☎ *(504) 465-3792/(800) 327-9633.*

Avis

☎ *(504) 464-9511/(800) 331-1212.*

Hertz
>   ☎ *(504) 468-3695/800-654-3131.*

For appropriate routes to take, and proper directions to all the following excursions, check with the local **AAA office**, ☎ *(504) 838-7500*, or the **Visitor's Information Center**, ☎ *(504) 566-5011/ (800) 672-6124.*

Great River Road

There are more plantations on Great River Road than Scarlett O'Hara herself could have ever dreamed of owning. However, before visions of hoopskirts and magnolia blossoms dance in your head, not all of Great River Road is an antebellum wonderland. In between the stately plantations are stretches of industrial grunge and rundown factory towns that bear absolutely no resemblance to the Old South as M.G.M. knew it. That is not to say that there are not some magnificent images that still remain. Today, they are best represented by the great historic plantations that have survived to bear witness to a way of life both gracious and grotesque by present day standards of civilization. No matter how spectacular the plantation, the slave quarters in the back stand as a grim reminder of a not quite so romantic "Tara."

It is possible to see one or two plantations in a half day tour from New Orleans but doing an "overnight" enables you to really visit them at your own pace as well as get a feeling for the country life that existed outside the European sophistication, and celebrated society of the city. Each great house has its own distinct personality and reflects the owner's way of life as well as his excesses. Most are done in the Greek Revival style while others are of the much more exuberant "Steamboat Gothics" done in bright color with all kinds of kitsch. Aaron Spelling could have taken a lesson or two from the extravagant dynasties which created them. (All of the plantations discussed charge an admission and are open daily, however it's best to call, just to be sure).

Destrehan Manor
>   *LA48 (P.O. Box 5) Destrehan, LA 70047;* ☎ *(504) 764-9315, 9:30 a.m.–4 p.m., daily. Admission $7 adults, $2 children.*
> Only 22 miles from New Orleans, Destrehan was built in 1787. It is the oldest plantation remaining in the Mississippi valley. A free black planter built the house in West Indian style. It has eight heroic columns across the front and a less formal rambling appearance than the plantations that would come later. The live oaks on the property are some of the longest living in the state.

San Francisco
>   *LA44 (P.O. Drawer Ax), Reserve, LA 70084;* ☎ *(504) 535-2341, 10 a.m.–4 p.m., daily. Admission $7 adults, $2.75 children.*
> You might think its name came from the Golden Gate city we all know and love, but in truth it was born out of the owner's complaint after its completion that he was *sans fruscin* which means "without a

cent." Who among us has not uttered these very same words after the contractor has left the scene of the crime? Through the years everyone has referred to it as San Francisco. The house is overwhelmingly ornate, built in the style of Steamboat Gothic with a lowered roof and intricate carved detail. The ceilings are lushly painted with frescoes. In a burst of wit, a ship's crow's nest was added to the top of the upstairs ballroom.

*Spectacular plantations are all along **Great River Road**.*

Oak Alley

3645 LA18, Vacherie, LA 70090; ☎ *(504) 265-2151, 9 a.m.–5:15 p.m., daily. Admission $7 adults, $3 children.*

This is the "big" one, the most famous plantation of them all, in Louisiana. The avenue of 28 live oaks, some over 300 years old that lead up to the magnificent house is of course how it got its name. You've seen it time and again in films about the South since it is the quintessential vision of the approach to a plantation. Most recently it was

Fielding
NEW ORLEANS
GREAT RIVER ROAD

Touring the stately examples of 18th and 19th century architecture scattered along the Mississippi is a trip back in time filled with fascinating history.

Mississippi River

Houmas House
40136 Highway 942, Darrow, LA
(504) 522-2262
This Greek Revival mansion built in 184❚ is furnished with period antiques. The movie *Hush, Hush Sweet Charlotte* was filmed here.

Houmas House

Nottoway

Nottoway
30765 Mississippi River Road (504) 545-2409
Completed in 1859, Nottoway is the largest plantation home in the South and is known as the White Castle of Louisiana.

Tezcuco

Laura

Oak Alley

Tezcuco
3138 Highway 44, Burnside, LA
(504) 562-3929
This gracious Greek Revival style raised cottage, built in 1855 is adorned with wrought iron trimmed galleries and ornate friezes and medallions.

San Francisco

**Highway 44, Garyville, LA
(504) 535-2341**
San Francisco, built in 1856, is
a galleried home in the old
Creole style, featuring
decorative ceilings, wood
graining and marbling.

Destrehan

**13034 River Road, Box 5,
Destrehan, LA (504) 764-9315**
Built in 1787 and eight miles from New
Orleans airport, this is the oldest
plantation left in the lower Mississippi
Valley. Scenes for *Interview With the
Vampire* were shot here.

*Lake
Maurepas*

*Lake
Ponchartrain*

San
Francisco

New
Orleans

■ Destrehan

*Lake des
Allemands*

Laura

**2247 LA Highway 18, Vacherie, LA
(504) 265-7690**
Laura consists of 12 original buildings
and slave quarters dating from 1805. It
is famous as the American home of
Br'er Rabbit.

Oak Alley

**645 LA Highway 18, Vacherie,
LA (800) 44-A-LLEY**
Built in 1837-39, Oak Valley is
an example of Greek Revival
architecture and is famous for
its 1/4 mile of 300-year-old oak
trees.

EXCURSIONS

used as Lestat's home in *Interview with a Vampire*. (Unfortunately not a sign of Tom Cruise or Brad Pitt remains). The house itself was built in 1839 and has 28 Doric columns that surround the veranda to echo the number of trees in the "alley." The sweeping porch with its tall glass windows and French doors is breathtaking. You can actually spend the night here amid all this splendor in several small cottages on the property.

Tezcuco

3138 LA44, Darrow, LA 70725; ☎ (504) 562-3929, 9 a.m.–4:30 p.m., daily. Admission $6 adults, $3.25 children.

Less formal but no less impressive, this 1850s beauty is done in the manner of the Louisiana Cottage, made of cypress wood and brick. The name Tezcuco is the Aztec word for rest (the mystery is how many Aztecs settled in Louisiana). It was one of the last plantations to be raised before the Civil War and was built almost exclusively by slaves. The wrought-iron galleries are particularly graceful. It's possible to spend the night in one of the cottages or in the main house itself.

Houmas House

40136 LA. 942, Burnside, Darrow, LA 70725; ☎ (504) 473-7841, 10 a.m.–5 p.m., daily. Admission $8 adults, $3 children.

This plantation is just about perfect in representing everyone's fantasy of the sweeping, impressive estates that are synonymous with the Romance of Dixie. You can almost hear the rustle of ballgowns on the veranda. The house is over two towering stories high, done in the Greek revival style, with 14 columns on both sides of its magnificent wings. Built in 1840, it originally included over 10,000 acres of live oaks and magnolia trees. It's most imposing detail is the spiral staircase that twists to the top of the house. The formal gardens alone are worth a visit.

Madewood

4250 LA, 308, Napoleonville, LA 70390; ☎ (504) 369-7151, 10 a.m.– 4:30 p.m., daily. Admission $5 adults, $2 children.

The story of this celebrated plantation house is fodder for a miniseries or a Harold Robbins novel. Act 1—Two brothers have a fight giving a whole new meaning to sibling rivalry. Act II—It's brother against brother, each trying to outdo the other in owning the most impressive dwelling. Act III—Madewood was clearly the winner in the *House Beautiful* contest but the brother who built it died of yellow fever before he saw it finished. Easily a "three handkerchief" epic.

The ceilings are more than 25 feet high in the Greek Revival showplace with a sweeping staircase leading to the bedrooms. If you close your eyes in the extravagant ballroom you can almost hear the music as the elegant couples swirl around the floor. Is that Ashley Wilkes over there in the corner? Best of all, you can stay in the main house yourself which is an experience not to be missed. Dinner is served by candlelight in the plantation dining room. How could anyone resist being Scarlett and Rhett for an evening? In the morning you'll be gone with the wind.

Nottoway

River Road, PO Box 160, White Castle, LA 70788; ☎ *(504) 545-2730,*
9 a.m.–5 p.m., daily. Admission $8 adults, $3 children.

The king of plantations in Louisiana. None of the others has the look
of a castle, which is what Nottoway has been likened to. Erected in
1859 to be the best of Greek Revival and Italianate architectures that
blend into a sumptuous mansion of 53,000 feet and 64 rooms. It was
saved from imminent destruction during the Civil War by a Union
officer who had visited there in better times. It was most recently
restored just a few years ago, so you simply can't leave without a look
at the ballroom. It's dazzling enough to be part of Versailles.

Lunch or Dinner

Cabin, The $$

Rtes. LA44 at LA.22; ☎ *(504) 473-3007.*
Cuisine: Sandwiches. Avg. $15–$30.
Hours: 7 a.m.–7 p.m., daily.

Funky, casual and historically correct since it is a converted slave quarter cabin with lots of po'boy sandwiches and Cajun specialties. If you
get here early enough there is a real down-home breakfast. Credit Cards:
All Major.

Lafitte's Landing $$$

Sunshine Bridge on LA70, Acalo Road; Donaldsonville; ☎ *(504) 473-*
1232.
Cuisine: Cajun. Avg. $40–$60.
Lunch: 11 a.m.–3 p.m., Tues.–Sat.
Dinner: 6–10 p.m., Tues.–Sat.

Another of the Pirate Lafitte's favorite pubs with a really good
French/Cajun menu. Credit Cards: All Major.

The Land of the Cajuns

Hold on to your "blackened redfish." If you think Cajun just
refers to food preparation on a menu, you're in for a wonderful
trip that will take you only a few miles from New Orleans. For-
mally Acadiana, known as l'Acadie, this area was settled by the
French Canadians in the early 1700s after the British made them
most unwelcome, and finally exiled them completely. The Brits,
being very shortsighted would never again know the joys of
good onion soup or a decent apple tart. If you're in a lyrical
mood you can reread "Evangeline" by Longfellow for a poetic
spin on the whole dust-up. The perfect solution for the French
Canadians was to settle in a place with strong ties to France.
Voila—Louisiana. What they didn't count on was the steamy,
soggy, bayous and swamps, definitely not the high rent district
of the territory. The good news was that fishing, trapping and
farming could not have been more rewarding. With the country
folk came country cooking with a different kind of French accent. The Creole sophisticates of New Orleans regarded their
rough and tumble country cousins, the Cajuns as suppliers of
fish or fur and little else. But to everyone's surprise, this hearty
group prospered, intermarried and formed their own communi-

ties. They spoke their own language ("French Provincial") kept their own customs and gloried in the philosophy of "Laissez les bons temps rouler" (let the good times roll) and the "good times" takes in a lot of territory. Cajuns revel in their spicy, rustic food, their endless parties and most of all their freedom.

There is no high season in Cajun country, so whenever you visit you're bound to stumble across some festival or cook-out. "Gumbo madness" goes on all year long. If you can do an overnight or even a weekend exploring the little towns that make up the hodge-podge of Cajun communities, that would be the best way to get an overview of this very unique aspect of the Louisiana experience.

Lafayette

The very center of the Cajun experience is in **Lafayette** which is their largest town. To get more familiar with the Cajun mystique you can visit the **Acadian Village** there. It covers about 10 acres with a bayou winding through its middle. There are small wooden footbridges, just as there would have been in the 1800s. The houses were moved to the village from their original locations so they cover a variety of Cajun architectural styles and furnishings. They have a gift shop with some terrific crafts that you won't necessarily see in the city. *(200 Greenleaf Drive, Lafayette, LA;* ☎ *(318) 981-2364. Admission)*

The **Acadian Cultural Center** depicts the history of the Cajuns through audiovisual exhibits that highlight their culture and customs. There is also a film about their exile from Canada. *(501 Fisher Road;* ☎ *(318) 232-0789)* Right next to the Cultural Center is **Vermilionville** which is yet another replica of a settlement, but this one is newer and covers more territory. Unlike the Acadian Village, it has food and artisan demonstrations as well as a dance pavilion and a restaurant. It's much more commercial than the older "village" but it's still great fun *(1600 Surrey Street;* ☎ *(318) 233-4077)*. **St. Martinville** is often referred to as "Paris on the Bayou." Lost in a time warp, it's an exquisite little town in the heart of Evangeline Country. In fact the very "Evangeline Oak" where the melancholy lovers used to meet is near the town square. The romance of "Evangeline" is definitely in the air here. In the 1750s **St. Martinville** was also an outpost for French officers who the King had sent to keep an eye on the Indians. They kept formal French culture alive at the outpost and thereafter it was referred to as a community of "Frenchmen from France."

The town that calls itself the Queen City of the Teche (Bayou Teche), is New Iberia. It was settled by Spanish immigrants from Malaga, and became a rollicking steamboat town until Yellow fever killed 25% of its population. It has more than recovered and today it's sugarcane country. If you arrive during the Sugar cane Festival in the fall of each year there are parades and Fais-

do-dos (Cajun dance parties) as well as sugar recipes demon-
strated right before you. This town is sweet-tooth heaven.

"WEBB-ED" BLISS

*In an effort to make his daughter's wedding the social event of the season
a doting father used as outdoor decorations giant webs, woven by industrial strength spiders, (where is Charlotte when you need her?) through
the trees leading to his house. When they were in place he had them
sprayed with gold and silver dust. Of course the town's arachniphobics
sent their regrets. There is a representation of all this weirdness at the
Petit Paris Museum.*

Avery Island is not only of the utmost importance to everyone
who loves a "hot" Bloody Mary, but to all of the Cajun population in Louisiana for whom Tabasco® sauce is mother's milk.
Avery Island grows the mega-hot peppers that give Tabasco®
sauce its oomph. The sauce was invented by a young hothead
named McIlhenny in the 1800s and his family runs the factory
that produces the Cajun "nectar" even today. It's possible to
take a tour of this hotbed of fiery flavor and then buy the "incendiary" product in the country store that adjoins the factory.
There is also an exotic Jungle Garden complete with a 1000
year-old Buddha, and a bird sanctuary spread over 200 acres.
(Avery Island; ☎ *(318) 365-8173*. Admission for Jungle Garden
(☎ *(318)369-6243)*.

Details
Lafayette Accommodations

Bois des Chenes   **$$**
  338 N. Sterling, LA 70501; ☎ *(318) 233-7816.*
  Ask for a suite in the 1820s plantation house. It's listed in the Histor-
  ical Register.

Hotel Acadiana   **$**
  1801 W Pinhook Road, Lafayette, LA 70508; ☎ *(318) 233-8120.*
  Small town hotel but very adequate as well as inexpensive. They have
  an executive floor that's much more upscale.

Lafayette Restaurants

Prudhomme's Cajun Cafe   **$$**
  ☎ *(318) 896-7964.*
  Cuisine: Cajun. Avg. $15–$30.
  Hours: 11 a.m.–10 p.m., Mon.–Sat.
  This is a must for fans of the Prudhomme family. Paul's sister Enola
  runs this wonderful cafe with the same brilliance that Paul is famous
  for in the city. Credit Cards: All Major.

Prejean's   **$$**
  ☎ *(318) 896-3247.*
  Cuisine: Cajun. Avg. $15–$30.
  Hours: 11 a.m.–10:30 p.m.
  They've won award after award for their Cajun cuisine. This is
  "dressed-up" Cajun with a touch of nouvelle thrown in for good

EXCURSIONS

measure. One of the best places to eat in Acadiana. Credit Cards: All Major.

St. Martinville Accommodations

Old Castillo Hotel

Place d'Evangeline, 220 Evangeline Boulevard; ☎ *(318) 394-4010.*
A charming B & B, with just five rooms so it might be wise to call ahead. Antiques and four-posters set the country-inn scene.

St. Martinville Dining

Le Place d'Evangeline　　　　　$$

Old Castillo Hotel, Place d'Evangeline, 220 Evangeline Boulevard;
☎ *(318) 394-4010.*
Cuisine: Creole. Avg. $20–$40.
Hours: Hotel hours.
The lovely inn has a lovely restaurant attached to it. A very comfortable room to dine in, with food to match. Credit Cards: All Major.

"Steamboatin' on the Mississippi"

To travel the great Mississippi river on a steamboat is to step back into Louisiana's history in the most memorable of ways. It's the perfect capper to your New Orleans experience. If you can devote two or three days to a cruise on one of the picturesque paddleboats that sail up and down the river, you will have the opportunity to see the country the way everyone did before the Civil War. Riverboats were made famous by a writer named Samuel Clemens who was so mesmerized by the romance and adventure of the great paddlewheelers that he changed his name to Mark Twain, the term the pilot used to measure the depth of the river. But travel was not their only purpose. Entertainment and elegant dining were all part of this extraordinary experience, just as it is today.

The best way to do a steamboat cruise is to save it for the end of your trip. They leave from New Orleans on various itineraries and return in from three to twelve days. One of the most popular routes incorporates the Great Plantations on River Road and goes as far as Natchez with shore trips included in the package. You can coordinate your return trip home with the end of your cruise.

The Delta Queen Steamboat Company which was founded in 1890 runs the big paddleboat cruises that are so popular today. They have three magnificent boats: the *Delta Queen*, the *Mississippi Queen* and the newest, largest of the three, the *American Queen*, which carries 436 passengers. As for accommodations, the staterooms on all the "Queens" are done in Victorian splendor with brass and dark wood paneling, crystal chandeliers and stained glass. It's almost like stopping in a turn of the century B&B. The public rooms have velvet, crystal and brocades as far as the eye can see. Blink twice and you'll think you're part of the cast of "Show Boat." True to the cruise "code of honor" the Queens serve four meals a day including tea and a moonlight buffet. In between meals, if there is any time left over you can attend calliope concerts, movies, lectures, or classes conducted by the "Riverlorian" who will beguile you with tales of the Mississippi. And of course there's wall to wall jazz as you sail into the past. Best of all is the "front porch" deck, a covered area where you can sit back and watch ole man river just keep rollin' along. In the words of Mark Twain "the face of the water in time, became a wonderful book...and it was not a book to be read once and thrown aside, for it had a new story to tell every day."

Musicians on the Mississippi Queen *keep passengers entertained.*

Details

Delta Queen Steamboat Co.
30 Robin Street, Wharf, New Orleans, LA 70130; ☎ *(800) 543-7637. Reservations:* ☎ *(800) 543-1949.*

AGENDA GUIDED TOURS

The riverfront trolley passes several famous attractions.

All tour prices are based on the type and the number of people participating. Call in advance for price—options available.

General Orientation

Gray Line

1300 World Trade Center; ☎ *(504) 587-0861.*
Various different half-day and full day tours of the city as well as the plantations out on River Road. They also have walking tours of the French Quarter and the Garden District. The best way to see any city is to walk it.

Magic Walking Tours

1015 Iberville Street; ☎ *(504) 593-9693.*
They have a host of different options including a cemetery tour as well as voodoo, haunted houses, vampire (only when the sun is out) and ghost-hunter tours. That about covers all the occult occupations in New Orleans.

Superdome

One Sugar Bowl Drive; ☎ *(504) 587-3810.*
(See Top Sights, page 21)

Southern Seaplane Inc.

☎ *(504) 394-5633.*

If you don't need a 747 to make you comfortable aloft, this is a heavenly way to see Gumbo Land.

Tourist Information Center

529 St. Ann Street; ☎ *(504) 561-1001.*

They will rent you a cassette for a do-it-yourself walking tour. It's a great way to get to know the Quarter at your own pace.

Tours by Isabelle

P.O. Box 740972, New Orleans, LA 70174; ☎ *(504) 391-3544.*

Tours by mini-bus (air-conditioned, of course). They take about three hours but they cover a lot of territory including the Quarter, the cemeteries and the Garden District.

Jean Lafitte National Park Service

419 Decatur Street; ☎ *(504) 589-2636.*

These wonderful people offer free walking tours conducted by National Park Service rangers. There are various itineraries around the city.

Hidden Treasure Tours

1915 Chestnut Street; ☎ *(504) 529-4507.*

By foot or by car they focus not only on the history but the architecture of an area. There is also a Woman's History tour, just in case Gloria Steinem is your traveling companion.

Louisiana African Odyssey

10985 N. Harrell's Ferry Road, Baton Rouge, LA 70816; ☎ *(504) 338-6309.*

Members of the tour are taken to Tulane University to visit the Amistad Research Center where a collection of documents pertaining to African-American culture are on view.

Cemetery Tours

Cukie's Travels, Inc.

☎ *(504) 882-3058.*

Cukie will give you an in-depth account of the cemetery scene in New Orleans. She walks you through two and drives you through the one that covers more than 150 acres.

Save Our Cemeteries

☎ *(504) 588-9357.*

Volunteers lead you through the most interesting of the lot, St. Louis No. I. They use this as an informative way to collect money for the preservation of these astounding places. The funds are needed for maintenance.

Swamp Tours

Chacahoula Tours

492 Louisiana Street, Westwego, LA 70094; ☎ *(504) 436-2640.*

Jerry Dupre is one of the most knowledgeable expedition leaders you could hope to have if you find yourself in the middle of a swamp. His flat bottom boat glides through the bayous while he enfolds the history of the swamp for you accompanied by some pretty swell scene stealers such as an alligator named Barbara who answers to her name.

Dr. Wagner's Honey Island Swamp Tour
☎ *(504) 242-5877.*
This tour covers over 70,000 acres of protected wildlife land. Your tour is led by Wagner himself who is a wetland ecologist.

Cukie's Travels
☎ *(504) 882-3058.*
The same indefatigable Cukie (of the Cemetery tours) has swamp tours run by members of her family. They all enjoy sharing the beauty of the swamp and as a bunch they're great fun.

Angella's Atachfalaya Basin Tours
☎ *(504) 667-6135.*
About two hours total with native Cajun guides.

Carriage Tours

Good Old Days Buggies
☎ *(504) 523-0804.*

Gay 90s Carriages
☎ *(504) 943-8832.*
If you're interested in a "tour de horse" both of the above will take you throughout the quarter in the most romantic of ways.

"Ooh! Bummer!"

Drawing by Booth; ©1995 The New Yorker Magazine, Inc.

Plantation Tours

Tours By Isabelle
☎ *(504) 391-3544.*
Small vans will take you on a variety of tours to the great Plantations. Some are full day, others just afternoon trips to Great River Road. Lunch is included.

New Orleans Tours, Inc.

☎ *(504) 587-1751.*

Half day tours of one of the great old River Road mansions with lunch sometimes included.

Gray Line Tours

☎ *(504) 587-0861.*

Nottoway Plantation and Houmas House are on the 7-1/2 hour tours. Oak Alley can be done on their half-day tours.

Varied Interests

Anne Rice Tours, New Orleans Tours

☎ *(504) 592-1991.*

This is the opportunity you've been waiting for if you want to go behind the scenes with some of Lestat's greatest fans. They'll take you to his favorite literary hot spots as well as his mommy, Anne Rice's house. You'd have to have bats in your belfry not to go.

Cradle of Jazz Tours

☎ *(504) 282-3583.*

Touring with "a beat" is done by a jazz historian who will take you back in history to the homes and hangouts of the Righteous and Famous.

Go Antiquing

☎ *(504) 899-3027.*

Customized shopping itineraries for shopaholics. Magazine Street is one of their prime destinations.

Tours Extraordinaire by Nancy

☎ *(504) 898-0602.*

She customizes anything you have in mind, expertly. She'll show you "the works."

Boat Tours

Moonlight Shrimping Tours

☎ *(504) 689-3213.*

Six hour trips to see up front, how the Cajuns get all their shrimp and crabs. The boat is a big "lugger" craft and they prepare a moonlight feast. Great fun.

Natchez

1340 World Trade Center; ☎ *(504) 586-8777.*

Two hour daytime cruises up the Mississippi with an optional buffet on this picturesque steamboat. In the evening they do a Jazz dinner cruise.

Creole Queen

☎ *(504) 529-4567.*

The Queen, which ia beautiful Paddlewheeler, gives you three full hours of narrated boat trip on "Ole Muddy." There is also a Jazz cruise in the p.m.

John James Audubon

☎ *(504) 586-8777.*

This delightful old sternwheeler goes from the Aquarium of the Americas to the Zoo and back again four times daily. It's a wonderfully scenic trip and add immeasurably to both sights.

AGENDA 1, 2, 3 DAYS IN NEW ORLEANS

St. Louis Cathedral is the oldest cathedral in the United States.

Agenda's One Day In New Orleans

The following is elemental New Orleans, a quick look at the city, to include at least two of my top three sights (you may not be in New Orleans during Mardi Gras) and just a whiff of the heady scent of Creole and Cajun cuisine. If you have only one day here, this is the best way to spend it.

Since it is an impossible task to get more than a taste of New Orleans in as brief a time as one day, the least frustrating route to take is to spend just a short while at each of your stops, no matter how hard it is to tear yourself away, because, in truth, you could easily devote days of fascinating exploration in this exciting city. Remember, this is just a taste, your next visit will be a banquet.

Morning

Café au lait and beignets are a New Orleans institution.

If you only have one breakfast in New Orleans then **Brennan's**, in the **French Quarter**, (see Restaurants, page 142) is the place to start off your day. Settle down to an order of eggs sardu with grits and top it off with a milk punch (and it certainly has one). Now that you've covered the most famous breakfast bases and you're on **Royal Street** you are in fine shape to explore the street that personifies the city's most elegant antiques scene. Then, walk just a few blocks over to **Jackson Square**, the heart of the **Vieux Carré** and probably the most historic area of the city. If you have time as you stroll around, stop into the **Cabildo** for a helping of the past as well as **St. Louis Cathedral** for a helping of tranquility. From **Jackson Square** you can head for the **French Market** to browse among the produce stands and the umpteen varieties of chiles and Cajun spices. Nibble a praline or two to tide you over to lunch. Whatever you do, resist the temptation to make a stop at the **Cafe Du Monde** no matter how much fun everybody looks like they're having; you're saving it for later. Besides, it's time for your first look at the **Mississippi**. The way to see it is from the **Moonwalk** which is right alongside the market on a raised levee promenade. The walk stretches all the way down to **Woldenberg Park**. By now you're probably hungry enough to eat a gumbo and a half. The best way to handle your only lunch in the **French Quarter** is to have the chef of the moment, Emeril Lagasse, prepare it in the bistro of the moment, **Nola**. (See Restaurants, page 148.) Wall to wall people scarfing down Emeril's superb goodies.

Afternoon

The cemeteries of the city are so fascinating and bizarre, not to mention historic, that they simply must be seen. You may think that with only one day at your disposal you should get "up close and personal" with the Vieux Carré, but trust me, the cemeteries are unforgettable. A tour should only take a couple of hours and you'll be back in time to rest your weary tootsies on the **St. Charles Streetcar**. You'll certainly need the "sit down," and the most scenic way to take a load off is by riding through the gorgeous **Garden District** to see how the other half lives. Take the streetcar up to **Riverbend** where you'll have gotten your second wind and can stroll around the boutiques and stop at the **Camellia Grill** (see Restaurants, page 135.) for a heavenly slice of pecan pie. Hop aboard the streetcar for the ride back to your hotel. Its last stop is on **Canal Street** which is near most of the hotels. Rest up, it's going to be a big night.

Evening

It's important to have an early dinner because the "mythic" **Bourbon Street** and **Preservation Hall** simply have to be on your agenda this evening. However, dinner should be just as spectacular since you'll have reserved a table at the signature restaurant of New Orleans, **Commander's Palace**. (See Restaurants, page 147.) If you book early you can top off dinner with a cup of their dramatically presented Cafe Brulot (coffee, Brandy, spices, flames, WOW) and be in a cab in time to join the crowds at **Preservation Hall**. Since the last set is played by 11 p.m. you'll have plenty of time to get a good look at **Bourbon Street** at its "liveliest." There is only one place to end this New Orleans day and that would have to be at New Orleans quintessential landmark, **Cafe Du Monde**. (See Restaurants, page 139.) Sink down at a table, inhale your fragrant café au lait, take a bite of your sugar drenched beignet and watch the world of "The Big Easy" go by.

Agenda for the Second Day of a Two-day Trip

Morning

Yesterday's whirlwind of sights and sounds, not to mention
tastes has again made an early start essential. Today you can join
the New Orleanians at one of their very favorite breakfast hangouts, the **Croissant D'Or**. (See French Quarter Best Bites,
page 75.) Get a copy of the *Times-Picayune*, order a slice of incredibly rich quiche or if you're feeling particularly wicked, a big
piece of French pastry, add a steaming cup of café au lait and
voila—you have become an instant native. After breakfast you
can begin to really explore the streets of the Quarter, don't try to
have a particular plan, wandering is the best way to get to know
the winding streets with their glorious old homes and tropical
gardens. See if you can peek into a courtyard or two for a magical
"look behind the tourist scene." You might take some time to
visit a few of the historic homes that are open to the public. The
Old Ursuline Convent on **Chartres Street** would be the perfect place
to reflect on that sinful slice of apple tart you just made disappear, especially in their beautifully restored chapel. Walk over to
Esplanade Avenue which borders the Vieux Carré and stroll
around the "picture postcard" **Faubourg Marigny** and then back
over to **Decatur Street** to explore the small flea markets and
quirky little shops on its upper stretch, at the end of the **French
Quarter**.

Afternoon

Since you're already on **Decatur Street** what better place for
lunch than the **Central Grocery** (See French Quarter Best Bites,
page 74.) and your "de-rigeur" introduction to the muffuletta
(no, that is not the southern version of the Macarena). Remember, just order a quarter sandwich per person. (The whole muffuletta could feed Uganda for a year.) After lunch, with charge
cards at the ready, walk over to **Camp Street**, right off **Canal
Street**. That is the magical route of the **Magazine Street** bus. Since
the whole world of "junque" awaits you it might be a good idea
to reserve the rest of the afternoon. You can hop on and off the
bus where the pickings seem the fattest. Keep in mind that there
are stretches in-between with questionable neighborhoods, so
when the shops thin down reboard the bus.

Evening

Since you've found the treasures of Kubla Khan during your
spree on **Magazine Street**, you have certainly earned a terrific
drink. Therefore you're off to **Napoleon House** (See Bars,
page 175.) for a very historic Pimms Cup in the midst of the
most historic bar in the city. But don't go for any of the "nib-
bles." You must have enough resolve to wait for dinner at **Galatoire's**, truly the most beloved of all the restaurants of New

Orleans **"Golden Age."** (See Restaurants, page 136.) After dinner you'll need some exercise and the **Moonwalk** in the moonlight has got to be the most romantic way to end the evening.

Agenda for the Third Day of a Three-day Trip

Cornstalk Fence is a famous French Quarter landmark.

Your third day may be your last (in New Orleans, that is). Three days seems to be the most popular length of stay for most visitors. So, this is "do or die" until you return to see all the rest of the "hot spots" you weren't able to squeeze in on the first two days of your trip.

Since you've covered most of "important" New Orleans briefly over the past two days, this would be the day to try to see some of the museums. While not as staggering in scope as the Louvre they are nonetheless major contributors to the artistic life of the city. Then on to the **Warehouse District**, headquarters for New Orleans' emerging art scene.

Morning

The day has to begin at **Mothers** because to leave New Orleans without sampling their mammoth breakfast platter would be unthinkable. Then back to the **St. Charles Streetcar** for a closer look at the **Garden District**. This time you'll have the energy to get on and off the streetcar for mini-walks that will give you an opportunity to see the magnificent houses in detail. Be careful to avoid areas that look questionable. Better still, take a walking tour. (Tours, page 195.) When you've smelled all the flowers in the **Garden District** you can continue on your outdoor odyssey to **City Park**. There you can admire the live oaks, draped with moss as well as some of the 30,000 other trees in the park. It also puts you right at the door of the **New Orleans Museum of Art** (see Top sights, page 26). After the museum, on your way back, you can wander over the Campuses of Loyola and Tulane Universities since they're back-to-back on St. Charles Avenue.

Afternoon

Lunch today is at **Uglesich's** (restaurants, page 138, take a cab) where you will receive, after a bit of a wait, the world's most luscious Oyster Po'Boy sandwich in the city. It will be hard to tear yourself away but the **Warehouse District** has enough shops and galleries to keep you busy for the rest of the year. A stop at the **Contemporary Arts Center** (see Districts, page 91) is a must. Then wandering from gallery to gallery is a treat you can now give your full attention. What better way to spend your last day in this fabulous city than looking at the work of its newest artists. The afternoon should end with one of the short, but definitely "sweet" river cruises that leave from in front of the **World Trade Center**. How can you even think of leaving without a good look at the **Mississippi**?

Evening

If you've denied yourself one of New Orleans' dynamite Hurricanes now's the time, and some of the best ones are mixed at **Lafitte's Blacksmith Shop** (see Bars, page 178). It's also close enough to **K-Paul's Louisiana Kitchen** (see Restaurants, page 144) so that a little staggering won't slow you down. Tonight is a Cajun dining experience so that you can leave the city with a salute to the "Big Gumbo." After dinner a return to **Bourbon Street** in order to make sure the last sounds you hear on your trip are the sounds New Orleans is most famous for, all that jazz.

Mardi Gras Agenda

Congratulations! If you're reading the Mardi Gras Agenda I will assume that you planned far enough in advance to actually get a reservation for the world's "Fattest Tuesday." I've already gone into the history and mystique of Mardi Gras (see Top sights, page 13.) so you are aware that many events during the dawn-to-dawn celebrations are very private affairs that can only be attended by members of Krewes or their guests, however there are still enough "Bons Temps" going on in the streets and the clubs to keep your dial turned up to frenzy for most of the duration. When the clock strikes midnight and Lent begins on Wednesday, with any luck at all, you should be as exhausted as any native New Orleanian.

The festivities really heat up during the four-day Carnival weekend that precedes Ash Wednesday. The most important parades take place then and the city is filled with glittering celebs from all over the world who come to participate as kings or float ornaments for the different Krewes. The very best vantage points for viewing are either **Canal Street** or **St. Charles Avenue**, both are major parade routes. On Carnival day itself revelers are fully costumed and at their chosen parade sites at 7 a.m. (Carnival is hard work), equipped with blankets, portable barbecues and enough ice in their coolers to last through hours of "happy hour.' The two most important parades of Mardi Gras, Zulu and Rex will soon take place and expectations have reached their peaks. At 9 a.m. the parades start and the fun never stops until midnight or you've passed out, whichever comes first.

If you really want to enter into the zany spirit of Mardi Gras you may want to bring a costume with you. Perhaps something that you would never dare to wear among people who actually know you. After all, Mardi Gras is fantasy time, and New Orleans is the least judgmental city on the planet. If once you've arrived, you feel empowered enough to become Batman or Marie Antoinette then head for the Mardi Gras Center, *831 Chartres Street;* ☎ *(504) 524-4384.* You can write for a brochure on Mardi Gras and a schedule of events from the New Orleans Convention and Visitors Bureau, *1520 Sugar Bowl Drive, New Orleans, LA 70112;* ☎ *(504) 566-5005/(800) 672-6124.*

When you check in at your hotel you can get a copy of the *Times-Picayune* newspaper which prints the parade route for each and every one.

If you are serious about attending Mardi Gras in New Orleans you must be prepared to reserve at least one (1) year in advance. Accommodations are sometimes sold out even further by regulars who do this craziness every year. Also be aware that everybody wants a slightly larger piece of the action at this peak time so prices will tend to be higher. That said, the only thing to do is have the time of your life if you decide to join the celebration. And remember, don't be bashful. Fight your way right up to the side of one of the most beautiful floats and yell up in your loudest voice: "Throw Me Somethin' Mista!"

Children's Agenda

Aquarium of the Americas is one of the five best in the country.

New Orleans was made for kids. It's **French Quarter** is a living museum for kids where they can experience the past as well as participate in the fun and games of a city where the grownups love them as much as the kids do. "The Big Easy" is just that when you bring the family. No sitting up straight, with a few exceptions, when the exquisite manners of the south may dictate a bit of restraint. But all eventualities considered, New Orleans is most always in the mood to kid around.

The following is an agenda in no particular order (since kids have unpredictable needs) which can be used to make up an exciting day for the biggest small fry.

Audubon Zoo
6500 Magazine Street; ☎ *(504) 861-5101.*
See Top Sights, page 22.

Aquarium of the Americas
1 Canal Street; ☎ *(504) 861-2537.*
See Top Sights, page 23.

Louisiana Children's Museum
420 Julia Street; ☎ *(504) 523-1357.*
See Museums, page 165.

Museé Conti Wax Museum
917 Conti Street; ☎ *(504) 525-2605.*
See Museums, page 165.

Children's Storyland Playground
City Park; ☎ *(504) 483-9381.*

Blaine Kern's Mardi Gras World
> Canal Street Ferry; ☎ (504) 362-8211.
> See Museums, page 165.

Louisiana Superdome
> 1500 Poydras Street; ☎ (504) 587-3810.

New Orleans Voodoo Museum
> 724 Dumaine Street; ☎ (504) 523-7685.

Children's Hour Book Emporium
> 3308 Magazine Street; ☎ (504) 899-2378.

Old Children's Books
> 734 Royal Street; ☎ (504) 525-3655.

Global Wildlife Center
> Louisiana Nature and Science Center, Brown Memorial Park, 11000 Lake
> Forest Boulevard (via 1-10E); ☎ (504) 246-5672.

Louisiana Toy Train Museum
> 519 Williams Boulevard; ☎ (504) 468-7223.

Gator Swamp Tour
> ☎ (504) 484-6100 or (800) 875-4287.

Angelo Brocato's Ice Cream Parlor
> 537 St. Ann Street; ☎ (504) 525-9676.

Hansen's Sno-Blitz—World's largest Sno Cones
> 4807 Tchoupitoulas Street; ☎ (504) 891-9788.

Accents on Arraignments
> 938 Lafayette Street, #410, New Orleans, LA 70113; ☎ (504) 524-1227.
> A remarkable service that will customize a special Mardi Gras experi-
> ence, "a kinder, gentler carnival," specializing in activities just for
> kids.

Christmas Agenda

Christmas in the "Crescent City" can be as festive and magical
as you want it to be. There are scores of events taking place all
over New Orleans that heighten the season even though they
may be conducted in a semitropical atmosphere. Of course snow
is unheard of, so the New Orleanian Christmas celebrations
would have been a great disappointment to Bing Crosby.

There are holiday events that take place during the entire
month of December when the city begins its extravagant display
of Christmas decorating, which includes its historic homes as
well as the parks and squares in every district. The **Moonwalk** and
the **Spanish Plaza** at **Woldenberg Park** are strung with hundreds of
illuminated globes and **City Park** has over 1 million lights decorating the glittering trees. It looks like a true fairyland. The
French Quarter's shops have a multitude of exotic gifts, some imported, that will remind you of the boutiques of Paris. The great
restaurants of New Orleans all have Christmas menus called
"Reveillon Feasts" which are made up of customary Creole holiday dishes. Of course there is caroling and performances of the
"Nutcracker" and most romantic of all, huge Christmas bonfires

on River Road in front of all the old plantations, on Christmas eve. They were begun by the planters to "light the way for Papa Noel." They are spectacular.

Since there are only a few department stores in New Orleans, the commercial decorating falls to the hotels and none do it more opulently than the **Fairmont**. Its entire lobby ceiling is covered with glistening snow white angel hair that drips with spun glass ornaments. It forms a magical tunnel that runs from one end of the block-long lobby to the other.

There is so much to do in New Orleans during the Christmas season that I've listed some of the highlights below. As with Mardi Gras, Christmas is a "hot" ticket so you must plan ahead. Some of the hotels have special packages that are lower in price, making the demand even greater. To get a list of dates for the holiday events I've suggested, you can write in advance to **A New Orleans Christmas**, *100 Conti St., New Orleans, LA 70130; (800) 673-5725* or **A New Orleans Christmas, French Quarter Festival**, *1008 N. Peters Street, New Orleans, LA 70116,* ☎ *(504) 522-5730.*

Angel Hair Christmas Lobby	Fairmont Hotel, Dec. 1–31.
Bonfire Adventure	Gray Line Tours, Dec. 24.
Brass Choir Concert	St. Louis Cathedral, Jackson Square, Dec. 6–20.
Candlelight Tour of Historic Homes	Gray Lines, ☎ *(504) 523-6722*, Middle of Dec.
Caroling in Jackson Square	Middle of Dec.
Celtic Christmas	O'Flaherty's Pub, *514 Toulouse Street*, Dec. 12–23.
Christmas Eve Bonfire Riverboat Race	Cajun and Creole Queen paddlewheelers boarding at LaSalle's Landing, ☎ *(504) 524-0814*, Dec. 24.
Christmas Eve Midnight Mass	St. Louis Cathedral, Dec. 24.
French Market Holiday Marching Bands	French Market, various days in Dec.
Kwanza	Celebrations all over the city, ☎ *(504) 827-0707*, Dec. 26–31.

AGENDA FOR TRAVEL ARRANGEMENTS

Jackson Brewery is a popular shopping spot for locals and tourists.

Having a successful trip requires as much planning and imagination as a successful marriage. Because travel is an equally maddening combination of pleasures and pitfalls, what you do *before* you go is your best insurance.

The first travel arrangement you make is in your head. Take a little time to decide what you want to do and see in New Orleans. Make your own agenda for the most important things, not just shopping or museums but which shops and what museums. Same thing with restaurants. *DO NOT* leave all of those choices to be made once you arrive. Why spend precious "Big Easy" minutes planning instead of experiencing? You can access all the information needed to make a decision before you go.

Once your travel reservations are confirmed, get a copy of the New Orleans *Times-Picayune, Where* or *New Orleans Magazine* at an out-of-town newsstand. Every city has them. Go to the library and find out what articles have appeared recently on New

Orleans. Contact the **New Orleans Convention and Visitors Bureau**, *1520 Superbowl Drive, New Orleans, LA 70112;* ☎ *(504) 566-5011/(800) 672-6124.* I promise that your advance planning efforts will pay off by allowing you to arrive in town with reservations at Commander's Palace and tickets to the Superdome.

New Orleans Weather

Of course you want to go to New Orleans during Mardi Gras. But be reasonable, New Orleans is just as exciting the rest of the year, especially April and May or September and October. The summer can be unbearable with temperatures and humidity both in the 90s. Steamy, soggy, and "too damn hot. "Beware!!! Denial isn't just limited to Egypt. The month that holds nothing but discomfort for travelers is August. The winter months are mild but damp, so the chill in the air is a biting one. Now that you know the grim facts, forget everything I've said! New Orleans is exciting every month of the year.

AGENDA FOR TRAVEL ARRANGEMENTS

Average Monthly Weather						
	Jan.	**Feb.**	**Mar.**	**Apr.**	**May**	**June**
High (°F/°C)	62/17	65/18	71/22	77/25	83/28	88/31
Low (°F/°C)	47/8	50/10	55/13	61/16	68/20	74/23
Rainfall (in./mm)	4.6/ 117	4.2/ 107	4.7/ 119	4.8/ 122	4.5/ 114	5.5/ 140
	July	**Aug.**	**Sept.**	**Oct.**	**Nov.**	**Dec.**
High (°F/°C)	90/32	90/32	86/30	79/26	70/21	64/18
Low (°F/°C)	76/24	76/24	73/23	64/18	55/13	48/9
Rainfall (in./mm)	6.6/ 168	5.8/ 147	4.8/ 122	3.5/ 89	3.8/ 97	4.6/ 117

Dress Code

Most New Orleanians like to dress casually most of the time except in their formal restaurants. It's part of their social identity. As a visitor you may not feel at ease being quite as informal as you might be at home, particularly in the evenings. If you're off to tea at a fashionable hotel, you'd probably feel more comfortable in a jacket (this may not be required, but ask) or a smart outfit. Perhaps the most appropriate phrase is "designer casual" (even if you're not from L.A.). For sightseeing around town, jeans or slacks are fine, but shorts in churches or theatres, in my opinion is "major tacky." You'll need a jacket or sweater from November through March because it cools down considerably in the evening. Your two most important travel aids: an umbrella, and a comfortable pair of shoes.

Travel Documents

All foreign citizens, even babies, need a valid passport to enter the U.S. for a stay of up to 90 days. If you intend to drive, you will need a valid license and an International drivers license.

Customs

U.S. Customs allows you to enter the country with 200 cigarettes, or 100 cigars, one liter of wine or one liter of hard liquor, or two liters of wine and gifts you wish to bring into the country with a value of no more than about $100 (at press time). Foreign tourists may bring in or take out up to $10,000 in U. S. foreign currency.

Foreign tourists are entitled to a refund check on taxes paid on any purchases made in the U.S. They must go to the Louisiana Tax Free Shopping Refund Center at the airport, to present receipts accompanied by their passports and airline tickets.

Money Madness

U.S. currency is based on the dollar. The paper notes are in the denominations of 1, 2, 5, 10, 20, 50, 100 dollars. The coins are: 1, 5, 10, 25, 50 cents and 1 silver dollar. There are 100 cents to every dollar.

In New Orleans most U.S. and foreign credit cards or traveler's checks are accepted everywhere, however always check with restaurants and clubs, just to make sure, since policies change. If you can, charge your purchases and meals to your credit cards. The rate of exchange is usually better, and it will help to have a record of what you have spent. If you plan to attend an antiques market or small bistro, try to take cash.

If you are a foreign visitor, it would be wise to convert about $100 into dollars before you leave for New Orleans so that when you arrive, you won't need to bother with money matters till you've reached your hotel and had some rest. Usually, I tell my readers to always try to change money at the bank rather than at the hotel since the rate will be better. Well, times are changing as well as money, we noted in several instances, the hotels were giving as good a rate because they usually don't add a service charge. Ask at the bank about the use of ATM machines for your cash needs. Some will take foreign credit cards, but not all. Foreign currency may be changed at **American Express**, *158 Baronne Street;* ☎ *(504) 586-8201.*

To Tip or Not To Tip

Restaurants around town do not add a service charge as they do in Europe, so tip 15 to 20 percent, which is the norm.

Cab drivers expect about 15 to 20 percent, and there is an extra charge for each piece of luggage.

Doormen—50¢ to a dollar for hailing a cab.

Bellhop—a dollar per bag or room service.

AGENDA REVELATION

T.I.P. originally stood for To Insure Promptness. There were boxes in restaurants and hotels with those initials. You deposited money and you received preferential service. TALK ABOUT THE GOOD OLD DAYS.!!!

Telephone Facts

A telephone card can be purchased at a newsstand or the post office. Most of the phones in the street take a 25¢ coin. All 800 numbers can be dialed free. (Your 25¢ coin will be refunded)

If at all possible, try to make your calls to home from the hotel lobby phone, or from street phones. If you call long distance from your room, the hotel imposes a horrific service charge that is out and out thievery. Sometimes it's as high as $5 or $6. So far, we haven't been able to "lick them," so the only thing we can do is not "join them."

Special New Orleans Festivals

Feb	Mardi Gras
March	Tennessee Williams / Literary Festival
April	French Quarter Festival
April	Jazz Festival
June	French Market Tomato Festival
July	New Orleans Wine and Food Experience
October	Gumbo Festival

"I've heard a lot about you—all nutty, of course."

Drawing by C. Borsotti; ©1995 The New Yorker Magazine, Inc.

LIST OF ATTRACTIONS

LIST OF HOTELS

LIST OF
RESTAURANTS

Restaurant	Price	Rating	Pg.
Acme Oyster House	$$$		75
Alberto's	$$		107
Angelo Brocato Confectionery	$		100
Antoine's	$$$	★	135
Arnaud's	$$$	★★★	137
Bayona	$$$	★★★	143
Bella Luna	$$$	★★★	149
Bistro	$$$	★★★	151
Bizou	$$$	★★★	138
Bluebird Café	$		100
Bon Ton Cafe	$$$		80
Bottom of the Cup Tearoom	$$	★★	153
Bozo's	$$		109
Brennan's	$$	★★	142
Brigston's	$$$	★★★	145
Bruning's	$$		112
Cabin, The	$$		189
Café Atchafalaya	$		89
Cafe Du Monde	$	★★★	139
Café Maspero	$		75
Café Sbisa	$$$		76
Camellia Grill	$	★★★	135
Caribbean Room	$$$		90
Casamento's	$$		89
Central Grocery Co.	$		74
Chacahoula Tours			196
Chart House	$$$	★	150
Christian's	$$$	★★	144
Clancy's	$$$		100
Coffee Pot Restaurant	$		74
Commander's Palace	$$$	★★	155
Commander's Palace	$$$	★★★	147
Court of the Two Sisters	$$	★★	155
Creole Queen	$$	★★★	150
Croissant d'Or	$		75
Croissant d'Or	$	★★★	153
Cukie's Travels, Inc.			196
Deanie's	$$		109
Dooky Chase	$$	★★★	139
Doug's Place	$$		95
El Liborio Cuban Restaurant	$$		80
Emeril's	$$$	★★★	145

223

Restaurant	Price	Rating	Pg.
Feelings Cafe	$$$		108
Frankie's Café	$$		100
Gabrielle	$$$	★★★	140
Galatoire's	$$$	★★★	136
Gautreau	$$$	★★★	143
Genghis Khan	$$$		99
Graham's	$$$	★★	146
Grill Room	$$$	★★★	151
Gumbo Shop	$$		76
Home Furnishings Store Café	$		90
House of Blues	$$	★★★	155
Howlin' Wolf	$$		95
Hummingbird Grill	$		80
Irene's Cuisine	$$$	★★★	136
Joey K	$		89
Kabby's	$$$	★	149
Kabby's	$$$	★	79
Katie's	$$		100
K-Paul's Louisiana Kitchen	$$$	★★	144
L'Economie	$$$		95
La Crepe Nanou	$$	★★	141
La Madeleine Bakery & Cafe	$		101
La Madeleine	$	★★	153
La Marquise	$		76
La Marquise	$	★★	153
La Peniche	$$		108
Lafitte's Landing	$$$		189
Le Jardin	$$$	★	150
Le Place d'Evangeline	$$		192
Le Salon	$$$	★★★	152
Louis XVI	$$$	★★	145
Louisiana Pizza Kitchen	$		75
Lucky Cheng's	$$$		74
Mandina's	$$		99
Mike's On The Avenue	$$$	★★	146
Montrel's Creole Cafe	$		108
Mother's	$	★★	138
Napoleon House	$	★★	140
New City Diner	$		80
Nola	$$$	★★★	148
P.J.'s Coffee & Tea Co.	$	★	153
Palace Cafe	$$	★★★	154
Palamer's Restaurant	$$		99
Parasol's	$		90
Pascal's Manale	$$$		101
Pearl	$		80
Pelican Club	$$$	★★	141

Restaurant	Price	Rating	Pg.
Peristyle	$$	★★	142
Petunia's	$$	★★	136
Pie in the Sky	$		89
Port Of Call	$	★★	137
Praline Connection Gospel and Blues Hall	$$	★★★	155
Praline Connection	$$	★★★	140
Prejean's	$$		191
Prudhomme's Cajun Cafe	$$		191
Red Bike	$		95
Rib Room	$$$		75
Rue de la Course	$		90
Save Our Cemeteries			196
Sazerac	$$$	★★	151
Semolina	$$		89
Sid-Mar's	$$		109
Snug Harbor	$		107
Tavern on the Park	$$$		100
Tavern on the Park	$$$	★	149
Tujague's	$$		75
Uglesich's	$$	★★★	138
Upperline	$$$	★★★	141
Vic's Kangaroo Cafe	$$		95
Warehouse Café	$		94
West End Café	$$		109
Zachary's	$$		101

INDEX

NEW FIELDING WEAR!

Now that you own a Fielding travel guide, you have graduated from being a tourist to full-fledged traveler! Celebrate your elevated position by proudly wearing a heavy-duty, all-cotton shirt or cap, selected by our authors for their comfort and durability (and their ability to hide dirt).

Important Note: Fielding authors have field-tested these shirts and have found that they can be swapped for much more than their purchase price in free drinks at some of the world's hottest clubs and in-spots. They also make great gifts.

WORLD TOUR

Hit the hard road with a travel fashion statement for our times. Visit all 35 of Mr. D.P.'s favorite nasty spots (listed on the back), or just look like you're going to. This is the real McCoy, worn by mujahadeen, mercenaries, UN peacekeepers and the authors of Fielding's *The World's Most Dangerous Places*. Black, XL, heavy-duty 100% cotton. Made in the USA. $18.00.

LIVE DANGEROUSLY

A shirt that tells the world that within that high-mileage, overly educated body beats the heart of a true party animal. Only for adrenaline junkies, hardcore travelers and seekers of knowledge. Black, XL, heavy-duty 100% cotton. Made in the USA. $18.00.

MR. DP CAP

Fielding authors have field-tested the Mr. DP cap and found it can be swapped for much more than its purchase price in free drinks at some of the world's hottest clubs. Guaranteed to turn heads wherever you go. Made in U.S.A. washable cotton, sturdy bill, embroidered logo, one size fits all. $14.95.

Name:

Address:

City:

State: Zip:

Telephone:
Shirt Name:
Quantity:

For each item, add $4 shipping and handling. California residents add $1.50 sales tax. Allow 2 to 4 weeks for delivery.

Send check or money order with your order form to:

Fielding Worldwide, Inc.
308 South Catalina Avenue
Redondo Beach, CA 90277

or order your shirts by phone,:
1-800-FW-2-GUIDE
Visa, MC, AMex accepted

Order Your Guide to Travel and Adventure

Title	Price	Title	Price
Fielding's Alaska Cruises and the Inside Passage	$18.95	Fielding's Indiana Jones Adventure and Survival Guide™	$15.95
Fielding's America West	$19.95	Fielding's Italy	$18.95
Fielding's Asia's Top Dive Sites	$19.95	Fielding's Kenya	$19.95
Fielding's Australia	$18.95	Fielding's Las Vegas Agenda	$16.95
Fielding's Bahamas	$16.95	Fielding's London Agenda	$14.95
Fielding's Baja California	$18.95	Fielding's Los Angeles	$16.95
Fielding's Bermuda	$16.95	Fielding's Mexico	$18.95
Fielding's Best and Worst	$19.95	Fielding's New Orleans Agenda	$16.95
Fielding's Birding Indonesia	$19.95	Fielding's New York Agenda	$16.95
Fielding's Borneo	$18.95	Fielding's New Zealand	$17.95
Fielding's Budget Europe	$18.95	Fielding's Paradors, Pousadas and Charming Villages	$18.95
Fielding's Caribbean	$19.95	Fielding's Paris Agenda	$14.95
Fielding's Caribbean Cruises	$18.95	Fielding's Portugal	$16.95
Fielding's Caribbean on a Budget	$18.95	Fielding's Rome Agenda	$16.95
Fielding's Diving Australia	$19.95	Fielding's San Diego Agenda	$14.95
Fielding's Diving Indonesia	$19.95	Fielding's Southeast Asia	$18.95
Fielding's Eastern Caribbean	$17.95	Fielding's Southern California Theme Parks	$18.95
Fielding's England including Ireland, Scotland and Wales	$18.95	Fielding's Southern Vietnam on Two Wheels	$15.95
Fielding's Europe	$19.95	Fielding's Spain	$18.95
Fielding's Europe 50th Anniversary	$24.95	Fielding's Surfing Australia	$19.95
Fielding's European Cruises	$18.95	Fielding's Surfing Indonesia	$19.95
Fielding's Far East	$18.95	Fielding's Sydney Agenda	$16.95
Fielding's France	$18.95	Fielding's Thailand, Cambodia, Laos and Myanmar	$18.95
Fielding's France: Loire Valley, Burgundy and the Best of French Culture	$16.95	Fielding's Travel Tools™	$15.95
Fielding's France: Normandy & Brittany	$16.95	Fielding's Vietnam including Cambodia and Laos	$19.95
Fielding's France: Provence and the Mediterranean	$16.95	Fielding's Walt Disney World and Orlando Area Theme Parks	$18.95
Fielding's Freewheelin' USA	$18.95	Fielding's Western Caribbean	$18.95
Fielding's Hawaii	$18.95	Fielding's The World's Most Dangerous Places™	$21.95
Fielding's Hot Spots: Travel in Harm's Way	$15.95	Fielding's Worldwide Cruises	$21.95

To place an order: call toll-free 1-800-FW-2-GUIDE
(VISA, MasterCard and American Express accepted)
or send your check or money order to:
Fielding Worldwide, Inc., 308 S. Catalina Avenue, Redondo Beach, CA 90277
http://www.fieldingtravel.com
Add $4.00 per book for shipping & handling (sorry, no COD's),
allow 2–6 weeks for delivery

International Conversions

TEMPERATURE

To convert °F to °C, subtract 32 and divide by 1.8. To convert °C to °F, multiply by 1.8 and add 32.

Fahrenheit	Centigrade	
230°	110°	
220°		
210°	100°	Water Boils
200°	90°	
190°		
180°	80°	
170°		
160°	70°	
150°		
140°	60°	
130°		
120°	50°	
110°	40°	
100°		
90°	30°	
80°		
70°	20°	
60°		
50°	10°	
40°		
30°	0°	Water Freezes
20°	-10°	
10°		
0°	-20°	
-10°		
-20°	-30°	
-30°		
-40°	-40°	

WEIGHTS & MEASURES

LENGTH

1 km	=	0.62 miles
1 mile	=	1.609 km
1 meter	=	1.0936 yards
1 meter	=	3.28 feet
1 yard	=	0.9144 meters
1 yard	=	3 feet
1 foot	=	30.48 centimeters
1 centimeter	=	0.39 inch
1 inch	=	2.54 centimeters

AREA

1 square km	=	0.3861 square miles
1 square mile	=	2.590 square km
1 hectare	=	2.47 acres
1 acre	=	0.405 hectare

VOLUME

1 cubic meter	=	1.307 cubic yards
1 cubic yard	=	0.765 cubic meter
1 cubic yard	=	27 cubic feet
1 cubic foot	=	0.028 cubic meter
1 cubic centimeter	=	0.061 cubic inch
1 cubic inch	=	16.387 cubic centimeters

CAPACITY

1 gallon	=	3.785 liters
1 quart	=	0.94635 liters
1 liter	=	1.057 quarts
1 pint	=	473 milliliters
1 fluid ounce	=	29.573 milliliters

MASS and WEIGHT

1 metric ton	=	1.102 short tons
1 metric ton	=	1000 kilograms
1 short ton	=	.90718 metric ton
1 long ton	=	1.016 metric tons
1 long ton	=	2240 pounds
1 pound	=	0.4536 kilograms
1 kilogram	=	2.2046 pounds
1 ounce	=	28.35 grams
1 gram	=	0.035 ounce
1 milligram	=	0.015 grain

cm	0	1	2	3	4	5	6	7	8

Inch	0	1	2	3